# The Norwegian–American Historical Association

*Lawrence O. Hauge,* PRESIDENT

*Allen Osmundson*

*25 Okt. 1986*

# Norwegian-American Studies

*Volume 31*

1986
The Norwegian-American Historical Association
NORTHFIELD, MINNESOTA

*In Honor of C.A. Clausen on His Ninetieth Birthday*

# Preface

In 1928 the Norwegian-language newspaper *Scandia* described a district on the West Side of Chicago as "Little Norway" because of its concentration of Norwegians and their churches, lodge halls, and places of business. The neighborhood was but one of a large number of easily identifiable ethnic enclaves in the Chicago landscape; the same situation existed in other cities such as Brooklyn, Minneapolis, and Seattle, where Norwegians settled in considerable numbers.

The present volume of *Studies*, the thirty-first in the series, contains twelve articles largely devoted to immigrant life in America's great cities. Due at least partly to a rural bias in Norwegian-American historiography, this picture of Norwegian immigrants does not readily surface. Consequently, it is our wish to provide a better balance by giving increased attention to the urban environment, while we take care not to neglect the study of other significant aspects of the Norwegian-American experience.

In the lead article John Higham reviews the scholarly debate about the immigrant impact on urban America. He then explores the issues and forces that mobilized some ethnic groups to mass action; it was a militant phase of their American experience that Higham sees as having been neglected by historians during the ethnic revival of the past decades, in part because of the conventions that governed the writing of ethnic histories. It is therefore conceivable that a closer reading of the sources will reveal involvement of Scandinavians in some of the many episodes of ethnic assertiveness. Except for the Finns, Nordic nationalities appear at present to be conspicuous by their near invisibility; if the latter is actually the case, we need to explain why.

Profiling the career of a Norwegian-American Minneapolis politician, Lars M. Rand, in the heavily Scandinavian sixth ward, Carl H. Chrislock shows how Rand through his political organization and by his own shrewdness responded to the divisions, needs, and interests within his constituency to advance his political ambitions. In the next essay Christen T. Jonassen interprets how transplanted ethnic value systems and attitudes, and also American patterns, influenced behavior and produced conflict as well as cooperation within the Norwegian Brooklyn community. Appropriately in this the centennial year of the Haymarket Affair of May 4, 1886, Arlow W. Andersen surveys contemporary Norwegian-American press opinion about this disturbing incident, which left the entire American labor movement with a taint of radicalism and violence.

The following three contributions employ various kinds of evidence to gain entry into the immigrant community. John R. Jenswold uses "America letters," specifically a collection uncovered accidentally in 1981, to document the experiences of Norwegian immigrant workers in the 1890s. Deborah L. Miller delivers a striking photographic essay on Norwegian Minneapolis—a first in this series—and suggests how photographs may aid historical inquiry. The role of the immigrant press is the subject of the article by Odd S. Lovoll, which, relying heavily on the Norwegian-language *Washington Posten*, delineates the contours and stages of development and adjustment in the Norwegian community in Seattle.

How the successful newspaper *Skandinaven* in Chicago fostered Norwegian immigrant literature through its professional publishing venture is detailed by Orm Øverland in an article treating the Norwegian-American book trade in the

1860s and 1870s. Ingrid Semmingsen recounts the life and career of a Norwegian-American humorist and dissident, Ole S. Hervin, known by his pseudonym as Herm. Wang; she believes that additional biographical studies of individuals such as Hervin will establish the existence of an influential liberal and intellectual element in urban centers, and thereby serve to broaden our conception of Norwegian Americans. Janet E. Rasmussen writes about the Norwegian pioneer feminist Aasta Hansteen and her years in America, 1880 to 1889; Hansteen was greatly affected by the more advanced American feminist movement and by extension its impact was felt on the corresponding movement in Norway. The hitherto unknown correspondence between O. E. Rølvaag and Marie Halling Swensen, of a distinguished family in Norway, as presented by Einar Haugen offers glimpses of a deeply moving and unique relationship that developed during the final years of Rølvaag's life.

The ethnic community stimulated artistic activity, and eventually the practitioners arranged exhibitions, some of them attracting participation on a national scale. Rolf H. Erickson demonstrates the value for scholarly investigation of the catalogs and checklists that were prepared on such occasions. C. A. Clausen continues his listings of recent publications, assisted for Norwegian titles by Johanna Barstad. Charlotte Jacobson contributes another installment on acquisitions, which makes evident that important documents are being collected, but which also reminds us of the need for renewed effort to collect and preserve such records before they are lost or destroyed.

The altered appearance of *Studies* reflects the beginning of our fourth ten volumes, and we are indebted to Nancy Leeper for the design. Again I wish to acknowledge with deep appreciation and admiration the services of my competent and genial editorial assistant Mary R. Hove, my treasured co-worker now for nearly seven years.

ODD S. LOVOLL
*St. Olaf College*

# Contents

# Norwegian-American Studies

*Volume 31*

# 1

# The Mobilization of Immigrants in Urban America*

*by John Higham*

Early in the twentieth century sociologists inaugurated the scholarly study of immigrant communities in urban America. A whole new world came into view, especially well disclosed in the masterpiece by William I. Thomas and Florian Znaniecki, *The Polish Peasant in Europe and America*.[1] Historians, however, paid no heed. The discovery of the immigrant as a major theme in American history was made later, in the 1920s, and made by historians with no interest in urban sociology. It was made not in great cities like Chicago or New York but rather in midwestern state universities by young scholars still close to a small-town or rural background, who had gained their essential vision of American history from Frederick Jackson Turner. Between the two world wars the "Turnerverein" (as it was affectionately called) was so preeminent in our discipline that a Greek from Milwaukee, Theodore Saloutos, made his reputation as a student of American agriculture and shifted only in the 1950s to the history of his own forebears. The immigrants who fired the

*This paper was originally presented at a conference at St. Olaf College, October 26–27, 1984, on "Scandinavians and Other Immigrants in Urban America." The present article is a revised version of the paper as it was published in the proceedings of that conference.

imagination of historians in the 1920s and 1930s were those whose odyssey could be understood as part of the westward movement — people who belonged to the earth like Ántonia Shimerda in Willa Cather's Nebraska and Per Hansa struggling to endure the Dakota plains. The pioneers of American immigration history, above all Marcus Lee Hansen and Theodore Blegen, gave an international sweep to the Turnerian theme of the impact of the natural environment on the people it receives. This approach connected American history with European history; yet it left the familiar motifs of the American story undisturbed.[2]

A specifically urban approach to immigration history — by which I mean a focus on processes of social interaction in a dense and complex milieu — awaited the discovery of urban sociology and anthropology by historians whose own roots were in the great cities. By the 1940s a new generation, for whom the Turnerian vision of the American past would no longer suffice, was emerging from the graduate schools. Among these "asphalt flowers" (to use the sobriquet some Turnerites applied to them) was Oscar Handlin. His doctoral dissertation, *Boston's Immigrants*, published in 1941, offered a model of how the insights and methods of sociology could be adapted to the materials of American history. Guided by a sociological understanding of ethnic communities, Handlin looked — as no historian had before — at how immigrants coped with the process of urbanization and how a major city changed under the stress of their coming.[3]

After this superb beginning, progress was curiously slow. In the next two decades only one comparable monograph attempted, as Handlin's had, to embrace the multiethnic structure of an American city at a significant moment of transition; and this second effort was an implicit warning of the difficulty of the task, for it touched on too many disparate matters to make a strongly focused argument. The tremendous complexity of the modern American city discouraged comprehensive studies. An adequate successor to *Boston's Immigrants* materialized only in 1962, when Handlin's student, Moses Rischin, published *The Promised City*, but limited his subject to the experience of a single ethnic group, the eastern European Jews.[4]

Several more of Handlin's early students studied immigrants in urban or industrial contexts, as did some of Merle Curti's.[5] Gradually scholars overseas—activated by the spread of American Studies and the widening horizons of modern history—were attracted to the history of European emigration. Sources were close at hand, and the subject touched their own national histories in vital ways. Although foreign scholars have written mostly about the backgrounds and movement of emigrants, their contribution has been essential and is being continually enlarged.[6] Leadership, however, remained in the United States, and in the late 1950s it visibly waned.

Addressing this problem some years ago, Rudolph Vecoli ventured a partial explanation. In that expansive era after World War II, Vecoli pointed out, dazzling opportunities for academic careers were opening up for urban Catholics and Jews who could identify themselves with a professoriat that had previously been out of reach. Instead of studying their own origins, these newly arrived academics demonstrated their fervent commitment to the goal of assimilation by giving ethnic history a wide berth.[7] To this I would add a further thought. The process of assimilation was in actuality proceeding so rapidly and widely in the 1950s that even some scholars who were *not* escaping from their origins became doubtful of the enduring significance of ethnic differences. In the atmosphere of the late 1950s I myself found ethnic history less interesting than I had a decade earlier, and moved away from it.

Another factor that retarded the development of immigration history in the 1950s and 1960s was the paradigm that shaped the general contours of American historiography during those decades. Reacting against an earlier fascination with deep-cutting social conflicts, leading historians now reveled in discovering underlying uniformities and similarities.[8] By incorporating the immigrants within a national consensus, historians stripped away much of their differentness.

If young scholars were first attracted to the story of the immigrants—as I was—because it vibrated with dramatic social contrasts, a perspective that reduced the salience of those contrasts could only be discouraging.

Three examples suggest how the erosion occurred. During the 1950s Oscar Handlin turned against the view of the immigrant as an ousider, "a foreign element injected into American life."[9] Instead, he cast the immigrant as a type of American, undergoing as all Americans have a painful but liberating transition to modernity and freedom. By the 1960s Handlin was writing mostly about the American character and American institutions, and so were his students.

One of the earliest of those students, Rowland Berthoff, had begun by studying British and Slavic coal miners in America. In 1960, after some years of unexciting toil, Berthoff found his own way to display the whole of American history against a medieval background. He has never gone back to the mines.[10] At the University of Minnesota two years later Timothy L. Smith launched a wide-ranging study of eastern European immigrants with special reference to their assimilation. His chief contribution was to trace the immigrants' pursuit of the American dream back to predisposing experiences in Europe, experiences that made their entry into an American mainstream virtually foreordained.[11] This approach stimulated some valuable research, but it yielded a history that was peculiarly free from conflict. After a decade of study of the history of migration, Smith returned to the history of religious beliefs.

Thus for several decades the leading scholars in American immigration history emitted an ambivalent message. They called for research in a new field that seemed strikingly different from what historians had customarily studied, yet the lessons they extracted from it simply reinforced the conventional wisdom. Historians brought a new group of characters onto the stage; but the new characters usually behaved in accordance with traditional scripts. Immigration historians needed a perspective that could accentuate the distinctiveness and therefore the differentness of their subjects.

Not until the late 1960s did such perspectives become widely available. Against a tumultuous background of riots and protests the consensus paradigm was severely shaken. A new insistence on the power and persistence of the ethnic bond came to the fore.

Again social scientists led the way. Nathan Glazer and Daniel P. Moynihan inaugurated in 1963 a sustained critique of the melting-pot idea, a critique that became more and more insistent in the late sixties and early seventies. *Beyond the Melting Pot* argued that Americans are not and never have been a single people. Ethnic differences, originating in peculiar cultural inheritances, become fortified in the course of time by diverse economic and political allegiances. Ethnic groups survive not only as cultural vehicles but also as interest groups.[12] Here was a perspective that young historians, disillusioned with the promise of assimilation and aroused by the collapse of consensus, had been waiting for.

The resulting production of specialized scholarship on dozens of American ethnic groups has been abundant; and most of this outpouring has concentrated on the urban world from which our younger historians now largely derive. Even some of the earliest immigrant groups — the Palatine Germans and the French Huguenots — have now been studied in urban settings.[13] It is not easy to say what general conclusions these studies yield, but four special features that many of them share may be identified.

*1. Intra-ethnic conflicts.* Historians during the last fifteen years have diligently explored many disputes and rivalries within groups previously seen as more cohesive: struggles between generations among the Japanese, between tongs and other rival societies among the Chinese, between secular nationalist and Roman Catholic leaders among the Poles, between Uptown and Downtown Jews, between socialist Finns and church Finns, and so on.[14] Ethnic scholarship flourished in the 1970s as a means of particularizing identities. It exposed the cleavages that abstract ideological labels had obscured — labels such as American, Catholic, Indian, Negro, or even German-American and Italian-American. What mattered now was the tangible community of shared experience within sub-groups like Italian-American working-class women or the members of a German Catholic parish. Accordingly, serious scholarship did not often substitute an idealized ethnic nationalism for the Americanism it was undercutting. Some of the more fervent ethnic studies programs failed to appreciate the double-edged character of this particularizing imperative which made the divisions within an ethnic sector as vivid and significant as its overall identity. But a recognition that internal conflict is part of the life of every community was widely characteristic of the scholarship of this period.

2. *Contrasting responses of different ethnic groups to the American milieu.* Until the 1960s immigration historians had generally avoided making comparisons between ethnic groups. Such comparisons were thought to be invidious, potentially inflammatory, and misleading in view of the presumed dominance of environment in human affairs. *Boston's Immigrants* had featured a striking cultural contrast between the Irish and the Yankees, but Handlin had thereafter shifted to a more inclusive style of generalization, and the contrast was not followed up. But the pluralist mood of the 1960s finally legitimized the explicit examination of ethnic differences, and Glazer and Moynihan in *Beyond the Melting Pot* provided a bold example of the attractions as well as the dangers of such inquiries.

Simultaneously the opportunity materialized to probe these ethnic responses to American life at an altogether new level of scholarly rigor. The sudden popularity of quantitative methods, which historians had not hitherto used, enabled them to investigate the strategies of different groups in a way that demanded a hearing. The ethnocultural school of political historians, springing from the pioneering work of Lee Benson and Samuel P. Hays in the early 1960s, made clear how the cultural and religious traditions of various groups affected their political behavior.[15] From the point of view of the immigration historian much of this work had an important limitation. It was designed to explain how the American political system has worked; it was not intended to contribute to a larger history of the ethnic groups, and thus it did not probe the relation of politics to other aspects of their communal life. But historians who are primarily interested in ethnicity have begun to do just that.[16]

Another quantitative discipline that has encouraged the comparative study of ethnic groups is historical demography. Beginning with Stephan Thernstrom's doctoral dissertation, *Poverty and Progress* (1964), historians learned how to use unpublished census schedules and other records of private life to reconstruct the decisions that immigrants and others made about the size and character of their families, the education of their children, and the work they did. Thernstrom showed that the Irish differed significantly from the older American working class in the trade-off they made between education and the acquisition of property. Josef Barton then showed that the Slovaks differed in similar ways from Italians and Rumanians, and so on.[17]

These quantitative studies of mobility and adaptation addressed a central question that had fueled immigration history from the beginning. How have immigrants joined in the American pursuit of success, and to what avail? Measuring the material and social advancement of one generation over the previous one was extremely fashionable for a few years but then seemed increasingly out of place in a climate of opinion that scorned the old myths of assimilation and progress. After the mid-seventies a reaction against mobility studies set in. This happened, I believe, because such studies demonstrated too much success to fit the prevailing critique of the melting pot. Mobility studies had been born out of a sympathy for failure as much as a respect for success; they had offered a means of putting defeat and achievement side by side. Pluralistic historians cooled rapidly toward such studies when Andrew Greeley and Thomas Sowell used them to demonstrate that all ethnic groups succeed in America sooner or later.[18]

3. *A search for ethnic continuities.* In challenging the homogenizing myth of the American melting pot, immigra-

tion historians in the last two decades have looked hard for distinctive traditions, customs, and capabilities that did not yield easily to assimilative pressures but instead sustained a group in its encounter with a new and alien land. None of our immigration historians has produced a study of cultural continuity that is as powerful as Lawrence Levine's *Black Culture and Black Consciousness* or as imaginative as Herbert Gutman's *The Black Family in Slavery and Freedom*,[19] but many have worked along the same lines. Some have examined sympathetically the continuities imbedded in religious beliefs and institutions. Others have shown how sturdily the immigrant family coped with the shocks of migration and how strongly it molded the next generation. In what may be the finest book in this mode, *From Italy to San Francisco*, Dino Cinel takes a dialectical approach to continuity and change, pointing to ways in which Italian emigrants strove to hold on to a crumbling world and in doing so found the strength to make a new one.[20]

Numerous historians have traced ethnic continuities into the sphere of work—some to explain the immigrants' choice of occupations, others to account for the way workers responded to the kind of discipline they encountered in factories and mines. Especially influential has been Herbert Gutman's theory that what he calls "premodern values," brought to industrial America by a constant influx of newcomers, account for much of the resistance of workers to employer demands.[21]

*4. The relation of ethnicity to class.* The fascination of many historians in the late 1960s and 1970s with questions of exploitation and injustice inevitably called attention to the problematic relation between ethnic loyalties and class struggles. Following up ideas that Gutman borrowed from E. P. Thompson, historians of labor and of radicalism have probed diligently for the contributions specific ethnic groups have made to wider movements of social protest.[22] This line of inquiry meets considerable resistance from more traditional Marxists, who regard the emphasis on culture and ethnicity as romantic traditionalism and propose that labor history should concern itself more largely with political and economic power.[23]

While labor historians have disagreed about the importance of ethnicity, as a group they have been fully aware of the significance of the issues it poses for them. Immigration historians have been more parochial. Few of them, at least until recently, have looked squarely at the problem of class. In the 1980s this situation has begun to change. Independently of one another, John Bodnar and Olivier Zunz have proposed what seem to me exciting new interpretations of the coalescence of previously distinct ethnic groups into a white working class in the twentieth century.[24] Their interest in class *formation* can lead us beyond the labor historian's preoccupation with class *antagonisms*. Nevertheless, it remains true that immigration historians, unlike their colleagues in labor history, have not yet joined in any ongoing debate or theoretical argument on the interaction in American history between ethnicity and class. Why this is so deserves an explanation.

A simple answer might be that the influence of Marxism and other economic theories has long given labor history an aggressively interpretive edge that immigration history does not have. Immigration history has drawn on the less systematic concepts of empirical sociology. For immigration historians the basic question has always been the question of assimilation—the extent and direction of it, resistance to it, and myths about it.[25] In asking this question immigration historians have ordinarily concentrated on the immigrants' behavior and have tended to view American society "as a constituted and integral whole."[26] Understanding the changing structure of the larger society has not been, for immigration historians, a major objective. For labor historians it has.

As a means of contrasting the intellectual antecedents of two fields that now find themselves occupying common ground in the study of the American city, this explanation will do well enough. But something more should be said to account for the special condition of immigration historiography in the 1960s and 1970s. Historians of American ethnic groups during those years were simply less interested in the shape and structure of the host society than their predecessors had been. Under the spur of the ethnic revival, historians turned inward. Each tended to become a specialist in one particular group. In studying the chosen group, scholars reaped a harvest of knowledge about specific ethnic institutions, responses, and attainments. As to how those phenomena might have altered a larger context, very little was said.

The exceptional attraction of this internal approach to immigration history in the period just past becomes dramatically apparent in looking back at the four features of the period that I have just reviewed. The study of intra-ethnic conflicts, the comparative study of immigrant reactions to the American environment, and the search for ethnic continuities: all three of these features gave priority to what was happening within the experience of particular groups. The fourth feature — relating ethnicity to class — leads outward from the ethnic community to the larger society; but most of that job was not done by immigration historians. All in all, it seems fair to say that during the ethnic revival the scholars who opened to us so much of the inner world of the immigrants left their impact on America largely unexamined. In the 1980s a renewed assessment of how immigration and ethnicity have affected other aspects of American life belongs near the top of the agenda of immigration historians.

II

Rather than survey the numerous ways in which the impact of immigrants on urban America needs reappraisal, I have chosen in the remainder of this essay to dwell on one that has never received the attention it deserves. People make themselves felt in a society on many different levels, some complex and subtle, others blatantly obvious; some fully intentional, others unplanned and unforeseen. The most forceful and outspoken demands for power or influence occur when previously apathetic or uninvolved people are aroused to feverish activity and intense commitment. This is what I mean by ethnic mobilization. It is a good place to begin to look at the immigrant as a causal agent in American history.

In recent years the concept of mobilization has come into fairly widespread use in political science and sociology to designate the process by which submerged elements in society attain political consciousness and begin to make political demands.[27] Historians have occasionally employed the term "ethnic mobilization" in talking in a very general way about the formation of group consciousness. One speaks, for example, of the "ethnic mobilization of what became America's immigrant peoples" as beginning "in their homelands."[28] For my purpose ethnic mobilization does not refer to the genesis of ethnic consciousness or to its earliest political expression. Instead, I have in mind a more advanced stage of militancy.

Not every ethnic group in America has experienced a militant phase, nor have all sections of a group participated in the militancy when it occurs. But mobilization can be a contagious process, and I shall therefore concentrate on those dramatic occasions in American history when two or more ethnic minorities have joined in a common struggle. On such occasions mobilization sweeps across some ethnic boundaries, then stops at others, and thus reveals like a bolt of lightning the geography of discontent. To study ethnic mobilization as historians have studied other recurrent phenomena, watching it rise and fall, spread and contract, and take new forms as it taps new demands, is to observe how insecure minorities have striven at certain times to shape the course of history.

Since mobilization requires an internal change in the people it activates, one might suppose that it should have attracted considerable interest during the ethnic revival. That it did not may be partly attributable to the conventions that govern the writing of ethnic histories. The prevailing historiographical convention assumes that each group has its own separate history. That history is thought to consist of certain prescribed stages, which vary little from one group to another. The common pattern begins with the origins of the group, the reasons for its departure from the homeland, and the form its migration took. The second stage is the creation of a community: finding an area of settlement, gaining a livelihood, and transplanting essential institutions. In the third stage the ethnic community matures. The historian accordingly devotes successive chapters to a topical treatment of various aspects of its developed life. The fourth and last stage concerns the survival and/or decline of the ethnic group in later generations. Mobilization can sometimes be discovered, if the reader ferrets it out, in aspects of the third stage and even the fourth; but the overall sequence of stages does not lead us to expect it. Quite the reverse: the history of each single group unfolds through an inner dialectic of growth and adaptation. Mobilization, however, springs from external incitements that strike a group in a particular state of ethnic readiness. To study mobilization is to study the foreign relations of ethnic groups with one another. It is to move decisively beyond the particularistic parameters of the immigration history inspired by the ethnic revival.

To readers of Scandinavian background a warning is in order. In what follows, the Finns are the only Scandinavian nationality who play a prominent role. Other Scandinavians are conspicuous by their near-invisibility. Although further investigation may show that I have unjustly neglected some Norwegian or Swedish involvement in inter-ethnic mobilization, on the surface the very limited participation of Scandinavian Americans in the great episodes of ethnic assertiveness seems an important and hitherto unnoticed feature of their American experience.

III

Mobilization depends crucially on leadership. It is hardly surprising that the earliest significant mobilization of European minorities occurred in the sphere in which a vigorous inter-ethnic leadership first came into being. Only in their religion did the immigrants in antebellum America have a leadership willing and able to challenge existing institutions. In the 1840s and 1850s Catholic immigrants rallied behind their priests and bishops to oppose the Protestant character of public education in towns and cities where they were sufficiently numerous to have some effect.

Surprisingly little is known about Catholic efforts to alter the public schools in the mid-nineteenth century or about the counter-mobilization of urban Protestants in the Know-Nothing movement. Although we now have good studies of the development of public education in those years and some valuable political analysis of the Know-Nothing party,[29] the basic confrontation of Catholic and Protestant has not been reexamined on a national scale since Ray Billington wrote *The Protestant Crusade* in 1938. What we know is that a tremendous surge in the growth of the Catholic population—increasing 142 percent in the 1840s alone—coincided with a growing belief among older Americans in the necessity of a unified public school system to maintain a stabilizing morality in a highly volatile society. The common school emerged in the mid-nineteenth century as one of the essential symbols of American nationality. Immigrant Catholic leaders, however, loathed the state schools that threatened to separate children from their parents and their pastors. In the early 1850s Catholic clergy and the Democratic legislators who represented them began to agitate for a cessation of Bible-reading in public schools and the allocation of a share of the public school funds to parochial schools so that the taxes Catholics paid could be used to support their own institutions.[30]

Nearly everywhere these demands were repelled. In the cities Protestants remained in control of the public schools. Although this first mobilization seemed to fail, the bloodshed and animosity it produced taught both sides a lesson in pragmatic accommodation. Catholic authorities were much more cautious thereafter about taking political initiatives. School boards, for their part, gradually made the public schools more attractive to Catholic parents by informal concessions on curricula and textbooks.[31]

Another major mobilization of immigrants in defense of their culture occurred from 1889 to 1893. This time the immigrant coalition was wider than it had been in the 1850s.

German Lutherans were roused and joined forces with Irish, German, Polish, and French-Canadian Catholics. The basic alignment of immigrants upholding their specific heritage against Protestant nationalists who insisted on greater cultural uniformity was unchanged, but the issues were broader. Prohibition was at least as important as the school question, which entailed for many Lutherans and Catholics a special struggle to retain their language. But the chief difference between the mid-century phase and this later phase of cultural mobilization was the strictly defensive character of the latter. By 1889 the immigrants were simply protecting the institutions they had painfully built in the preceding decades.

Why did the school problem revive in the late eighties, unprompted by the kind of initiatives that immigrant leaders had taken in the 1850s? One explanation stresses Anglo-Protestant alarm at a vigorous expansion of the Catholic school system, which the bishops had ordered at the Third Plenary Council of Baltimore in 1884.[32] Another explanation, one that accounts better for the prominence of German Protestants in the new mobilization, is that the outside world was closing in on ethnic enclaves in a sudden, unexpected way.

Two sets of demands for greater state control of private life converged on Republican state legislators in the late 1880s. One set, originating among evangelical Protestant women and reformers, called for some form of local or statewide prohibition of the liquor traffic. According to Richard Jensen, the prohibition question became the paramount local issue, year in and year out, throughout most of the Midwest and large parts of the East.[33] A second set of demands, though less noisy, was actually more explosive. It came from professional educators who wanted more effective supervision and centralization in education. Compulsory school laws, already enacted in half the states, had never been enforced. At least partly to enforce school attendance and prevent child labor, Illinois and Wisconsin in 1889 enacted laws requiring children to attend a school approved by their local board of education. The laws further stipulated that certain basic subjects should be taught in English.[34] To ethnic groups whose survival might depend on the local autonomy American institutions had always allowed, prohibition and the regulation of private schools seemed frontal attacks on their culture and their rights as parents.

The new school legislation envisaged only limited regulation. Why it deeply outraged vast numbers of immigrants may be hard to understand unless one bears in mind the wider alarm in late nineteenth-century America over a loss of independence and a decline in local autonomy. Old-stock Americans as well as immigrants felt that great forces beyond their control were invading their communities.[35] The intrusive, centralizing state that evangelical Republicans sponsored presented to Catholic and Lutheran minorities a threat similar to that which the "trusts" were beginning to pose to other Americans. Through the Democratic party the immigrants rallied to defend their "personal liberty."

Their triumph was stunning but short-lived. Beginning in 1889 with dazzling victories in Iowa and New Jersey, the Democrats swept state after state where temperance and school issues were central. They repealed the new school laws in Illinois and Wisconsin, turned back the prohibition movement, and in 1892 rolled up huge majorities in German, Swedish, Italian, Polish, and Bohemian districts.[36] For the time being, the parochial schools and the saloons were safe. After repelling the Republican onslaught, though, the immigrant coalition quickly broke up. Quarrels between the major ethnic groups within the Catholic Church, having subsided somewhat with the united front of the early nineties, flared up with new bitterness. In politics the depression of 1893 sidetracked evangelical moral reform and turned attention to national economic issues on which there was no ethnic consensus.[37] The party loyalties of many immigrant voters weakened. When the depression lifted, the political system of the northern states was firmly in the grasp of a nationally oriented middle class. In most of the larger cities outside the South the Republican party had gained a clear predominance. Among the ethnic groups that had supported the

Democratic party so vigorously in the early nineties voting
now declined substantially; the newer immigrants entering
the United States voted even less.[38] The mobilization of ethnic dissent by a major political party was out of the question
for a generation.

So the cultural battles of the nineteenth century subsided
in a tolerable truce, and ethnic militancy shifted to different
terrain. While the political defense of religion and culture
slackened, many immigrants threw themselves into movements for control of the workplace. They endeavored to
mobilize as a class. Whether to join in the struggle or to stand
aloof was the first critical decision that the new immigrants
from southern and eastern Europe had to make after deciding
to stay in America.

At least from the 1840s European immigrants had decisively shaped the American labor movement. Since many
northern European immigrants arrived in America with experience in industrial crafts and with a well developed class
consciousness, they joined trade unions readily and rose
quickly to leadership. The Germans, for example, comprised
36 percent of the Chicago trade unions in 1886, though they
were only 22.5 percent of the Chicago working class.[39] But
while the immigrants brought stamina and dedication to
American unions, disharmony between ethnic groups discouraged industry-wide organization. Working-class action
was confined to the narrow and immediate objectives of au-
tonomous craft unions. In 1897 just 2 percent of those gain-
fully employed outside of agriculture were organized.

By the turn of the century this modest figure doubled; a
momentous change was under way. Between 1897 and 1919,
two great waves of unrest rippled through the motley ranks
of semiskilled and unskilled workers from southern and eastern Europe. Total union membership in the United States
soared from 447,000 to more than five million, or about 16
percent of the labor force outside of agriculture.[40] The first of
the two waves of unrest, extending from 1897 to 1904, began among the Slavic coal miners in the anthracite fields of
eastern Pennsylvania, where the uncharacteristic persever-

ance of the strikers apparently owed a good deal to a legacy
of peasant insurgency which rebellious priests who formed
the Polish National Catholic Church brought from Galicia.[41]
The second wave began in 1909 among immigrant steel
workers at McKees Rock, Pennsylvania, and among Jewish
and Italian women in the shirtwaist shops of New York.
Here again the embattled workers had at the outset, within
their own ethnic groups, leaders who brought experiences
and radical convictions from the Old World. The McKees
Rock workers included several veterans of European radical
movements, who constituted themselves an executive committee to stiffen the equivocal stand of the American skilled
workers. The shirtwaist-makers gained the backing of the
rising socialist movement on the lower East Side and most especially of new emigrés who came to America after the failure of the Russian Revolution of 1905.[42]

To stress radical leadership is inevitably to call attention
to the gathering strength of the Socialist party during these
years, and particularly to the importance of its foreign language federations. The largest of the federations, proportion-
ately, were Finnish, Slovenian, and Jewish. They grew not
because of, but almost in spite of, the national leadership of
the Socialist party, which did little in the early years of the
twentieth century to cultivate its new-immigrant constituen-
cies. Their activation sprang directly from European socialism through the migration of young Marxist firebrands who,
on fleeing to the United States to escape arrest or military service, established the first socialist clubs and newspapers for
their respective nationalities.[43] World War I brought this immigrant radicalism to a culmination. The foreign language
federations swelled to 35 percent of Socialist party membership in 1917, then to 53 percent in 1919. Carried over into
peacetime, the apocalyptic mood of the war years nerved the
immigrant masses to attempt against all odds to unionize the
steel industry.[44] When the great steel strike of 1919 failed,
immigrant radicalism collapsed. The era of class mobilization
was over.

How shall we account for the fervent militancy of those

years? Obviously the presence of dynamic leadership will not by itself explain the tremendous response that came forth from hundreds of thousands of vulnerable little people, who put their livelihood, and in some cases their lives as well, on the line. Historians are far from having answers to such questions, but there may be an intriguing clue in the curious fact that a third type of ethnic mobilization emerged in the climactic years of class mobilization and reached a peak at the same time. This was nationalist mobilization.

At various times in American history members of one or another ethnic group have organized to affect the destiny of their homeland.[45] These efforts may be intense, but ordinarily they occur separately and have only scattered, episodic effects. The First World War was unique in exciting passionate nationalist movements among a dozen ethnic groups simultaneously, each resonating to the others and all together awakening in the usually fatalistic immigrant masses a level of collective expectation that was unprecedented. Thousands of Poles, Serbs, Czechs, Slovaks, and Jews returned to the Old World to fight for the nationalist cause, many of them in special units whose exploits were followed eagerly by their compatriots in America. Although the number of German-American publications declined, the rest of the foreign-language press increased about 20 percent between 1914 and 1918. Nationalist heroes like Ignace Paderewski, the famous Polish pianist, and Thomas Masaryk, the exiled philosopher-statesman of the Czechs, toured American cities. In Washington ethnic lobbying designed to influence the peace settlement became, for Jewish Zionists, Ukrainians, Yugoslavs, Italians, Greeks, and others, a new style of politics.[46]

None of these mobilizations was more impressive than that of eastern European Jews in behalf of a Jewish homeland in Palestine. For almost two decades before World War I little Zionist societies had been helpless in the face of the Jewish immigrants' overwhelming preoccupation with their new American home. "America is our Zion," intoned the principal Jewish spokesmen, to which the socialists added, "The world is our fatherland." But the outbreak of war created such enormous needs for relief, both in Palestine and in eastern Europe, that anxiety about divided loyalties was swept aside. In this context of concern for fellow Jews dislocated by war, Zionism acquired an American relevance. Linking itself with the Wilsonian ideal of national self-determination, the goal of a Palestinian homeland for Jews suddenly seemed almost as American as apple pie. It gained the endorsement of President Wilson, widespread public sympathy, and the fervent support of the Jewish immigrant masses, who began through Zionism to exercise a new influence in American Jewish affairs.[47]

Similarly among American blacks the First World War transformed a previously inconsequential ethnic nationalism into a spectacular mass movement. Through Marcus Garvey the flickering vision of an African homeland suddenly became, in the black ghettoes of America, a palpable prospect. Like the socialist agitators who came in the same years from southern and eastern Europe, Garvey arrived in 1916 from Jamaica to proselytize among West Indians in Harlem. His primary object was to gain support for a conservative racial improvement society he had founded at home. Only after the United States entered the war did Garvey comprehend the messianic power of the nationalist idea. Identifying Africa as the subjugated homeland of blacks everywhere, Garvey began to link the redemption of his race in America to the creation of a powerful black state in Africa. "The Irish, the Jews, the East Indians and all other oppressed peoples are getting together to demand from their oppressors Liberty, Justice, Equality," he pointed out, "and we now call upon the four hundred millions of Negro People of the world to do likewise."[48] Before Garvey, the principal black protest movements had not reached much beyond an educated elite. It remained for a flamboyant Jamaican immigrant — attuned to the international scale of the ethnic ferment in American cities — to galvanize a million urban blacks into collective action.[49]

One of the attractions of nationalist mobilization was the usually welcome visibility it gave to ethnic groups yearning for greater recognition on the crowded stage of American life. Rallying opinion and raising funds for overseas projects produced countless public demonstrations: receptions for representatives from the homeland, mass meetings to pass resolutions and secure pledges, musical festivals to display a cultural heritage, and, above all, parades. In reporting these events, general-circulation newspapers were sometimes noticing for the first time the local presence of an entire community that had earlier been largely invisible.[50] After the United States entered the war, government agencies worked to orchestrate the ethnic campaigns in the interest of a united war effort; that led to still greater visibility. When Liberty Loan officials in 1918 organized a monster Fourth of July parade up Fifth Avenue in New York, the notion of demonstrating the loyalty and affinity of every nationality to the American cause proved so popular that the original roster of forty-four participating groups expanded to sixty-four. A ten-hour procession, numbering altogether 109,415 marchers and 158 bands, included American Indians, Haitians, Liberians, Japanese, Zionists for the Jewish Nation, Parsees, Russians, Carpathians, and Americans of German Origin. The Poles won first prize for the best floats, but the judges also commended the Assyrians, the Bolivians, and the Americans of German Origin.[51]

In this wartime tumult of reverberating patriotisms, what scope was left for the mobilization of a working class along lines of economic self-interest? The standard view of American history, with its heavy emphasis on the repression of dissent during the war years, suggests that class action was sharply contained. It is true that the war brought governmental intervention and manipulation here too; but whether that vitiated labor's organizing drive is another question. While federal authorities scourged the socialists and syndicalists who opposed the war, the great majority of unions received unprecedented governmental support. After a pause on the eve of the war, the mobilization of immigrant labor resumed at a high level through unionization of war industries. The appointment of many labor leaders to governmental boards and commissions gave the labor movement a new kind of civic recognition, which prompted some unions to claim (to the disgust of employers) that Uncle Sam was on their side.[52]

Even the illiberal aspects of wartime nationalism did not immediately dampen the fervor of class mobilization. To be sure, nationalism competed against a radical class consciousness for the loyalty of the immigrant masses; a deadly enmity divided nationalists from socialists in many ethnic groups. But the rivalry temporarily stimulated both forms of consciousness. In the 1917 municipal elections Socialist candidates running on anti-war platforms made heavy gains in large industrial cities like New York, Chicago, and Cleveland, where European immigrants were strongly entrenched.[53] The class and nationalist mobilizations of the Progressive Era drew a common strength from a basic urge to change the world. Both movements inspired a collective vision—one promising to realize in a new way the old dream of America, the other to redeem the homeland as well. The two awakenings shared a millennial hope, and thus each contributed to the ambiance in which the other flourished.

It is little wonder, then, that ethnic radicalism and ethnic nationalism went down in a common defeat in 1919 and 1920. For a decade thereafter both labor union membership and the number of strikes dwindled year by year.[54] Within the various ethnic groups radical organizations withered; nationalist agitation virtually collapsed. Even the Zionist movement, now greatly shrunken, survived only by becoming a purely philanthropic venture. Most historians have attributed the decline of radicalism to repression, while blaming war-weariness and factional quarrels for the fading of homeland issues.[55] But simultaneous demobilization on both fronts points also to a common cause: a general surrender of grandiose ideals.

What remained for the immigrants and their children was their lives in America. Although limited in many ways by prejudice, poverty, and cultural barriers, the southern and eastern European groups gradually acquired—through home ownership, naturalization, and education—a modicum of stability and social integration. By the end of the 1920s a second generation, born in America, substantially outnumbered the immigrants themselves in most of the new-immigrant communities. As the second generation moved out of the narrow world of its parents, it became the spearhead of the last and greatest mobilization of European immigrants. To use the language of the day, this was a mobilization of New Americans, pushing for wider access and fuller acceptance in the world around them.[56]

The origin of this last mobilization lay in an experience no previous generation of European immigrants had undergone. The New Americans grew up in a country that had turned decisively against large-scale immigration, a country that no longer wanted any more of their kind. The American-born children of the immigrants felt the stigma of inferiority more keenly than their parents, for the children were largely Americanized and had little consciousness of an older heritage.[57] Thus the New Americans sought dignity and inclusion, and to a remarkable degree during the 1930s and 1940s they attained these goals. They succeeded in part because their dissatisfactions converged with the economic discontent of other significant groups. But that convergence in turn was fashioned by the instrumentalities of earlier ethnic mobilizations, now reshaped and connected: the Democratic party and the labor movement.

The new mobilization began in 1928 as a powerful revival of opposition to prohibition on the part of urban Democrats. Astute observers could sense, however, that the immense enthusiasm for Alfred E. Smith in the cities where the foreign stock congregated expressed not only a cultural protest against "puritan" morality but also a wider yearning to escape from social subordination and to claim for their own kind a full civic recognition. "Here is no trivial conflict," wrote Walter Lippmann. "Here are the new people, clamoring . . . and the older people, defending their household goods. The rise of Al Smith has made the conflict plain, and his career has come to involve . . . the destiny of American civilization."[58]

If the dramatic urban turnout for Smith had simply been a cultural mobilization in defense of a traditional way of life, it would have ended with the repeal of prohibition and the onset of new issues, just as the mobilization of the late 1880s dissipated in 1893. This time, however, the mobilization did not end. The turnout for Democratic candidates in the foreign-stock districts of major cities continued to soar, especially through an outpouring of new voters who had been too apathetic or too young to vote before 1928.[59] Even the foreign-language press, in which Republican interests were strongly entrenched, moved decisively into a reconstructed Democratic party. The number of foreign-language Republican newspapers dropped from 57 percent of those identifying with some party in 1923 to 40 percent in 1932. Over the same span of time socialist and other radical journals declined from 30 to 16 percent of the total. Democratic newspapers increased from 11 percent to 43 percent. Four years later, in 1936, the Democratic preponderance became overwhelming.[60]

In recapturing many cities from Republican control the New Americans contributed a crucial element to the election of Franklin D. Roosevelt. Victory at the polls supplied the impetus to resume unionization of the mass-production industries. Roosevelt's triumph in 1932 led swiftly to a federal guarantee of the right of workers to organize and bargain through their own representatives. This awakened the ravaged unions and stirred in unorganized workers a fitful, uncertain courage to test anew their collective strength. "The President wants you to join the union," organizers told the Slavic miners in the Appalachians.[61]

But a second and stronger demonstration of electoral might was necessary to unleash a major economic mobilization. When labor unrest in 1933-1934 produced only minimal changes, aspiration and militancy flowed back into the political system. Not until Roosevelt's spectacular reelection in 1936 by majorities that reached from 70 to 80 percent in the most heavily ethnic cities did the New Americans become fully conscious of their power.[62] Just two weeks after the election, mass sit–down strikes began in the automobile industry. During the following year the American labor movement made the greatest gains in its history.[63]

In contrast to previous ethnic mobilizations, that of the New Americans is difficult to classify. Its varied initiatives appeared sometimes as cultural, sometimes as political, sometimes as economic. They often blended indistinguishably with those of other disadvantaged elements that were also bent on reducing inequalities of power and origin. Yet the basic concern of the New Americans was not equality. It was incorporation, and that is why the militant self–assertion that impelled their mobilization was infused with a passionate Americanism. The Congress of Industrial Organizations appealed to workers with fluttering American flags and patriotic songs that invoked visions of national fraternity. Even the Communists enthusiastically adopted the language of Americanism. In 1936 the *New York Times* noted that the unrest in the steel industry was part of the same "nation-building . . . process" that was putting husky young men with Slavic and Italian names on the leading college football teams. The workers in the steel mills, the *Times* reflected, were growing more discontented as they grew more American.[64]

To view the industrial and political struggles of the 1930s in this ethnic perspective goes far toward clarifying the paradoxical mixture of conservatism and protest that distinguished the American New Deal among the major responses in the Western World to the Great Depression.

## Notes

[1]William I. Thomas and Florian Znaniecki, *The Polish Peasant in Europe and America*, 5 vols. (Chicago, 1918).

[2]Allan H. Spear, "Marcus Lee Hansen and the Historiography of Immigration," in *Wisconsin Magazine of History*, 44 (Summer, 1961), 258–268; Carlton C. Qualey, "Marcus Lee Hansen," in *Midcontinent American Studies Journal*, 8 (Fall, 1967), 18–25. A more sympathetic account, full of new information and insight, is Moses Rischin, "Marcus Lee Hansen: America's First Transethnic Historian," in Richard L. Bushman *et al.*, eds., *Uprooted*

*Americans: Essays to Honor Oscar Handlin* (Boston, 1979), 319–347. For Blegen's rural sympathies see especially his collected essays, *Grass Roots History* (Minneapolis, 1947), and his personal memoir, "The Saga of Saga Hill," in *Minnesota History*, 29 (December, 1948), 289–299. Another member of this early group of immigration historians was George M. Stephenson, who like Hansen came from a small town in Iowa and was a student of Frederick Jackson Turner. Stephenson's *A History of American Immigration, 1820–1924* (Boston, 1926), although the first survey of the subject by a professional historian, was less important than his later work, *The Religious Aspects of Swedish Immigration: A Study of Immigrant Churches* (Minneapolis, 1932).

[3]For a fuller assessment of Oscar Handlin's *Boston's Immigrants: A Study of Acculturation* (Cambridge, Massachusetts, 1941) see my review of the revised edition (Cambridge, 1959) in *New England Quarterly*, 32 (September, 1959), 411–413.

[4]Moses Rischin, *The Promised City: New York's Jews 1870–1914* (Cambridge, Massachusetts, 1962), is reexamined as a classic work in *American Jewish History*, 73 (December, 1983). Compare with Robert Ernst, *Immigrant Life in New York City, 1825–1863* (New York, 1949).

[5]Handlin's students included Rowland T. Berthoff (discussed below), Arthur Mann, Barbara M. Solomon, and J. Joseph Huthmacher. On Curti's interest in the immigrant theme see Merle Curti and Kendall Birr, "The Immigrant and the American Image in Europe, 1860–1914," in *Mississippi Valley Historical Review*, 37 (September, 1950), 203–230. Among Curti's students who were drawn to immigration history were Edward G. Hartmann, Rudolph Vecoli, A. William Hoglund, and myself.

[6]The special contribution of overseas scholars is suggested in *Perspectives in American History*, 7 (1973), titled "Dislocation and Emigration: The Social Background of American Immigration."

[7]Rudolph Vecoli, "Ethnicity: A Neglected Dimension of American History," in Herbert J. Bass, ed., *The State of American History* (Chicago, 1970), 70–88. I have also relied on Vecoli's indispensable historiographical conspectus, "European Americans: From Immigrants to Ethnics," in William H. Cartwright and Richard L. Watson, Jr., eds., *The Reinterpretation of American History and Culture* (Washington, D.C., 1973), 81–112.

[8]John Higham, *History: Professional Scholarship in America* (Baltimore, 1983), 212–232.

[9]Oscar Handlin, "Immigration in American Life: A Reappraisal," in Henry Steele Commager, ed., *Immigration and American History: Essays in Honor of Theodore C. Blegen* (Minneapolis, 1961), 10. This essay elaborates programatically the point of view Handlin first stated in *The Uprooted: The Epic Story of the Great Migrations that Made the American People* (Boston, 1951).

[10]Rowland Berthoff's early work was *British Immigrants in Industrial America, 1790–1950* (Cambridge, Massachusetts, 1953) and "The Social Order of the Anthracite Region, 1825–1902," in *Pennsylvania Magazine of*

*History and Biography*, 89 (July, 1965), 261–291; the later work began with "The American Social Order: A Conservative Hypothesis," in *American Historical Review*, 65 (April, 1960), 495–514.

[11]Timothy L. Smith, "New Approaches to the History of Immigration in Twentieth-Century America," in *American Historical Review*, 71 (July, 1966), 1265–1279; "Immigrant Social Aspirations and American Education, 1880–1930," in *American Quarterly*, 21 (Fall, 1969), 523–543; "Religion and Ethnicity in America," in *American Historical Review*, 83 (December, 1978), 1155–1185.

[12]Nathan Glazer and Daniel P. Moynihan, *Beyond the Melting Pot: The Negroes, Puerto Ricans, Jews, Italians, and Irish of New York City* (Cambridge, Massachusetts, 1963). See also Glazer's later reflections on the book and the context in which it was written: "Pluralism and Ethnicity," in *Journal of American Ethnic History*, 1 (Fall, 1981), 43–55.

[13]Stephanie Grauman Wolf, *Urban Village: Population, Community, and Family Structure in Germantown, Pennsylvania, 1683–1800* (Princeton, 1977); Jon Butler, *The Huguenots in America: A Refugee People in New World Society* (Cambridge, Massachusetts, 1983).

[14]Roger Daniels, "The Japanese," and Robert F. Berkhofer, Jr., "Native Americans," in John Higham, ed., *Ethnic Leadership in America*, (Baltimore, 1978), 36–63, 119–149; Stanford M. Lyman, *Chinese Americans* (New York, 1974); Victor R. Greene, *For God and Country: The Rise of Polish and Lithuanian Ethnic Consciousness in America 1860–1910* (Madison, Wisconsin, 1975); Arthur A. Goren, "Jews," in Stephan Thernstrom, ed., *Harvard Encyclopedia of American Ethnic Groups* (Cambridge, Massachusetts, 1980), 571–598: Michael G. Karni and Douglas J. Ollila, eds., *For the Common Good: Finnish Immigrants and the Radical Response to Industrial America* (Superior, Wisconsin, 1977). See also articles in June Drenning Holmquist, ed., *They Chose Minnesota: A Survey of the State's Ethnic Groups* (St. Paul, Minnesota, 1981).

[15]Lee Benson, *The Concept of Jacksonian Democracy: New York as a Test Case* (Princeton, 1961); Samuel P. Hays, *American Political History as Social Analysis* (Knoxville, Tennessee, 1980); Samuel T. McSeveney, "Ethnic Groups, Ethnic Conflicts, and Recent Quantitative Research in American Political History," in *International Migration Review*, 7 (Spring, 1973), 14–33.

[16]Edward M. Levine, *The Irish and Irish Politicians* (Notre Dame, 1966); Ronald H. Bayor, *Neighbors in Conflict: The Irish, Germans, Jews, and Italians of New York City, 1929–1941* (Baltimore, 1978); Edward R. Kantowicz, *Polish-American Politics in Chicago, 1880–1940* (Chicago, 1975).

[17]Stephan Thernstrom, *Poverty and Progress: Social Mobility in a Nineteenth-Century City* (Cambridge, Massachusetts, 1964) and *The Other Bostonians: Poverty and Progress in the American Metropolis, 1880–1970* (Cambridge, Massachusetts, 1973); Josef Barton, *Peasants and Strangers: Italians, Rumanians, and Slovaks in an American City* (Cambridge, Massachusetts, 1975); Thomas Kessner, *The Golden Door: Italian and Jewish Immigrant Mobility in New York City, 1880–1915* (New York, 1977); Clyde and Sally

Griffen, *Natives and Newcomers: The Ordering of Opportunity in Mid-Nineteenth-Century Poughkeepsie* (Cambridge, Massachusetts, 1978). See also John Bodnar, Roger Simon, and Michael P. Weber, *Lives of Their Own: Blacks, Italians, and Poles in Pittsburgh, 1900–1960* (Urbana, 1982), and Jay P. Dolan, *The Immigrant Church: New York's Irish and German Catholics, 1815–1865* (Baltimore, 1975).

[18]Andrew M. Greeley, *The American Catholic: A Social Portrait* (New York, 1977); Thomas Sowell, *Ethnic America: A History* (New York, 1981).

[19]Lawrence Levine, *Black Culture and Black Consciousness: Afro-American Folk Thought from Slavery to Freedom* (New York, 1977); Herbert Gutman, *The Black Family in Slavery and Freedom, 1750–1925* (New York, 1976).

[20]Randall M. Miller and Thomas D. Marzik, eds., *Immigrants and Religion in Urban America* (Philadelphia, 1977); Richard L. Ehrlich, ed., *Immigrants in Industrial America, 1850–1920* (Charlottesville, 1977); Dino Cinel, *From Italy to San Francisco: The Immigrant Experience* (Stanford, 1982).

[21]Herbert Gutman, *Work, Culture, and Society in Industrializing America: Essays in American Working-Class and Social History* (New York, 1976); Wayne G. Broehl, Jr., *The Molly Maguires* (Cambridge, Massachusetts, 1965). On occupational choices, see Caroline Golab, *Immigrant Destinations* (Philadelphia, 1978); Virginia Yans-McLaughlin, *Family and Community: Italian Immigrants in Buffalo, 1880–1930* (Ithaca, 1978); Humbert S. Nelli, *The Business of Crime: Italians and Syndicate Crime in the United States* (Chicago, 1976).

[22]Eric Foner, "Class, Ethnicity, and Radicalism in the Gilded Age: The Land League and Irish-America," in Foner's *Politics and Ideology in the Age of the Civil War* (New York, 1980), 150–200; Dirk Hoerder, ed., *American Labor and Immigration History, 1877–1920s: Recent European Research* (Urbana, 1983); Melvyn Dubofsky, *When Workers Organize: New York City in the Progressive Era* (Amherst, Massachusetts, 1968). See also David Brody's pioneering monograph, *Labor in Crisis: The Steel Strike of 1919* (New York, 1965).

[23]David Montgomery, "Gutman's Nineteenth-Century America," in *Labor History*, 19 (Summer, 1978), 416–429; Elizabeth Fox-Genovese and Eugene D. Genovese, "The Political Crisis of Social History: A Marxian Perspective," in *Journal of Social History*, 10 (Winter, 1976), 205–220.

[24]John Bodnar, "Immigration, Kinship, and the Rise of Working-Class Realism in Industrial America," in *Journal of Social History*, 14 (September, 1980), 45–65, and *Workers' World: Kinship, Community, and Protest in an Industrial Society, 1900–1940* (Baltimore, 1982); Olivier Zunz, *The Changing Face of Inequality: Urbanization, Industrial Development, and Immigrants in Detroit, 1880–1920* (Chicago, 1982).

[25]Notice, for example, the title of Milton Gordon's extremely influential theoretical essay, *Assimilation in American Life: The Role of Race, Religion, and National Origins* (New York, 1964). The renewed importance of alternative theories of assimilation in the general studies published in the last several years is noted in John Higham, "Current Trends in the Study of

Ethnicity in the United States," in *Journal of American Ethnic History*, 2 (Fall, 1982), 5–15.

[26]John B. Jentz and Hartmut Keil, "From Immigrants to Urban Workers: Chicago's German Poor in the Gilded Age and Progressive Era, 1883–1908," in *Vierteljahrschrift für Sozial- und Wirtschaftsgeschichte*, 68 (1, 1981), 97.

[27]Karl Deutsch, "Social Mobilization and Political Development," in *American Political Science Review*, 55 (September, 1961), 493–514; Hubert M. Blalock, Jr., *Toward a Theory of Minority-Group Relations* (New York, 1967), 109–133, 139–142, 176–180.

[28]Smith, "Religion and Ethnicity in America," 1165–1167.

[29]Recent scholarship is expertly synthesized in Carl F. Kaestle, *Pillars of the Republic: Common Schools and American Society, 1780–1860* (New York, 1983). On nativism, see Michael F. Holt, "The Politics of Impatience: The Origins of Know-Nothingism," in *Journal of American History*, 60 (September, 1973), 309–331; and Jean H. Baker, *Ambivalent Americans: The Know-Nothing Party in Maryland* (Baltimore, 1977).

[30]Holt, "Politics of Impatience," 323–324; Vincent P. Lannie, "Alienation in America: The Immigrant Catholic and Public Education in Pre-Civil War America," in *Review of Politics*, 32 (October, 1970), 503–521. See also "The Catholic Church Blunders, 1850–1854," a commonly overlooked chapter in Ray Allen Billington's *The Protestant Crusade, 1800–1860: A Study of the Origins of American Nativism* (New York, 1938), 289–321. My statistics on Catholic population are from Gerald Shaughnessy, *Has the Immigrant Kept the Faith? A Study of Immigration and Catholic Growth in the United States, 1790–1920* (New York, 1925), 189, which shows for the 1840s the highest growth rate of any decade in the nineteenth or twentieth centuries.

[31]Charles Shanabruch, *Chicago's Catholics: The Evolution of an American Identity* (Notre Dame, 1981), 24–25, 28–30; James W. Sanders, *The Education of an Urban Minority: Catholics in Chicago, 1833–1965* (New York, 1977), 22–25, 125. See also Kaestle, *Pillars of the Republic*, 170–171. The bloodiest incident is reported by Wallace S. Hutcheon, Jr., "The Louisville Riots of August, 1855," in *Register of the Kentucky Historical Society*, 1971, 150–172.

[32]Daniel F. Reilly, *The School Controversy (1891–1893)* (Washington, D.C., 1943); Sanders, *Education*, 33–35.

[33]Richard J. Jensen, *The Winning of the Midwest: Social and Political Conflict, 1886–1896* (Chicago, 1971), 70. See also Paul Kleppner, *The Third Electoral System, 1853–1892: Parties, Voters, and Political Cultures* (Chapel Hill, 1979), 298–356.

[34]Shanabruch, *Chicago's Catholics*, 59–62; *Proceedings of the National Educational Association, 1891*, 393–398; Roger E. Wyman, "Wisconsin Ethnic Groups and the Election of 1890," in *Wisconsin Magazine of History*, 51 (Summer, 1968), 269–294. For a concurrent struggle in Massachusetts, see Robert H. Lord et al., *History of the Archdiocese of Boston in the Various Stages of Its Developments, 1604 to 1943*, 3 (New York, 1944), 110–133.

[35]Here I have adapted and extended the familiar argument in Robert

H. Wiebe's *The Search for Order, 1877–1920* (New York, 1967), 44–55.

[36]John M. Allswang, *A House for All Peoples: Ethnic Politics in Chicago, 1890–1936* (Lexington, Kentucky, 1971), 25–33; Jensen, *Winning of the Midwest*, 89–177; Thomas C. Hunt, "The Bennett Law of 1890: Focus of Conflict Between Church and State in Education," in *Journal of Church and State*, 23 (Winter, 1981), 69–93.

[37]Shanabruch, *Chicago's Catholics*, 76, 93–104; Frederick C. Luebke, "German Immigrants and American Politics: Problems of Leadership, Parties, and Issues," in Randall Miller, ed., *Germans in America: Retrospect and Prospect* (Philadelphia, 1984), 67–68.

[38]Paul Kleppner, *Who Voted? The Dynamics of Electoral Turnout, 1870–1980* (New York, 1982), 57–58, 68–80; Carl N. Degler, "American Political Parties and the Rise of the City: An Interpretation," in *Journal of American History*, 51 (June, 1964), 46–49. See also the detailed case study in Marc Lee Raphael, *Jews and Judaism in a Midwestern Community: Columbus, Ohio, 1840–1975* (Columbus, 1979), 123–128.

[39]Hartmut Keil, "The German Immigrant Working Class of Chicago, 1875–90: Workers, Labor Leaders, and the Labor Movement," in Dirk Hoerder, ed., *American Labor and Immigration History, 1877–1920s: Recent European Research* (Urbana, 1983), 162–163; David Montgomery, "The Irish and the American Labor Movement," in David Noel Doyle and Dudley Edwards, eds., *America and Ireland, 1776–1976: The American Identity and the Irish Connection* (Westport, Connecticut, 1980), 205–218. There are perceptive overviews in Mike Davis, "Why the U.S. Working Class Is Different," in *New Left Review*, September–October, 1980, 3–44, and David Brody, "Labor," in Stephan Thernstrom, ed., *Harvard Encyclopedia of American Ethnic Groups*, (Cambridge, Massachusetts, 1980), 609–618.

[40]Leo Wolman, *The Growth of American Trade Unions 1880–1923* (New York, 1924), 33, 85. My percentages are calculated from figures on nonfarm workers in United States Bureau of the Census, *Historical Statistics of the United States, Colonial Times to 1970* (Washington, D.C., 1975), 134.

[41]Victor R. Greene, *The Slavic Community on Strike: Immigrant Labor in Pennsylvania Anthracite* (Notre Dame, 1968), 106, 141, 155; Ewa Krystyna Hauser, "Ethnicity and Class in a Polish American Community" (Ph.D. dissertation, The Johns Hopkins University, 1981), 13–27, 71–85.

[42]Melvyn Dubofsky, *We Shall Be All: A History of the Industrial Workers of the World* (Chicago, 1969), 203–205; Irving Howe, *World of Our Fathers* (New York, 1976), 290–304.

[43]Charles Leinenweber, "The American Socialist Party and 'New' Immigrants," in *Science and Society*, 32 (Winter, 1968), 1–25; Melvyn Dubofsky, "Success and Failure of Socialism in New York City, 1900–1918: A Case Study," in *Labor History*, 9 (Fall, 1968), 361–375; Karni and Ollila, *For the Common Good*, 14–15, 65–71, 94–95, 132, 168–175. A similar beginning of Croatian socialism in America is described in *Radnicka Straza*, August 12, 1910, and January 7, 1914, in Chicago Foreign

Language Press Survey, Reel 8, I E (Immigration History Research Center, University of Minnesota).

[44]Nick Salvatore, *Eugene V. Debs, Citizen and Socialist* (Urbana, 1982), 285–286; David Brody, *Labor in Crisis: The Steel Strike of 1919* (Philadelphia, 1965), 71–75, 113–114.

[45]For example, Thomas N. Brown, *Irish-American Nationalism, 1870–1890* (Philadelphia, 1966).

[46]Joseph P. O'Grady, ed., *The Immigrants' Influence on Wilson's Peace Policies* (Lexington, Kentucky, 1967); Robert E. Park, *The Immigrant Press and Its Control* (New York, 1922), 309–312; M. M. Stolarik, "The Role of American Slovaks in the Creation of Czecho-Slovakia, 1914–1918," in *Slovak Studies*, 8 (1968), 7–82; Kantowicz, *Polish-American Politics*, 110–115.

[47]Melvin I. Urofsky, *American Zionism From Herzl to the Holocaust* (Garden City, New York, 1975), 117–245; Naomi W. Cohen, *American Jews and the Zionist Idea* (n.p., 1975), 3–24.

[48]Circular [1918], reproduced in Robert A. Hill, ed., *The Marcus Garvey and Universal Negro Improvement Association Papers*, 1 (Berkeley, 1983), 315.

[49]According to the best available estimate, Garvey's movement at its height enrolled a million members in the United States and perhaps as many more in other countries. Its only rival as a protest organization, the National Association for the Advancement of Colored People, reached a peak of 91,000 members around the same time. Emory J. Tolbert, *The UNIA and Black Los Angeles: Ideology and Community in the American Garvey Movement* (Los Angeles, 1980), 3.

[50]Hauser, "Ethnicity and Class," 165–168.

[51]American Scenic and Historic Preservation Society, *Twenty-Fourth Annual Report, 1919*, 125–129; George Creel, *How We Advertised America* (New York, 1920). There is a particularly vivid record of ecstatic mobilization in the pages of the Czech-American daily, *Denni Hlasatel*, 1917–1918, in Chicago F. L. Press Survey, Reel 2, I G.

[52]Alexander M. Bing, *War-Time Strikes and Their Adjustment* (New York, 1921), 236–240; Wolman, *Growth*, 34–37.

[53]A. William Hoglund, "Breaking with Religious Tradition: Finnish Immigrant Workers and the Church, 1890–1915," in Karni and Ollila, eds., *For the Common Good*, 30–41, 58–59; James Weinstein, *The Decline of Socialism in America, 1912–1925* (New York, 1969), 145–162.

[54]United States Census Bureau, *Historical Statistics*, 178–179; Irving Bernstein, *The Lean Years: A History of the American Worker, 1920–1933* (Boston, 1960), 83–143, 334–357.

[55]Allswang, *House for All Peoples*, 117–118; William Preston, Jr., *Aliens and Dissenters: Federal Suppression of Radicals, 1903–1933* (Cambridge, Massachusetts, 1963).

[56]Louis Adamic, "Thirty Million New Americans," in *Harper's*, 169 (November, 1934), 684–694; United States Census Bureau, *Historical Statistics*, 116–118. How the initiative of second-generation immigrant workers

gradually enabled the older first-generation Slavs to overcome fear and submissiveness is sensitively examined by Peter Friedlander, *The Emergence of a UAW Local, 1936–1939: A Study in Class and Culture* (Pittsburgh, 1975).

[57]Louis Adamic's impressions on this point were very widely shared, as Richard Weiss points out in "Ethnicity and Reform: Minorities and the Ambience of the Depression Years," in *Journal of American History*, 66 (December, 1979), 583–584.

[58]Quoted in J. Joseph Huthmacher, *Massachusetts People and Politics 1919–1933* (New York, 1969), 154.

[59]For evidence of the mobilization of a new generation of voters in heavily "ethnic" cities, see Kristi Andersen, *The Creation of a Democratic Majority, 1928–1936* (Chicago, 1979), 30–38, 105–114.

[60]"Analysis of Foreign Language Publications . . . 1923," and Press Release, Foreign Language Information Service, November 7, 1932, in Archives of American Council for Nationalities Service (Immigration History Research Center, University of Minnesota); *New York Times*, August 10, 1936, 6.

[61]Irving Bernstein, *Turbulent Years: A History of the American Worker 1933–1941* (Boston, 1969), 37–46, 92–171, 217–316.

[62]Sidney Fine, *Sit-down: The General Motors Strike of 1936–1937* (Ann Arbor, 1969), 96, 330–332, 338–341.

[63]United States Census Bureau, *Historical Statistics*, 178.

[64]Roy Rosenzweig, " 'United Action Means Victory': Militant Americanism on Film," in *Labor History*, 24 (Spring, 1983), 274–288; *New York Times*, July 10, 1936, 18.

# 2

# Profile of a Ward Boss: The Political Career of Lars M. Rand*

*by Carl H. Chrislock*

During the last weekend of September, 1913, a doleful message passed by word of mouth through the Cedar-Riverside neighborhoods of south Minneapolis: "The barefoot boy is dead." Further identification of the departed one was unnecessary. Nearly all established residents of the sixth ward knew—or thought they knew—that fourteen years earlier Alderman Lars M. Rand had delivered a speech containing a startling autobiographical revelation: "Forty-two years ago on the rocky coast of Norway there was born of poor but honest parents a barefoot boy. Who was that boy? That was me, Lars M. Rand."[1] Whether Rand actually said what was attributed to him on that occasion is uncertain. In any event, the barefoot boy image remained attached to him long after memories of other aspects of his career had faded.[2]

During his twenty-year tenure on the Minneapolis city council—from 1890 through 1910—Lars Rand collected a number of other images. Journalists occasionally identified him as "the little alderman"—in physical stature he was short and in later years his girth expanded. Some dubbed him "the

---

*This article is a much expanded version of a paper presented at a conference at St. Olaf College, October 26-27, 1984, on "Scandinavians and Other Immigrants in Urban America."

*The Minneapolis Journal,* Sunday, December 30, 1906. Courtesy of the Minnesota Historical Society.

little Norwegian," and although his physique did not conform to Nordic stereotypes his friends insisted that he was a courageous, resourceful modern-day Viking. Viking symbolism is, of course, a double-edged instrument. One cartoon carrying the caption, "This missed being by a thousand years or so," portrayed Rand as a brutal chieftain in Viking attire imperiously commanding two hapless slaves to fetch him his supper.

Rand was not reticent with respect to his ethnic background. On one occasion he responded to harsh attacks from the opposition by telling his audience: "Your humble servant was born on the coast of Norway, with the rocky hills upon

*The Minneapolis Journal*, Sunday, December 30, 1906. Courtesy of the Minnesota Historical Society.

one side and the angry waves of the blue ocean on the other." This declaration inspired a cartoon depicting "the infant Lars" perched dangerously on a narrow ledge between a turbulent sea in the foreground and a massive rock formation in the back. Incidentally, the lad was wearing wooden shoes.[3]

Although these images helped to shape the Rand legend, they do little to illuminate the real Lars Rand. His outstanding trait was an uncanny ability to wield power within two chosen spheres, the sixth ward and the Minneapolis city council. Within the sixth ward his power base was built on two foundations: tight control of the ward's Democratic organization and strong appeal to sixth ward voters, an appeal extending well beyond the Democratic electorate. Within the city council his dominance was less impressive than in the sixth ward—Democratic aldermen were always in the minority throughout the twenty years that Rand was a council member—but his influence was considerable. Thanks to his mastery of parliamentary procedures, Rand frequently succeeded in manipulating council processes to serve his ends. His superior skill as a legal craftsman was highly valued by colleagues seeking to draft ordinances of dubious constitutionality. Finally, he was a shrewd negotiator who on a number of occasions managed to initiate the formation of bipartisan "combines" that effectively negated control of the council by its perennial Republican majority.

Rand's many critics admired his capacities as a vote getter and municipal legislator. Their case against him focused not on competence but on two other complaints: his electioneering tactics and his allegedly total commitment to the parochial interests of the sixth ward at the expense of the city's broader concerns. On the occasion of his retirement in 1910, the *Minneapolis Journal* summed up the critics' case in an editorial titled "A Hero of the Ward System." According to the *Journal*, Rand's political durability was attributable to the stagnant character of the sixth ward, and to the fact that he was personally acquainted with most of his constituents. "He was," continued the editorial, "an ideal alderman of the ward type. If that were the best type, he would have been one of the best aldermen, but as it is a type characteristic of about the worst kind of local government, Alderman Rand need be subjected to no greater criticism than that he was part of a bad system." After paying tribute to Rand's ability, the editorial concluded on a note of regret: "It is a pity that he did not have the city as his constituency."[4]

No response by Rand to this evaluation of his career is on record. However, one may assume that he would have reacted with a spirited defense of the "ward system." Throughout his aldermanic career he posed as the uncompromising champion of the immigrants and "workingmen" of the sixth ward, disadvantaged groups whose interests could not safely be entrusted to the city's "Puritan-Yankee elite." Precisely how much of this pose was demagogic cant and how much a reflection of sincere commitment is difficult to determine. But it can be affirmed that Lars Rand belonged to a species that, according to conventional wisdom, was rare within Scandinavian America: the urban ward boss.

There was nothing in Lars Rand's background to prefigure the emergence of an urban politician. He was born on January 24, 1857, on the Rand farm in Nordfjord, an area relatively untouched by the feeble beginnings of modernization in mid-nineteenth-century Norway. Available sources reveal little about Rand's boyhood. It is known that in 1874 or 1875 his father, Mathias Rand, accompanied by Lars's mother and a large flock of children—minus the eldest son, who remained in charge of the family property in Nordfjord—responded to the lure of America, emigrated, and settled in Chippewa Falls, Wisconsin. Whether Lars took passage on the same vessel as the family or migrated either shortly before or after is unclear. In any case, the family established a permanent home in Chippewa Falls and Lars, now approaching his late teens, was on his own.

In the months immediately following his arrival in the new land, young Rand worked at a succession of temporary jobs, most of them agricultural, in Wisconsin, Iowa, and Minnesota. One of his employers, Harald Thorson, the well-known Northfield, Minnesota, banker and benefactor of St. Olaf College, was impressed by the young man's potential. In later years Rand credited Thorson with encouraging him to further his education and also with teaching him the ways of the world. Carl G. O. Hansen recalled Rand remarking "in a facetious vein" that "Harald Thorson and I have sold more blind horses and crippled cows than any two men in the state of Minnesota."[5]

However much he may have valued the relationship with Harald Thorson, Rand soon moved from Northfield to Winona, Minnesota, where he secured employment as janitor in a bank. While working at this job, he completed a course of study at Winona State Normal School. By this time he had decided to become a lawyer, and in preparing for this profession he studied law in the offices of two prominent Winona attorneys. In 1884 he gained admission to the bar, and in the same year was elected municipal judge—a post which in jurisdictional terms was a justiceship of the peace, but which permitted Rand to use the proud title "judge," as he occasionally did when corresponding with prestigious individuals. Two years earlier he had married Jane Beebe, whom Carl G. O. Hansen characterized as "a refined woman of old American stock."[6] By all accounts the marriage was a happy one: Rand watchers tended to be critical of the alderman's political morality, but not of the quality of his family life.

It is not difficult to understand why Rand, in 1885, decided to move to Minneapolis. In the 1880s the city was an exploding metropolis dominated by two thriving industries, timber and flour. It also held front rank in the grain trade. The population, too, was growing apace: from 1880 to 1890 it more than tripled—from 47,000 to nearly 165,000. Scandinavian immigrants, particularly Swedes and Norwegians, but more of the former than the latter, accounted for a healthy percentage of this increase. One can speculate that this influenced Lars Rand's decision to seek his fortune in Minneapolis. Upon arriving in the city, Lars and Jane took up residence at 1920 Fourth Street South, in the heart of the sixth ward, the most "Scandinavian" of the city's thirteen wards. Its boundaries ran west and northwest from Riverside Park along Seventh Street South to Tenth Avenue South, thence east along Tenth Avenue to the Mississippi River, and from there along the southwesterly bend of the river to Riverside Park.

To some extent, popular perception exaggerated the

Scandinavian character of this area: the ethnic composition of the so-called Bohemian Flats, a community located under the Washington Avenue bridge on the west bank of the Mississippi, was predominantly Slovak but also included a mixture of Czech, Irish, Polish, and French inhabitants, along with a number of Scandinavians. Nevertheless, Scandinavian concentration in the sixth ward was impressively high in the late nineteenth and early twentieth century. According to the Minnesota State Census of 1895, 6,437 of the ward's 15,519 residents were foreign-born Scandinavians: 4,056 Swedes, 2,186 Norwegians, and 195 Danes. If the American-born children of Nordic immigrant parents had been classified as Scandinavian, the total obviously would have been much larger.[7]

The Scandinavian presence was highly visible on the streets and avenues of the sixth ward. Washington and Cedar avenues, the ward's principal commercial thoroughfares, were lined with shops owned by Scandinavian entrepreneurs; and businesses operated by non-Scandinavians frequently displayed signs announcing, "Scandinavian spoken here." The ward also was a center of intense Scandinavian cultural and social activity. Dania Hall, located on Fifth and Cedar, Normanna Hall on the corner of Third Street South and Twelfth Avenue, and Peterson Hall, a third-floor auditorium above the H. O. Peterson dry goods store on Thirteenth Avenue and Washington, provided meeting places for a host of organizations. Such notables as Knut Hamsun lectured in Dania, and Kristofer Janson, the well-known Unitarian clergyman and author, presided over bazaars in Peterson Hall.[8]

Notwithstanding its reputation as a notorious saloon stronghold, the sixth ward could also be called the cradle of Scandinavian Lutheranism in Minneapolis. The Augsburg Seminary campus, on the corner of Seventh Street and Twenty-First Avenue, was on its border; and three of the city's significant "mother" churches, Augustana Lutheran, Trinity Lutheran, and Our Saviour's Lutheran, were initially located within the ward's boundaries. During Rand's aldermanic tenure, two prominent churchmen, Sven Oftedal, an

Augsburg Seminary professor, and M. Falk Gjertsen, Trinity Lutheran's longtime pastor, played an active role in civic affairs.

Even before the sixth ward achieved full stature as a center of Scandinavian life and activity, its desirability as a residential area began to decline. Two factors were primarily responsible, industrial encroachment and the so-called patrol limits. Well before 1890, multiple railroad trackage diagonally bisected the northern part of the ward, a development that displaced homes, created an intolerable smoke nuisance, and encouraged a proliferation of spurs and warehouses along the railroad right-of-way. The patrol limits, established by the Minnesota legislature of 1884, defined the boundaries within which liquor dispensaries and saloons could be licensed. The ostensible purpose was to confine the liquor trade to areas within walking distance of police precinct stations, thereby facilitating the difficult task of enforcing liquor ordinances. Whether or not they accomplished this goal, the patrol limits had a significant impact on the neighborhoods immediately within and adjoining their boundaries. Writing in 1903, Lincoln Steffens described them as running "along the river front, out through part of the business section, with long arms reaching into the Scandinavian quarters, north and south."[9] The southern arm followed Washington Avenue to Seven Corners, and from there along Cedar, assuring these two thoroughfares an extraordinarily high concentration of bars and saloons.

These two adverse factors—industrial encroachment and proliferation of saloons—contributed to a gradual alteration of the sixth ward's class structure. Upwardly mobile Scandinavians moved to more desirable locations farther south. Following a familiar pattern, incoming immigrants of other nationalities moved into some of the vacated sixth ward residences. However, a considerable Scandinavian population, consisting of those unable or unwilling to move as well as incoming Nordic immigrants who arrived in large numbers in the early 1900s, remained until well into the twentieth century. Again following a familiar pattern, the perception of the ward as a Scandinavian area was reinforced by the continued presence of Scandinavian churches and businesses, neither of which immediately followed the migration of their more affluent compatriots.[10]

Soon after settling in Minneapolis, and before becoming securely established in the practice of law, Lars Rand plunged into Democratic politics, seeking and winning election as a delegate to the Minnesota Democratic convention of 1886. At the convention he was more than a nominal participant. Despite his youth and recent appearance on the scene, he was appointed chairman of the convention's platform committee.[11] Apparently he had placed himself in the good graces of Michael Doran, who a few years earlier had established himself as leader of the Minnesota Democratic organization. Although available sources fail to disclose information on Rand's connection with Doran, it is known that Doran was actively recruiting promising young Scandinavians into the party in the hope of broadening its narrow Nordic base.[12]

The Democratic state ticket, headed by Dr. Albert Alonzo Ames and running on a platform emphasizing "personal liberty" (code word for opposition to anti-liquor and other "sumptuary" legislation), lost the fall election by an extremely narrow margin. The Minneapolis city elections, which up to 1887 were held in the spring, had produced happier results: the Democrats captured both the mayoralty and a majority on the city council. In distributing the patronage now available to it, the council appointed Seagrave Smith, a respected jurist and staunch Democrat, as city attorney. Smith in turn appointed Rand to be his assistant.

As assistant city attorney Rand developed the reputation of being a "law and order" prosecutor, which within the context of municipal court jurisdiction meant being "tough on drunks." He also acquired an intimate knowledge of the inner workings of Minneapolis city government and the complexities of the city charter, knowledge that would stand him in good stead following his election to the council. However, his tenure as assistant city attorney was brief: in the next election Minneapolis Republicans recaptured control of the council, whereupon Rand resigned and entered into a law partnership with Henry J. Gjertsen. Notwithstanding Rand's and Gjertsen's opposing partisan affiliations—Gjertsen was an active Republican—the partnership continued for many years and, by all accounts, prospered.[13]

Entry into private law practice did not diminish Rand's involvement in politics; and as the campaign of 1890 approached, a combination of factors enhanced Democratic prospects. Municipal elections were now held on the same date as federal and state elections, an arrangement that to some extent linked the fortunes of Minneapolis Republicans to those of the national and state GOP administrations, both of which were highly unpopular.[14] On the municipal level, the unpopularity of the scandal-ridden GOP administration headed by Mayor E. C. Babb further depressed Republican hopes. It is not surprising, then, that a mood of hopeful optimism animated the Minneapolis Democratic convention when that body met on August 27. Philip B. Winston, a native of Virginia and one of the relatively few Democrats in the upper echelons of the city's business community, was selected to head the ticket; and Kristian Kortgaard, a Norwegian-American banker, was nominated for city treasurer —"in deference to the Scandinavian element," as the *Minneapolis Journal* remarked.[15] The platform extolled the hallowed Democratic "personal liberty" ethos; endorsed the eight-hour day for public employees; called for strengthening the powers of the mayor; and accused the Babb administration of favoritism to the city's "privileged classes."

In the separate ward conventions following adjournment of the city convention proper, the aldermanic candidates were named. Rand, of course, was nominated by his sixth ward colleagues. The extent to which he was obliged to fight for the honor is uncertain. Contemporary journalistic accounts suggest that the proceedings were cut and dried. On the other hand, James Gray recalled years later that a spirited contest preceded Rand's nomination, and that the decisive factor in his favor was the support of top party leaders who had come to value the young attorney's effectiveness as a party orator.[16]

In any case, the November election brought considerable joy to Minneapolis Democrats. A *Minneapolis Journal* headline reporting that "Minneapolis has gone Democratic all the way" succinctly summed up the outcome, although the incumbent Republican governor William R. Merriam won statewide by a paper-thin plurality.[17] In the sixth ward, Rand buried his Republican opponent Fred Youngren in an avalanche of votes: the official count was Rand, 2,252; Youngren, 516.[18] The size of Rand's margin suggests that his victory cannot be attributed solely to the strength of the 1890 Democratic tide, although that certainly helped. One can perhaps assume that the celebrated Rand electioneering tactics — torchlight parades enlivened by spirited band music, emotionally charged mass meetings in Normanna Hall, and demonstrations organized with the mission of disrupting opposition meetings — also played a role. Unfortunately for the historian, political reporters failed to cover Rand as fully in 1890 as later when his prominence made his activities more newsworthy.

The Democratic sweep on the city council of 1890 failed to produce a Democratic majority. Democrats captured a number of seats formerly held by Republicans, but not a sufficient number to overcome Republican predominance among the holdovers. At that time, an aldermanic term ran for four years; each of the city's thirteen wards was represented by two members, whose terms expired in alternate even-numbered years.[19] The city council was the real center of authority in city government. Next to power over the purse, its most significant prerogative was a commanding control over patronage. A recent charter amendment had vested authority over the police department in the mayor's office, but the council reigned supreme, unhampered by a merit system, over the other branches of city government except those under the supervision of elected boards. As in all legislative bodies, the status and prestige of the individual council

member—including ability to influence the flow of patronage—depended to a considerable degree on his committee assignments. Following each biennial election, the council
would choose a president who in turn would appoint the various committees. His selections were subject to council confirmation, which usually was a matter of course, since the
president was the chosen leader of the council majority.

As a freshman member of the council minority, Rand began his aldermanic career in a modest but by no means incon-
spicuous role. His appointment to the committee on licenses
and police was less important than it would have been before
the police department was placed under mayoral authority,
but the council floor was a forum well suited to his oratorical
talents. In the first year of his incumbency, he emerged as the
eloquent champion of several causes dear to the "workingmen" of the sixth ward, notably the eight-hour day. He also
led a successful fight to defeat a council resolution that would
have given preference in city employment to full-fledged
citizens over "first-paper" citizens—a victory that in the opinion of James Gray "gave Rand his first opening."[20] At the
same time he cultivated the reputation of being incorruptible
by announcing that he would never accept a streetcar pass.[21]

In his first year on the council, Rand also forged an alliance that in the near future would have a significant impact
on Minneapolis politics. Among the Democrats winning
election to the council in 1890 was an ex-butcher of German
background, Joseph L. Kiichli. Born in 1854 or 1855, Kiichli
had come to Minneapolis in search of fame and fortune in
1873. Eventually he established a small meat-processing
plant in north Minneapolis. Evidently the enterprise
prospered, but by 1886 Kiichli concluded that small operations like his could not compete with giants like Armour.
Acting on this conviction, he shifted from meat to real estate
and politics. He lost his first bid for aldermanic honors; but
in 1890 his grip on the political process of the third ward,
coupled with the strong Democratic tide of that year, yielded
him victory.[22]

Kiichli and Rand had much in common. Both were loyal

Democrats, firmly committed to their party's creed of personal liberty; and both were of immigrant background. Their wards also shared similarities. Like the sixth, the third was heavily populated by first-generation immigrants, many of them day laborers. And both wards were blessed or cursed with a heavy concentration of saloons, a reality that no third or sixth ward alderman could safely ignore.

Problems relating to the regulation of the liquor trade provided the basis for the first major cooperative venture between Kiichli and Rand. For many years the issue of Sunday closing had agitated the Minneapolis public. State law appeared to require saloons to close on Sundays. However, depending on how the law was read, it also seemed to require other businesses—confectionaries, for example—to suspend operations on the Sabbath. Representatives of the liquor industry professed a willingness to keep their establishments closed on Sundays if the closing law was uniformly applied; until it was, they could in good conscience remain open.

Unimpressed by this logic and convinced that the police were not enforcing the law with sufficient vigor, a group of zealous Sabbatarians organized the Minneapolis Law Enforcement League for the purpose of mobilizing private initiative in the cause of Sunday closing. In the autumn of 1891, "spotters," ostensibly working under the auspices of the league, organized systematic patrols of the saloon districts. Upon discovering a suspected violation, they would swear out a complaint against the alleged offender, a tactic that challenged law enforcement officials to take action. According to the *Minneapolis Journal*, whose editorial policy strongly supported Sunday closing, the league campaign was approaching its goal by late October. On October 26 the newspaper reported that on the previous day, a Sunday, most of the city's saloons were closed, and that "saloon matters are approaching some sort of a crisis, and the worm is about ready to turn."[23]

Indeed it was, but not in the direction anticipated or desired by the *Journal*. As the weeks passed, some citizens unconnected with the liquor trade began to suspect that the

Minneapolis Law Enforcement League's campaign was cross-
ing the boundaries of legitimacy and becoming a nasty vigi-
lante crusade.[24] Not surprisingly, members of the city council's personal-liberty faction shared this view; and encouragement from those interests whose economic welfare was at
stake no doubt reinforced their inclination to move against
the spotters. However, there was a problem. The council
president, a Republican, was disinclined to challenge the
league; and theoretically the Republican majority on the
council was pledged to follow his leadership. The task of the
ten personal-liberty Democrats was to induce a sufficient
number of Republicans to join them and form an ad hoc
majority committed to action against the spotters.

Under the leadership of Rand, Kiichli, and James C.
Haynes, a future Democratic mayor of Minneapolis, such a
majority emerged during a stormy council meeting on
February 12, 1892. At 10:30 p.m., following completion of
a lengthy but mostly routine agenda, the presiding officer
declared the meeting adjourned. Fifteen council members, ten
Democrats and five Republicans — a clear majority — voted to
prolong the session in order to consider a liquor ordinance
drafted by Rand; nine aldermen voted to adjourn. A confusing succession of amendments, motions, points of order, and
other parliamentary maneuvers followed; but, throughout,
the fifteen to nine division held firm. The end result was
passage of the so-called Rand ordinance, one of the most
controversial measures ever passed by a Minneapolis city
council.[25]

Although it endorsed Sunday closing in principle, the
Rand ordinance took the bite out of this endorsement by
limiting authority to file complaints against suspected liquor
law violators to police officers, thus undercutting the Minneapolis Law Enforcement League's campaign. In a message
affirming that law enforcement was the responsibility of constituted authorities, Mayor Winston signed the ordinance.
Evidently the mayor accepted the reality that Sunday closing
was as difficult to enforce as the statutes against prostitution.
Under police supervision the problem could be contained and

managed by permitting discreet violations on the understanding that blatant flouting of the law invited police retribution.[26]

As one might expect, Minneapolis Sabbatarians declined
to accept the Rand ordinance gracefully. Instead they waged
what turned out to be an eight-year battle in the Minnesota
courts to invalidate it on constitutional grounds; their final
victory was won in 1900 when the Minnesota Supreme
Court ruled that the ordinance was indeed unconstitutional.
While this was a defeat for Rand, he could take a degree of
comfort from the opinion of some observers that the durability of his handiwork—attested to by the extraordinary
effort required to undo it—was a tribute to his legal craftsmanship.[27]

The animated discussion provoked by the Rand ordinance made the alderman's name well known throughout
Minneapolis. It also marked him as a staunch friend of the saloon. Such a reputation did not improve Rand's relations with
the vocal total-abstinence, anti-saloon sector of the city's
Scandinavian community. At a meeting of the South Minneapolis Total Abstinence Society called to protest enactment
of the ordinance, Reverend M. Falk Gjertsen focused his attack on the two Norwegian aldermen who had backed it.

"It brings a deep blush to my cheek," declared Gjertsen,
"when two of my countrymen, one a Democrat [Rand] and
one a Republican [C. H. Blichfeldt]—and God knows there
is little difference between them—are on the city council and
vote for this ordinance . . . God have mercy on a man who
will shame his friends, and dishonor his home, his word, his
church, and his pastor." A brief biographical sketch of Rand
published a year later by a Swedish-American writer delivered a similar indictment in somewhat less emotional language: "As a member of the city council of Minneapolis,
[Rand] became very unpopular with the temperance loving
element, because of his obnoxious liquor ordinance."[28]

Although Gjertsen undoubtedly was the most popular
Scandinavian clergyman in the sixth ward, his attack on Rand
did not seriously threaten the latter's political fortunes. Rand

was, of course, not up for reelection in 1892; but he did want a compatible sixth ward colleague on the council, a goal he achieved. With Rand's backing, Andrew Anderson, a Swedish American, won the Democratic nomination and also the final election. He won reelection in 1896, but was defeated for renomination in 1900 in the city's first primary election. It could be said of Andrew Anderson that he was obscure before becoming an alderman and remained so while in office. In effect, his presence on the council placed Rand in control of sixth ward representation with everything that this implied.[29]

Minneapolis Democrats hoped to gain control of the city council in the 1892 election, but the electorate frustrated this hope. The new council was Republican by a margin of fourteen to twelve.[30] When it organized in January, 1893, the Republican majority elected Dr. H. W. Brazie, a respected physician, to the council presidency. Brazie's performance soon demonstrated that medical experience does not necessarily sharpen the skills needed to exercise effective political leadership. His committee assignments antagonized members of his own caucus, and minority members—Rand in particular—were offended by what they felt was his cavalier style in presiding over council meetings.[31]

These discontents created the setting for the famous Kiichli-Rand coup of March 10, 1893, a coup executed at a regular council meeting. At 8 p.m. Rand gained the floor and proceeded to make a speech. "We Democrats," he declared, "believe in democratic principles, in rotation of offices. One man, a Republican, has held the office of president for three months. It is now time for him to step down so that the rest of us can have our turn. I therefore move that the presidency be declared vacant." Before the Brazie people could recover from the impact of this bombshell, Rand took charge of the roll call. With the backing of the twelve Democratic aldermen and two anti-Brazie Republicans, the motion prevailed.[32]

Following passage of Rand's motion, a comprehensive plan to reorganize the council unfolded. Kiichli was elected president, and choice committee assignments were divided among the Democrats and the two insurgent Republicans. Rand, whose previous committee assignments had been less than satisfactory from his point of view, was appointed chairman of the public grounds and buildings committee, a post that "gave him virtual control of the labor in . . . city hall." He also was made a member of the committee on gas, fire department, and railroads, "which in those days were all important." Implementation of this carefully planned design was not achieved in a few minutes. The council remained in session until 3 a.m. on the morning of March 11. Proceedings were marked by a succession of parliamentary maneuvers on both sides. According to one calculation, Rand introduced 144 motions in the course of the meeting.[33]

The Kiichli-Rand coup evoked a furious reaction from the Republican press. The *Minneapolis Journal* likened it to a "Mexican revolution" and predicted that it would impair the city's credit in the national money markets. "The performance last night," continued the *Journal*, "was a high-handed piece of business that should have resulted in handing some of the members of the council over to the police." The Brazie faction appealed to the courts, alleging that the March 10 proceedings had been irregular and that Brazie had been wrongfully deprived of the council presidency. Significantly, the Minnesota Supreme Court upheld Kiichli's title to the post. As Carl G. O. Hansen put it, "There was not a [legal] flaw in the Democratic attack."[34]

The election of 1894, which reduced the council's Democratic bloc from twelve to six and increased Republican representation to twenty, terminated the Kiichli council presidency. Kiichli was not one of the remaining six; he had chosen to make what turned out to be an unsuccessful race for the legislature.[35] Rand, on the other hand, won a magnificent reelection victory, swamping his Republican opponent by a vote of 1,697 to 889.[36] Although less impressive than his 1890 triumph, Rand's performance in 1894 should be judged within the context of the universal disaster suffered by the

Democratic party that year—disaster in large part attributable to the "Cleveland depression." In Minnesota the Democratic vote for governor fell from around 95,000 in 1892 to about 50,000 in 1894, and Hennepin county was again a Republican stronghold.

Rand's landslide victory in the face of these odds invested him with an aura of invincibility. While somewhat exaggerated, this "superman" image was not completely illusory. The alderman's agility in parliamentary situations, both on the floor and behind the scenes, assured his continued mastery of the sixth ward Democratic organization. More important, an overwhelming majority of sixth ward voters firmly believed that Rand was their friend. Beyond the Rand rhetoric, which consistently and persuasively stressed the alderman's commitment to the "workingman," was the reality that he controlled a vast patronage pool. Not all the jobs at his disposal were lucrative—many, in fact, were menial and low-paying—but in a time of high unemployment such as the nation was experiencing in 1894, a job was a job, especially in low-income neighborhoods.

In addition, the Rand organization provided free entertainment at a time when austere sixth ward family budgets severely limited expenditure for the amenities of life. A Rand rally may have contributed minimally to public enlightenment, but its mix of spirited band music and demagogic oratory, spiced with the alderman's brand of humor, was good entertainment. Occasionally, too, libations flowed; legend has it that on election eves free beer was dispensed on the Bohemian flats. Critics raised questions about how Rand, who personally was not wealthy, paid for these spectacles, implying that the saloon proprietors of the ward picked up the tab. No conclusive answers to these questions were forthcoming, but clearly financial stringency never handicapped a Rand election campaign.[37]

The ethnic factor also worked for Rand. As already noted, he made no secret of the fact that he was born "on the rocky coast of Norway." But he took care to avoid the impression that his organization was an exclusive Norwegian or even Scandinavian club. The roster of his associates in the 1890s included not only an Anderson and a Hagman, both Swedes, but also a Flaherty, a Sweeney, and, above all, a Matt Walsh. Unlike those Scandinavians who insisted that the Nordic-Irish relationship was adversarial, Rand stressed immigrant solidarity; in his view, all immigrant groups shared an interest in maintaining a common front against the power of the city's "Puritan-Yankee elite."[38]

The 1894 victory marked Rand as a possible candidate for higher honors. In commenting on the outcome of the election, *Folkebladet*, a church paper published in the ward, characterized Rand as the "most formidable Democrat in the state."[39] This was an exaggeration, but Rand's role in state politics was expanding. In 1894 he toured Minnesota on behalf of the state ticket. Given the dismal electoral prospects in that year, this was a thankless task. Perhaps that was why in addressing a small crowd in Princeton Rand chose to focus on Ohio instead of Minnesota. Unfortunately, his account of the Ohio situation was factually incorrect, an embarrassing reality fully exposed through a series of questions put to Rand by Robert C. Dunn, editor of the *Princeton Union*. The speaker responded in characteristic style: "Say, Bob, stop asking me such damn fool questions and I'll treat you when the meeting is over." Dunn then abandoned the interrogation and, as he recalled years later, "Lars made good at the close of the meeting, but he made no converts in the cause of democracy [Democratic party] that evening."[40]

On a more significant level, Rand was moving into closer association with the anti-Doran wing of the Minnesota Democratic party, a group opposing the conservative hard-money stance of the Cleveland administration and its staunch friend, Michael Doran. Hitherto the alderman had avoided conspicuous identification with any of the factions battling for control of the state party, but at the 1894 state convention he backed the renomination of State Auditor Adolph Biermann, whose defeat was being sought by the Doran people. After the convention adjourned, the anti-Doran faction strengthened its position by gaining the upper hand in a reorganization of the state central committee. Rand was appointed a member of that body.[41]

Two years later the victory of free silver and the nomination of William Jennings Bryan for the presidency by the Democratic national convention enabled the anti-Doran group to gain full control of the Minnesota Democratic organization. Suddenly Democratic prospects seemed to brighten. A fusion ticket backed by Minnesota Democrats, Populists, and silver Republicans, and headed by ex-Congressman John Lind, a silver Republican, entered the race. Dissatisfaction with the administration of incumbent Republican governor David M. Clough coupled with the popularity of Swedish-born Lind encouraged a belief that the fusionists might triumph in Minnesota. This perception was, of course, mistaken. They lost on both the state and the national level. Although Lind nearly defeated Clough, William McKinley won over Bryan by a more decisive majority than anticipated.[42]

Rand's role in the 1896 campaign was relatively modest but not insignificant. He was in charge of arrangements for the Minnesota Democratic convention which met in Minneapolis on August 4. Despite a rumor that Doran's friends would attempt to disrupt it, the convention completed its business in an atmosphere of harmony.[43]

Following adjournment of the state convention, Minneapolis Democrats turned to the problem of naming a city ticket, a process involving delicate negotiations with Populists and silver Republicans. Because of their senior status in the coalition, the Democrats demanded the right to name the mayoral candidate, and presently a "Rand for mayor" movement surfaced. But the alderman emphatically refused to be considered; he insisted "that it should be the duty of every loyal Scandinavian Democrat to keep his name off the Democratic ticket in order not to injure John Lind's candidacy for governor." He added that he "would remain a volunteer in the Democratic ranks and devote [his] time and attention to the election of the Bryan-Lind fusion ticket."[44] Other considerations undoubtedly strengthened his disinclination to run for mayor. For one thing, he possibly doubted his own electability: the Rand ordinance and his participation in the Kiichli coup did not enhance his popularity in the city's "Yankee" wards. For another, recent history indicated that a Democratic mayoral candidacy in a presidential year was virtually doomed. In any case, Rand kept his promise to campaign for Bryan and Lind, both of whom carried the sixth ward. He also was a Democratic member of the three-party conference committee set up to negotiate the city fusionist ticket. The committee named Alexander T. Ankeny, a respected lawyer, as its candidate for mayor. In the final election, Ankeny lost to Robert Pratt, the incumbent Republican mayor.

The intense emotion generated in the 1894–1896 period by Populism, free silver, labor unrest, and Bryanism tended to obscure the emergence in 1894 of a significant urban reform movement. Elitist in orientation and enthusiastically supported by elements within the business community, this movement aspired to streamline, centralize, and professionalize city government, a transformation that required first of all the elimination of machine politics and its attendant evils. The reformers also claimed that their program sought to restore power to the "people," a claim based on the assumption that a professionalized and centralized bureaucracy, divorced from partisan politics, would be more responsive to the popular will than a decentralized system within which the ward boss was sovereign.

In Minneapolis, the Kiichli-Rand coup of 1893 undoubtedly heightened interest in the emerging reform movement. Augustus Luther Crocker, a prominent Minneapolis real-estate broker, represented the Minneapolis Board of Trade at the Philadelphia convention of 1894 that founded the National Municipal Reform League. In December of the same year, the league held a second convention in Minneapolis; and before long an organization calling itself the Good Citizenship League appeared on the Minneapolis scene.[45]

Meanwhile the Minneapolis city council was coming to

terms with the outcome of the 1894 election. Its top-heavy Republican majority (twenty to six) may have encouraged reformers to hope that the aldermen would respond positively to their program. However, the 1895–1896 council session demonstrated that a less than cohesive Republican majority was incapable of serving the cause of municipal reform. Although the "combine" organized by Kiichli and Rand lacked the support needed to stage another coup, its influence remained strong, even in the absence of Kiichli.[46]

In 1896 the Good Citizenship League launched a determined effort to defeat Kiichli, who was attempting a comeback, and to retire several aldermen whose records fell short of their standards. The effort was less than successful. Two of the targeted aldermen suffered defeat, but Kiichli won in the third ward, and the Democratic minority gained three seats, for a total of nine. In assessing the election's outcome, the *Minneapolis Times*, a newspaper supporting the Good Citizenship League, remarked that "Kiichli, Rand et al will probably help to parcel out the big chairmanships. Good Citizenship aldermen are in the minority." The record of the 1897–1898 council basically confirmed this expectation.[47]

Two years later, when Rand was up for reelection, the reformers concentrated much of their fire on him. In mid-October, rumors of a Rand "scandal" surfaced. The most serious charge alleged that employees of the sixth ward street commissioner, a Rand appointee, had been compensated from the city treasury for work done on a small acreage owned by Rand on the shores of Lake Amelia (Nokomis); affadavits signed by the employees in question added credibility to the charge. Although the sums involved were small, Rand chose not to ignore the accusation. Instead he called a mass meeting in Normanna Hall at which he made a speech vehemently denying any wrongdoing. Before adjourning, the Normanna meeting approved a motion calling for the appointment of a "tripartisan" committee charged with the responsibility of investigating the allegations. The makeup of the committee was announced immediately after approval of the resolution. By whose authority the committee had been appointed remained unclear, a point not lost on Rand's critics.[48]

A few days later a "citizens' mass meeting," obviously organized by Rand's opponents, made copies of the employees' affadavits available for inspection. Neither Rand nor his Republican opponent was present, and the audience was divided in its sympathies. A Rand supporter emphatically declared: "Alderman Lars Rand is a boy of the boys; he is a boy of the boys and he does not forget the boys. I am a Republican and I shall vote for him. I ask all the men here to vote for him." Another member of the audience viewed Rand from a different perspective, saying, "The heelers and the workers who are on the payrolls are kept busy, but the alderman can't afford to put in water mains or sewers. Citizens are obliged to wait for years and then put in their own."[49]

Shortly before election day the "tripartisan" investigating committee presented its findings to a second Rand-sponsored meeting. To no one's surprise, the alderman was exonerated of wrongdoing: one of the employees had indeed received a check drawn on the city treasury shortly after having worked on Rand's property, but this check was overdue compensation for his work as a city employee. Following presentation of the report, Rand made a speech which, as usual, evoked strong audience approval.[50]

As election day, 1898, approached, Good Citizenship Republicans persuaded themselves that Rand could — and probably would — be defeated.[51] As it turned out, the contest was not even close. Rand prevailed over his Republican opponent by a vote of 1,172 to 681. A moderate Democratic tide in the state election may have helped to swell Rand's total. In the race for governor, John Lind (who also won statewide) trounced William H. Eustis in Minneapolis, partly, it seems, because Eustis suffered the reputation of being a "Swede hater." James Gray, a prominent journalist and anti-machine Democrat, was elected mayor, and the partisan division in the new city council was sixteen Republicans and ten Democrats.[52]

In 1900 Lars Rand's aura of invincibility showed signs of fading. Under the presidency of John Crosby, of the famous milling family, the Minneapolis city council was responding more positively to municipal reform causes than any of its immediate predecessors. A case in point was its enactment of the famous Wine Room ordinance.

Wine rooms were lounges separated from the bar by a wall and connected by a door, wherein customers of both sexes could fraternize, often, it was alleged, to negotiate illicit relationships. In early 1900 the Anti-Saloon league initiated a campaign to close these "dens of iniquity" and prevent their reemergence. Soon a formidable coalition of groups—including, among others, the WCTU, a society called the Women's Improvement League, an interdenominational ministerial committee, and some twenty congregations—joined the battle. The unifying theme of the crusade was a charge that wine room proprietors, consciously or unknowingly, were parties to a conspiracy seeking the debasement of young women.[53]

The response of the city council to the anti-wine room campaign differed markedly from its stance in the "spotter" controversy eight years earlier. In mid-March Alderman David P. Jones introduced an ordinance outlawing the wine rooms. A month later the council's ordinance committee recommended passage, and when the recommendation reached the full council that body approved the measure on a straight party-line vote. Both within the ordinance committee, of which he was a member, and on the council floor, Rand vigorously opposed the ordinance, arguing that it improperly and possibly unconstitutionally infringed on the fundamental rights of "certain citizens and property owners." However, Rand's eloquence, parliamentary savvy, and negotiating skill were insufficient to break Republican solidarity. And notwithstanding virtually solid Democratic opposition, Democratic mayor James Gray signed the measure into law.[54]

Before the wine room controversy crested, the political future of Joseph Kiichli became uncertain, a development that also had implications for Rand's political fortunes. In late

January the third ward alderman announced his intention not to seek another term. Political writers responded to the announcement skeptically. Perhaps Kiichli was expecting a groundswell of support that would give his candidacy the appearance of a draft. If so, he was disappointed; many third ward Democrats, it seems, had come to feel that his leadership was excessively heavy-handed and autocratic. For the next six months Kiichli's status remained uncertain; in mid-July he unequivocally withdrew from the aldermanic race.[55]

The probable impact of Kiichli's retirement on Rand invited speculation. One political writer implied that the sixth ward alderman may not have been entirely displeased. According to this writer, Rand had "pocketed his Viking pride on many an occasion when he would have loved to break away from the Kiichli rule and give the council a sample of his own leadership." On the other hand, Rand's effectiveness had owed much to the alliance with Kiichli.[56]

Rand also faced new challenges in the sixth ward. At the behest of Minneapolis Republicans, the Minnesota legislature of 1899 had enacted a direct primary law applicable to Hennepin county. Henceforth all legislative, county, and municipal officials within Hennepin's boundaries were to be nominated by a direct vote of the people rather than by the traditional caucus-convention system. Obviously, this reform diminished the ability of the ward boss to name his party's candidates; managing an electorate was more difficult than manipulating a convention. Rand was equal to the challenge: his candidate for the sixth ward Democratic nomination in 1900, Harry A. Lund, a Swedish-American attorney, prevailed in the primary. However, Lund lost in the final election to Nels J. Nelson, a successful Swedish-American businessman.[57]

It was a serious setback for Rand: now he would be obliged to share control of sixth ward patronage with a Republican colleague within a Republican-dominated city council. It also involved payment of a wager. Before the election Rand and one Louis Lere had agreed that if Lund won, Lere would transport Rand by wheelbarrow from Twenty-Second Avenue and Riverside to Washington and Tenth Avenue—a distance of approximately a mile and a half—and if Nelson won, Rand would do the same for Lere. Since Nelson won, Rand was of course the loser.

Rand's discharge of his wager attracted city-wide attention. On the appointed day, and long before the scheduled hour of departure, the announced route was crowded with onlookers. Promptly at two p.m. Lere, who weighed 206 pounds, climbed into the wheelbarrow and Rand took charge of the vehicle. Ahead of the wheelbarrow, two horse-drawn carriages transported a group of Cedar-Riverside dignitaries. Behind it a corps of standard bearers carried placards proclaiming, among other things, "Lars takes his medicine," and "This machine has lasted ten years and is good for two years more." The famed Normanna band added a musical dimension to the procession. Along the route spectators shouted good-natured comments: "Who says we haven't a laboring man for alderman?" "This is a friend of labor," and "It's contract labor this time." Meanwhile Rand struggled valiantly to reach his goal and in this he succeeded. The festivities ended at Tenth and Washington with a typical Rand speech.[58]

Notwithstanding his display of exuberance while paying off the wager, Rand was momentarily despondent in the aftermath of the 1900 election. A solid Republican council majority was likely to favor the patronage claims of Nels Nelson over those of Rand, and how Rand would fare when the 1901 council committees were selected appeared uncertain.[59] However, his despondency turned out to be short-lived. A patronage disagreement with Nelson was resolved on Rand's terms. More important, he fared very well with respect to committee assignments. In reporting on the organization of the new council, the *Minneapolis Journal* commented: "Everyone is more or less surprised at the good showing Alderman Rand made in the committee list. He got places on the police, fire department, and ordinance committees . . .

Ordinance and fire department are both good committees and the wonder is how he worked it."[60]

Undoubtedly, the key to Rand's good fortune was the working relationship he managed to establish with David P. Jones, the new council president. Two years later, when Democratic dissatisfaction with Jones's committee appointments generated rumors of plans to instigate an 1893-style coup, Rand—who again held membership on the ordinance and fire department committees—told a *Journal* reporter: "I'm entirely satisfied. I got just what I wanted on the committees. Mr. Jones is a gentleman and a scholar and a first-class presiding officer. He has never denied any request of mine."[61]

Although Rand and Jones were at odds on important issues (Jones, it will be recalled, sponsored the anti-wine room ordinance), there was a basis for cooperation between the two. Apparently Rand no longer contemplated organization of another "combine"; his main concern was serving the interests of the sixth ward, an objective that dictated, among other things, access to patronage. From Jones's standpoint, generosity to Rand in that area was cheap insurance against the reemergence of a hostile bipartisan coalition within the council. Moreover, as the months passed, a virtual collapse of Mayor Albert A. Ames's administration created a gap that only the city council could fill. Under the circumstances, Jones needed all the solidarity that he could muster.

Dr. Albert Alonzo Ames was a veteran of many political wars. Several times the voters of Minneapolis had elected him mayor on the Democratic ticket, and in 1886 Minnesota Democrats nominated him for governor. In the course of his career, Ames had acquired a double image. On the one hand he was perceived as a compassionate physician who administered free medical care to those unable to pay. On the other hand, good government advocates regarded him as the most venal and corrupt politician in the state. By the end of the 1890s his status within the Democratic party had deteriorated and it appeared that his political career was over.

Ironically, the Hennepin county primary law enabled Ames to stage a comeback. After announcing his conversion to Republicanism, he filed for mayor in the 1900 GOP primary, captured the nomination, and defeated James Gray, the Democratic incumbent, in the final election.

Upon taking office in January, 1901, Ames instituted a reign of corruption unparalleled in Minneapolis history. His first act was the appointment of his brother, Fred W. Ames, as police chief. Mayor Ames then instituted a massive purge of the police department, affirming an intention of creating a "Republican police force." What emerged was a police force that not only tolerated criminal behavior but actively participated in and profited from it. Fortunately, venality on such a scale sowed the seeds of its own destruction. Facing prosecution on numerous charges, Ames fled Minneapolis in August, 1902. The gap created by his departure was filled by council president Jones, who assumed the title of acting mayor. Notwithstanding the brevity of his stint — until January, 1903, when James C. Haynes took office — Jones managed to repair much of the damage inflicted on city government by the Ames gang.[62]

Rand's role in the Ames crisis is obscure; conceivably, untapped sources might disclose significant participation behind the scenes. In any case, the Rand-Jones relationship remained intact. As noted earlier, Rand was delighted with his 1903 committee assignments. His allegiance to the Democratic party precluded supporting Jones's successful candidacy for mayor in 1904; but an eloquent speech on the occasion of Jones's "graduation" from alderman to mayor in early 1905 radiated Rand's sincere respect and friendship. In reporting the ceremony, the *Minneapolis Journal* commented: "The presentation was made by Lars M. Rand, the patriarch of the city council, who in graceful language and with felicitous sentiment made one of the neatest speeches ever heard in the council chambers."[63]

The designation of Rand as city council "patriarch" (some called him "dean," others "nestor") suggests that the alderman was beginning to be viewed as an elder statesman. In terms of years he was still relatively young: forty-eight in

1905. But a fifteen-year career on a city council with a tradition of frequent turnover set him apart. Moreover, time had had a mellowing impact on Rand. His sixth ward machine continued to function essentially as it had from the beginning, and he still staunchly defended the ward's saloon interests, but the possibility that he would organize a conspiracy to overthrow the ruling council majority now seemed remote.

Although this altered stance promoted smoother relations with the city council's Republican establishment, the more zealous municipal reformers remained unappeased. In 1902 they had contested Rand's reelection by backing the candidacy of John F. Dahl, the Republican nominee. Dahl, a promising young Norwegian-born attorney, was a formidable contender, but Rand repeated his 1894 and 1898 triumphs. At the conclusion of the campaign, enough cash remained in the Rand coffers to finance a festive victory celebration in Dania Hall.[64]

A year later the reformers created the Minneapolis Voters' League. Modeled on the Chicago Municipal League, the new organization promised "to encourage a clean, businesslike handling of city affairs." For the present, it planned to concentrate its efforts on improving the city council, a priority dictated by the council's key role in city government on both the legislative and the administrative levels. In advance of primary and general elections and with the assistance of a paid staff, the league proposed to disseminate information relating to the qualifications and shortcomings of aldermanic candidates. While recommendations would on occasion be made, the organization's founding statement professed confidence in the ability of voters to decide wisely on the basis of the information supplied by the league.

The charter membership roster of the Minneapolis Voters' League reads like a register of the city's elite. John Crosby was the organization's first president. Other prominent families represented included Atwater, Belden, Bovey, Chute, Carpenter, DeLaittre, Dunwoody, Heffelfinger, Loring, Pillsbury, Washburn, and Wyman. A few Scandinavians were on the list, notably Sven Oftedal of Augsburg Seminary and Andreas Ueland, a prominent attorney. Stiles P. Jones, a journalist who had served as David P. Jones's secretary while the latter was acting mayor, was the organization's secretary. Stiles Jones, who apparently was not related to David Jones, had systematically investigated the Chicago model, thereby gaining the reputation of being an expert in the area of municipal reform.[65]

Although Rand was not up for reelection in 1904, the first year the Voters' League participated in the campaign, he nevertheless came under indirect attack. The organization's pre-primary evaluation of Nels Nelson, the other sixth ward alderman, charged that Nelson was "handicapped by lack of ideals of public service and official closeness to his colleague Alderman Lars M. Rand. Although opposed to [Rand] politically, he shapes his official action according to [Rand's] counsel." The manifesto issued on the eve of the final election reiterated the point. Nelson, it asserted, was "too much under Rand's influence for his own and the city's welfare."[66]

Notwithstanding this unfavorable review, Nelson won reelection, thanks in part to Rand's relative inactivity on behalf of the Democratic candidate. Meanwhile the league began preparations for a massive attack on Rand which the reformers confidently hoped would terminate the alderman's career.

The attack was launched in September, 1906, shortly before that year's primary election. A general report, released to the press on September 11, coupled a critique of the city council with recommendations for reform. Too many council members, the report charted, were "drones, deadweights, and gangsters." The report was especially critical of the "alderman who considers his own ward and constituents to the exclusion of the larger and more important interests of the city at large." Street construction, sidewalk maintenance, and street cleaning should be removed from ward jurisdiction and "assigned to the city engineer or other competent authority." Such a change, the report argued, "would result in better streets and lower ward taxes."[67]

The league released its so-called "candidates report" on

September 20. The assault on Rand was particularly brutal. After reviewing his career, the report characterized him as "an oily . . . unscrupulous ward boss" who had "been a dangerous influence in city affairs during all his sixteen years . . . in the council." The report further charged him with "vigorously" backing "the interests of the saloon, the brewery, and every other influence contributing to 'wide open' municipal conditions." It added that while Rand posed "as a champion of the people" he was "in reality a most useful agent of the railroads and public service corporations." Fortunately, the report concluded, sixth ward Democrats had a choice: Peter Gunderson, an anti-machine Democrat, was contesting the alderman's renomination, and he deserved the vote of every right-thinking member of the party.[68]

To no one's surprise Rand trounced Gunderson in the primary. However, the final election posed a considerably more formidable challenge. John Peterson, the Republican candidate, was an energetic organizer and effective orator who stressed his own strong commitment to the progressive Republicanism of President Theodore Roosevelt; and the appearance of several well-known Minneapolis progressives at Peterson rallies enhanced the credibility of this claim. Meanwhile a group of volunteers calling itself The Young Men's Equality Club conducted a door-to-door canvas of the ward in an effort to convince all voters that Lars Rand was an unworthy public servant.[69]

The league issued its final manifesto a week before election day. This document repeated most of the charges contained in the pre-primary report, adding that Rand was "interested in his ward and its people only as a means of making a fat living for himself." This was manifestly unfair. When Rand died in 1913, he left an estate of $32,475 — approximately $25,000 in securities, the remainder in real property — not a pauper's legacy but hardly evidence of "fat living."[70] The allegation that he served as a "useful agent" for liquor and public utility interests is more difficult to assess. No one could reasonably doubt his friendliness to the sixth ward saloon complex. On the other hand, Rand vigorously denied partiality toward the public service corporations. His rhetoric certainly supported this denial, but "secret covenants secretly arrived at" sometimes take precedence over rhetorical claims.[71]

The stridency of the Voters' League probably generated a backlash that benefited Rand. And it certainly is true that the alderman was provoked into using every campaign tactic that had served him in the past; he very much wanted to win. Nevertheless, confidence within the Peterson camp grew; Republican activists persuaded themselves that Rand's campaign was coming apart. The election failed to vindicate such optimism: Rand won with a vote of 1,026 to Peterson's 805; a third-party candidate running on the Public Ownership (Socialist) ticket polled 116 votes. Although his margin of victory was narrower than in previous council races, Rand had demonstrated again—this time in the face of enormous odds—his hold on the sixth ward electorate.[72]

Shortly after the 1906 election, Rand declared that he probably would not seek another council term, adding, "unless the Voters' League attacks me."[73] Although political writers responded skeptically to this declaration, it turned out to be an honest statement. It seems, too, that Rand's intention to leave the council lessened his zest for aldermanic responsibilities. His council committee assignments in 1907 were on a par with those he had held earlier; but in 1909 his long tenure on the ordinance and fire department committees ended.[74] Meanwhile, Rand was seeking council approval of an appropriation to finance construction of a municipal bath house on Riverside Avenue. Ultimately this project materialized, but not until after Rand left office.[75]

One day before the filing deadline for the 1910 primary election, Rand ended speculation about his immediate future. "Four years ago," he declared, "I announced that I would not seek a renomination unless forced to do so by the Voters' League. The Voters' League has let me alone, although I have waited until the last day for filing to give the league a chance. I am not satisfied to retire [unless] I can go without retiring under fire. Another reason I have for ending my political career is to give more attention to the practice of law and to private affairs. I go out of the council at peace with all my colleagues and city officials and with only friendliness for everyone, excepting always the Voters' League."[76]

Minneapolis newspapers responded to the announcement with a spate of articles and editorials reviewing and interpreting Rand's career. This is not surprising. After all, as one journalist put it, Rand's incumbency on the council began when most of his present colleagues were "barefoot boys." Moreover, and for better or worse, his influence had had a significant impact on city government. Inevitably, too, friends and supporters organized banquets in his honor; and when he appeared at a campaign rally on behalf of his chosen aldermanic successor, who would lose the final election, the audience's enthusiasm focused on Rand rather than on the candidate.

At the expiration of his term, Rand moved from the sixth ward into a Prospect Park residence in the second ward, a more affluent neighborhood than the one he left. His friends in the sixth ward, it was said, did not view this as an act of desertion, but as a shrewd move designed to broaden his political base preparatory to running for mayor. Whether Rand planned to make a bid for the mayoralty is uncertain. Chronic health problems plagued him the last two years of his life to an extent not realized by his followers. Therefore his death on September 27, 1913, at the age of fifty-six, was all the more shocking because unexpected.[77]

Lars Rand may not deserve an exalted place within the Scandinavian-American pantheon, but he does deserve more attention than he has up to now received. For twenty years the Rand organization was a significant entity within the Cedar-Riverside institutional structure. It provided a predominantly immigrant constituency with jobs, entertainment, and sociability. It also helped to integrate this constituency into the American political system. And to a degree not easily measured, it probably enhanced immigrant self-

*The Minneapolis Journal*, Sunday, December 30, 1906. Courtesy of the Minnesota Historical Society.

respect. The spectacle of an immigrant politician holding his own against the massed opposition of the Minneapolis power structure must have been encouraging.

As pointed out earlier, Rand sought to avoid the impression that his machine responded solely to Scandinavian interests; instead he wished to be seen as the champion of the entire sixth ward immigrant constituency. At the same time he frequently expressed pride in his own Norwegian background, and some observers suspected that he exaggerated his Nordfjord accent while addressing campaign rallies. He also held membership in such organizations as the Odin Club and the Sons of Norway. However, he preferred not to make speeches in the Norwegian language.

A faux pas committed early in his career may explain this reluctance. At a meeting held to promote a cultural project, Rand, speaking in Norwegian, sought to advocate "uplift of the Norwegian people." Knowing that the Norwegian word for "lift" was *heve*), he evidently reasoned that adding the prefix *opp* would be equivalent to "uplift." Unfortunately for Rand, the Norwegian word *oppheve* means "abolish." Hence the alderman appeared to be calling for abolition of the Norwegian people.[78]

For obvious reasons, the relationship between Rand and Scandinavian prohibitionists, a vocal element within the Nordic community, lacked intimacy. However, one suspects that even zealous Scandinavian supporters of total abstinence resented the more strident Yankee assaults on the Norwegian alderman. *Folkebladet*, a relentless crusader against "demon rum," occasionally sniped at Rand, but in 1906 it pointedly abstained from participation in the Minneapolis Voters' League's crusade to unseat him. Seven years later, on the occasion of the alderman's death, the same newspaper gave his career a review that on balance was less negative than might have been expected.

Rand, asserted *Folkebladet*, "was an extraordinarily cunning politican who always sought to accommodate majority opinion within his ward, which he succeeded in doing to such a degree that no one in the city's history has served as long as he on the council. One could always find Rand opposing the money power [*pengemagten*] and supporting the saloons. His resourcefulness was remarkable, and his close friends admired his compassion for the victims of misfortune."[79]

## Notes

[1] *Minneapolis Tribune*, September 28, 1913; see also *Minneapolis Journal* and *Minneapolis Tidende*, same date. All three survey Rand's career.

[2] Writing in the 1950s, Carl G. O. Hansen, in *My Minneapolis* (Min-

neapolis, 1956), 136, noted that he had heard the barefoot boy story "sprung only a short while ago."

[3]James Gray, "Aldermen Come and Go but Lars Rand Goes on Forever," in *Minneapolis Journal*, December 30, 1906. This feature story is a helpful source of information about Rand. James Gray was a well-known journalist and Democratic politician. He was mayor of Minneapolis from 1899 to 1901, midway in Rand's aldermanic career.

[4]*Minneapolis Journal*, September 1, 1910.

[5]Hansen, *My Minneapolis*, 133.

[6]Hansen, *My Minneapolis*, 136.

[7]Alfred Söderström, *Minneapolis minnen* (Minneapolis, 1899), 89–92. On Bohemian Flats, see M. Mark Stolarik, "The Slovaks," in June Drenning Holmquist, ed., *They Chose Minnesota: A Survey of the State's Ethnic Groups* (St. Paul, 1981), 354.

[8]On Cedar-Riverside at the turn of the century, see Hansen, *My Minneapolis*, 145–152; and John G. Rice, "The Swedes," in *They Chose Minnesota*, 263.

[9]Lincoln Steffens, *The Shame of the Cities* (1904; reprinted New York, 1948), 71.

[10]A profile of the sixth ward appearing in the *Minneapolis Journal*, November 5, 1900, suggested that the area was becoming a "problem" ward. Housing conditions were crowded and sanitation facilities inadequate. "It may be absurd," commented the *Journal*, "to talk of relieving slum conditions in Minneapolis — we are so much better off than some cities — but why wait until conditions grow as bad as elsewhere before attempting reform?"

[11]Martin Ridge, *Ignatius Donnelly: The Portrait of a Politician* (Chicago, 1962), 249.

[12]Peer Strømme, *Erindringer* (Minneapolis, 1923), 286.

[13]Gray, "Aldermen Come and Go"; and Hansen, *My Minneapolis*, 134.

[14]For a detailed analysis of the Minnesota political situation in 1890, see Carl H. Chrislock, "The Politics of Protest in Minnesota, 1890–1901, from Populism to Progressivism" (Ph.D. dissertation, University of Minnesota, 1954), 100–142.

[15]*Minneapolis Journal*, August 28, 1890.

[16]*Budstikken*, September 3, 1890; *Folkebladet*, same date; Gray, "Aldermen Come and Go."

[17]*Minneapolis Journal*, November 5, 1890.

[18]*Folkebladet*, November 12, 1890.

[19]When the city council organized in January, 1891, E. G. Potter, the Republican candidate for council president, received fourteen votes. Eleven aldermen voted for John T. McGovern, the Democratic contender, and one alderman cast a blank ballot. *Budstikken*, January 7, 1891.

[20]Gray, "Aldermen Come and Go."

[21]*Folkebladet*, February 11, 1891.

[22]See *Minneapolis Journal*, January 29, 1900, for a brief biographical sketch of Joseph Kiichli.

[23]See also *Minneapolis Journal*, November 16, 1891.

[24]*Budstikken*, February 3, 1892.

[25]For accounts of February 12 council session, see *Minneapolis Journal*, February 12, 13, 1892; *Budstikken*, February 17, 24, 1892. In its obituary article on Rand, the *Minneapolis Tribune* for September 28, 1913, called his speech in favor of the ordinance "notable."

[26]*Minneapolis Journal*, February 20, 1892; *Budstikken*, February 24, 1892.

[27]For stories on the prolonged and complex litigation precipitated by the Rand ordinance, see *Minneapolis Journal*, April 26, 1892, January 23, February 5, 1895, November 22, 1900.

[28]*Budstikken*, March 9, 1892; O. N. Nelson, *History of the Scandinavians and Successful Scandinavians in the United States*, 1(Minneapolis, 1893), 564.

[29]Gray, "Aldermen Come and Go."

[30]*Minneapolis Journal*, November 9, 1892.

[31]*Budstikken*, March 1, 1893.

[32]*Budstikken*, March 15, 1893.

[33]Gray, "Aldermen Come and Go"; *Minneapolis Journal*, March 11, 1893.

[34]Hansen, *My Minneapolis*, 134.

[35]*Minneapolis Journal*, November 7, 1894.

[36]*Minneapolis Journal*, November 8, 1894.

[37]*Minneapolis Tribune*, September 28, 1913; Gray, "Aldermen Come and Go."

[38]The roster of participants in the sixth ward Democratic convention in 1894 reveals a striking mix of Irish and Scandinavian names, among them Matt Walsh, James Sweeney, John Flaherty, Harry Lund, John Hagman, Andrew Anderson, and Joseph Phillips. *Minneapolis Journal*, September 18, 1894.

[39]*Folkebladet*, November 14, 1894.

[40]*Minneapolis Journal*, October 6, 1913, quoting *Princeton Union*.

[41]*Minneapolis Journal*, September 6, 21, 27, 1894.

[42]On 1895 campaign in Minnesota, see George M. Stephenson, *John Lind of Minnesota* (Minneapolis, 1935), 105–129.

[43]*Minneapolis Journal*, July 23, August 3, 5, 1896.

[44]*Minneapolis Journal*, August 6, 1896.

[45]*History of Minneapolis: Gateway to the Northwest*, 2(Chicago, 1923), 78.

[46]*Minneapolis Times*, October 25, 29, 1896.

[47]*Minneapolis Times*, November 6, 1896.

[48]*Minneapolis Journal*, October 20, 22, 1898; *Folkebladet*, October 26, 1898.

[49]*Minneapolis Journal*, October 28, 1898.

[50]*Folkebladet*, November 2, 1898; *Minneapolis Journal*, November 1, 1898.

[51]On November 5, 1898, a few days before the election, the *Minneapolis Journal* carried a story titled "Farewell to Rand."

[52]*Minneapolis Journal*, November 10, 1898; *Minneapolis Tidende*, November 11, 1898. On statewide campaign, see Stephenson, *John Lind*, 140–158.

[53]*Minneapolis Journal*, March 5, 10, 12, 1900.

[54]*Minneapolis Journal*, March 15, April 12, 14, 17, 1900.

[55]*Minneapolis Journal*, January 29, February 20, July 16, 1900.

[56]*Minneapolis Journal*, February 1, 1900.

[57]*Minneapolis Journal*, November 7, December 22, 1900.

[58]*Minneapolis Journal*, November 8, 9, 10, 1900.

[59]*Minneapolis Journal*, December 24, 1900.

[60]*Minneapolis Journal*, January 9, 1901.

[61]*Minneapolis Journal*, January 8, 1903.

[62]On Ames scandal, see Steffens, *The Shame of the Cities*, 63–97.

[63]*Minneapolis Journal*, January 3, 1905. See also *Minneapolis Tribune*, September 28, 1913.

[64]*Minneapolis Journal*, November 5, 11, 1902.

[65]*Minneapolis Journal*, December 5, 23, 1903.

[66]*Minneapolis Journal*, August 18, November 3, 1904.

[67]*Minneapolis Journal*, September 11, 1906.

[68]*Minneapolis Journal*, September 20, 1906.

[69]*Minneapolis Journal*, October 29, 1906.

[70]*Folkebladet*, October 8, 1913.

[71]*Minneapolis Journal*, October 30, 1906.

[72]*Minneapolis Journal*, November 8, 1906.

[73]Gray, "Aldermen Come and Go."

[74]*Minneapolis Journal*, January 8, 1907, January 5, 1909.

[75]*Minneapolis Journal*, September 28, 1913.

[76]*Minneapolis Journal*, August 31, 1910.

[77]*Minneapolis Tribune* and *Minneapolis Tidende*, September 28, 1913.

[78]Hansen, *My Minneapolis*, 136; *Folkebladet*, January 20, 1892.

[79]*Folkebladet*, October 1, 1913.

# 3

# The Norwegian Heritage in Urban America: Conflict and Cooperation in a Norwegian Immigrant Community

*by Christen T. Jonassen*

Did you, I wonder,
Know the land came with you? Did you sense
Norway's irrevocable immanence
In bone and blood and mind?
Did you perceive that more than you had spanned
Ocean and continent — [1]

*Ted Olsen*

The cultural heritage that the immigrant brings is intangible and invisible, yet pervasive and real, and often produces dramatically visible cultural products and behavior. It is neatly packaged in a marvel of miniaturization in the brain and expressed in the personality of the immigrant. It is evident in many ways and is far too complex in all its ramifications to be adequately described in this brief article. The author has developed elsewhere the proposition that the principal components of the Norwegian cultural heritage are the Viking, Christian, and scientific-humanistic value systems.[2] The Norwegian value system is thus seen as a special synthesis of these three world views as they are modified by the collective historical experience of the Norwegian people within a unique physical environment. If an examination can be limited in time and space to some crucial aspect of a community's life, much can be learned about how the Norwegian heritage was influential in shaping that community's social structure and processes. This essay will therefore focus on *conflict* and *cooperation* in a Norwegian immigrant community as a way of ascertaining the operation of some important aspects of the Norwegian heritage in a large American city.

It cannot be claimed that all Norwegian immigrant communities, or all urban ones, or even the same community, will exhibit the same characteristics at all times, but this study is presented as a record and illustration of how the Norwegian heritage fared and was reflected in one Norwegian-American urban community at one time and in one place. Those who are familiar with the Norwegian heritage in Norwegian communities in Europe and America will recognize similar elements of it operating in different settings.

In 1946–1947 the Brooklyn Norwegian immigrant community had probably reached its maximum development. It was a unique historical era; World War II had just ended victoriously and Norwegian consciousness had been raised to a fever pitch of awareness by the German occupation of the homeland and the struggle to free it from the Nazi yoke. What was true of the community then does not necessarily describe present conditions, but that moment in history presents a unique opportunity to observe certain aspects of the Norwegian heritage in an urban American environment.

In 1940 New York City had the largest urban population of Norwegian stock in the United States, 54,530. The next largest was Minneapolis with 42,557. New York City Norwegians were then concentrated in Brooklyn, where the United States Census counted 20,714 persons born in Norway and 14,700 born in the United States to Norwegian parents. Stranded Norwegian sailors and refugees not counted by the 1940 census swelled the population of the Norwegian colony.

The distinguished historian Theodore Blegen noted long ago that "one of the principal Norwegian-American economic, professional, and cultural centers is to be found in

Brooklyn. The eastern city . . . is a lively center of Norwegian institutional and social activity . . . it represents fresher contacts with Norway than do the settlements of the Middle West."[3] Yet this group has received comparatively little attention in the general histories of Norwegian settlement. One work, by A. H. Rygg, however, deals exclusively with Norwegians in New York and is a valuable source of historical data.[4] A comprehensive sociological study of the community in 1947 by the author of the present essay attempted to ascertain the reciprocal effect of the Norwegian heritage and the American urban environment on the nature of the colony and the behavior of its citizens.[5] Much of the material presented in this article is drawn from that study.

As compared to the settlements in the Midwest, the Brooklyn community was unquestionably more oriented to the sea and seafaring. Perhaps it was also more Norwegian, since its population was constantly renewed by immigrants and visitors from Norway. Speaking of the colony as it was in the nineteenth century, Rygg said, "There was always a strong whiff of the briny sea over the Norwegian colony in these early days. Most of the people encountered had either been or still were sailors, or they were employed in shipyards, on harbor vessels, or in business having to do with shipping. In consequence thereof, a strong atmosphere of the sea prevailed."[6] A survey of occupations of Norwegian men in Brooklyn made by *Nordisk Tidende* in 1941 showed that this occupational orientation was still predominant then.[7]

In a community as heavily laden with seafarers one might expect some of them to exhibit characteristics of their Viking ancestors. Many were world-rovers, proudly independent and self-sufficient, following a masculine life-style of hard work, vigorous sports, and hard drinking. At the same time Norwegians in Norway and some of the Norwegian immigrants were strongly influenced by Christianity in the tradition of such fundamentalist evangelists as Hans Nielsen Hauge, Gisle Johnson, and Ole Hallesby. To this volatile ideational mix in the colony were added the ideas of immigrant journalists and intellectuals who rejected Christian fundamentalism in the name of the humanism of Bjørnstjerne Bjørnson, Henrik Ibsen, and Arnulf Øverland. With so much to divide them, what bound these Norwegians together enough to enable them to form and sustain a viable community?

CONFLICT

When people are willing to sacrifice and fight for something, one can be sure that it is of vital importance in their lives. Social conflict colors social relations and reveals in contrasting behavioral hues ideologies and values that motivate actions and create social structures.

It should not be assumed that all members of a community are always engaged in conflict. Conflict is intermittent and usually involves only a minority at any one time.

Three principal points of conflict were discernible within the Brooklyn community: the conflict between the first and second generations, the conflict between the "Neo-Vikings" and church-centered people, and the conflict between the Christian value system and that of scientific humanism. These conflicts cut across kinship and associational lines.

The conflict between the first and second generations was essentially a conflict between Norwegian values as incorporated in the value-attitude system of the parents, who were born and bred in Norway, and the value-attitude system of their children, who were strongly influenced by American peer groups and the American schools. It was not that the children wished to deny their Norwegian background; on the contrary, they were for the most part proud of it.[8] But differences arose concerning the practical aspects of everyday living. And the children were incapable of appreciating and understanding the values to which many of their parents clung with emotional obstinacy. The parents were able to convey to their children an intellectual knowledge of many things Norwegian, but the deeper emotional attitudes did not survive the transfer. This caused friction and lack of sympathy. A second-generation Norwegian defined the situation in a slightly different way: "The first generation was so occupied with making a living that they did not have time to sit down and evaluate the culture from which they sprang. The attitude of their neighbors was, forget the old world. And the American schools set out to make us one hundred percent American."[9]

Areas of conflict developed in the home. The Norwegian parents had been brought up in a home with strict discipline, where the father was completely dominant and the children obeyed immediately and without question. They had had very definite duties and responsibilities to live up to and perform. These first-generation parents were inclined to bring up their children in the same way. But the children soon learned that, generally speaking, their American friends had much more freedom and fewer responsibilities, and were not so strictly disciplined. Conflict therefore arose between these points of view, and at best the result was compromise, often after considerable unpleasantness. The older Norwegians had a certain attitude toward their homes and found it difficult to accept the "hotel" attitude that was so prevalent around them.

Another point of conflict involved education. In the Norway of the parents, a person was considered an adult at fourteen, and was at that time expected to take on adult responsibilities. Any boy not able to do so might be considered something less than a man, a burden to others, and a weakling who could not take care of himself. In America, economic dependence had been continued to eighteen, to twenty-two or even longer, as it has been to a large extent in modern Norway. Although Norwegians loved their children and were convinced of the value of an education, the old view persisted, making parents reluctant to extend education, and the children, who sensed this attitude, reluctant to accept it even if it had been offered. Up until about 1945, college-educated second-generation Norwegians in the community were something of a rarity. In more recent times, there has been a considerable change of attitude on the part of many parents, and more and more young men and women of Norwegian background are going to colleges and professional schools.

Another source of conflict between generations was the use of the Norwegian language. This was apparent especially in the churches, where the Norwegian language was being forced out. As the first generation aged and the control of the church passed to the second generation, they, who spoke English and considered themselves American, were not interested in maintaining the Norwegian language. As it became apparent that Norwegian must go, the old people waged a bitter fight to keep it. For them the Norwegian language evoked thousands of unexpressed memories. An immigrant speaking of the use of Norwegian in the churches said: "There the sermon was in Norwegian, and the hymns were the ancestral expressions of a mystic power, a comfort and consolation in distress, a continuum from childhood in Norway, filled with sentimental and warm memories."[10] But for the second generation it meant little, and they could not see why they should pay another minister just to have it around.

The same problem was encountered in the clubs and lodges, but there a conflict based on age also entered the picture. Many organizations such as Bondeungdomslaget (The Farmer Youth Association) had been started by young men and women years before. The original members of the Bondeungdomslaget were no longer either farmers or youths and their interests had changed. They were now more interested in a good dinner than a cross-country run, more inclined to talk than to dance. But the second generation coming into the group were interested in the kinds of things—athletics, dances—that set the blood coursing more quickly, and they were more inclined to pursue these activities in American than in Norwegian ways. The original society had been organized to cater to the interests of one age group only; it now had to decide whether it would provide for different interests.

Conflict also arose about morals and behavioral norms: what was "sin" and what was not "sin." Many Norwegians were members of deeply religious pietistic sects and what to these parents was "sinful" and "worldly behavior" was, to the children associating with American friends, just exercising their inalienable right to a good time. They could not understand why dancing, roller skating, or going to the movies should make one a candidate for eternal hellfire.

This conflict of values between the first and second generations appeared within every church congregation, the second generation wanting a more liberal attitude and the first generation obstinately and passionately opposing any change. A pastor, in his annual report in 1946, wrote of the problems of his church:

"We realize . . . that there are still more difficulties to be overcome in the future. Bethelship Church is a bilingual church. We must face honestly the fact that as time passes on, and no new immigration takes place, our work will gradually go over to English. From a psychological point of view this is a delicate process which must be led in a wise and careful way. The English group must try to understand the elder Norwegian group who for years have carried the responsibility for the church. On the other hand, it is necessary that the Norwegian group meet the English group with concession and deference, realizing that the younger generation might have differences of opinion and attitudes on many questions".[11]

Though modern Norwegians do not esteem such nasty Viking habits as raiding and pillage, they do admire other qualities traditionally attributed to the Vikings, such as courage, tenacity, self-sufficiency, and physical prowess. Like the Vikings, many are not averse to feasting and fighting. In this sense they are "Neo-Vikings." In the Brooklyn community studied, they were bound to clash with the Christians, who stressed mildness, sobriety, and selflessness in a life devoted to achieving the end of all existence, eternal salvation.

The battle for men's souls is graphically depicted in the history of the Bethelship Church, which started its work in an old ship, the *Henry Leeds*, bought for $65 and tied up at convenient docks in Manhattan and Brooklyn. A street scene in the early settlement was described thus in a church history:

"In 1905 it was decided to buy 57 Rapelye Street. It was an old brick building about one hundred feet from the corner of Columbia Street and Hamilton Avenue—the so-called 'Grimstadhjørnet.'* Sin was unveiled there in all its rich colors. It offended many, but caused other multitudes to be saved. There was opposition to the church meetings and some tried to disrupt them. There were saloons next door to the mission and right across the street. The one next door very soon had to close its doors, and the one across the street was always changing owners. However, many attempts were made to disrupt the meetings. One time two Italian singers were hired, who together with a howling phonograph sought to create as much noise as possible from the second story of the saloon. But the louder they sang and played the stronger sounded the testimonials and the evangelical songs. Crowds were attracted by the unusual din, which caused many who otherwise would never have come around to receive a wound in the soul by the double-edged sword which was being swung with such power."[12]

There had always been a fundamental conflict between the "Neo-Viking" way of life on the one side and the asceticism of the religious fundamentalists on the other. Most of the time there was no direct contact between the two worlds. To go from one world to the other one had to go through the major psychological upheaval involved in "conversion" and "rebirth," and churches arose which specialized in this rite of passage. Sometimes, however, the protagonists of both ways of life existed within the same family, which created an almost intolerable situation for the individuals involved. It was not too unusual for the wife to be a devout Christian and the husband a hard drinker who had no use for Christianity or "saved" Christians.[13] She had probably married him in the mistaken hope of converting him. In such cases the two acted as constant goads on each other, which led to a life of prolonged marital warfare.

*"Grimstad corner": a hangout for immigrants from Grimstad, a town in Norway.

In the community, although there was no organized so-cial contact, there was interaction between these groups. The very existence of the saloons and the behavior of the "Neo-Vikings" stimulated the more religious to create associations that later developed into the twenty-one churches of the community. Furthermore, the "Neo-Vikings" were there as "horrible examples" to be thundered against in Sunday morn-ing services. Thus, paradoxical as it may seem, the saloon was a factor in sustaining the church, since the saloon gave a dra-matic *raison d'etre* for the church's existence. The church had a similar effect on the saloon. The constant aim of the mis-sions was to make the saloon group see the error of its ways and to point out the horrible fate of eternal hellfire in store for its habitués if they persisted in their way of life. The tech-nique of "conversion" was to create so much anxiety that the individual would alter his old habits and experience a "re-birth." But if the process was only partially successful, it sim-ply created a tension which demanded more alcohol for relief.

Those who were not *kristelig* (saved), tended to look upon the church group as "joy killers" and bluenoses, and ac-cuse them of being judgmental, self-righteous hypocrites. And at times the "saved" looked upon the "Neo-Vikings" with something that could hardly be described as "Christian love." It was "righteous wrath," because the saloon group persisted in "throwing away God's gift of grace." Some of those who were on the receiving end of this wrath called these church people "the fierce Christians."

Perhaps the most irreconcilable conflict in the commu-nity was that between the evangelical religious fundamen-talists and the "scientific humanists." Their differences were so basic that disagreements cut right across life patterns and affected all aspects of life. Humanism runs counter to super-naturalism, which interprets history as the actualization of di-vine providence. Humanism looks to man rather than to God as the agent of creation, who, by the application of intelli-gence and will, can control his fate.

In the Brooklyn community the protagonists of these

two ways of life had for years been conducting ideological warfare. The pages of *Nordisk Tidende* bore constant evidence of the two groups' sniping at each other. One avowed Christian wrote, "There is a spiritual conflict in this world between God and Satan. They both want our souls. No human being in this world can be neutral. The decision is personal and is of immediate concern."[14]

Another individual complained that free utterance was taboo in Norwegian–American newspapers because the editors had been given the "scientific" facts too late in life and "have not been able to throw off the influence of theological dogma." He explained that when children are conditioned to believe that "the Holy Writ" is the word of the creator they are not able later on to think independently. He then went on to review the scientific evidence for the theory of evolution.[15]

A contrary opinion was expressed by the Christian who wrote: "Science has thrown light on many things, but the 'theory of evolution' is an attack on the Bible by atheists. In no place do they profess their belief in an almighty, eternal, and sinless God. If the expression 'the survival of the fittest' can be used correctly, then it is the blessed Bible which through the ages has 'survived' all attacks of the unbelievers."[16]

The opposing points of view were represented in *Nordisk Tidende* by two columnists. Paradoxically, the scientific humanist, who certainly was concerned mainly with the things of this world, used for his column a title that had biblical connotations, "The Text for the Day" (*Dagens Text*); while the pastor who wrote the column on the church page, more concerned with heavenly things, gave his column an English name, "This World of Ours". Each one had his loyal and disputatious public.

One correspondent wrote: " 'Dagens Text' by Roedder is without doubt the best thing in *Nordisk Tidende*. When one looks at the slop which is served each week on page ten [the church page], then one might think that they would not begrudge those who like sound common sense and reasoning this little piece of Roedder's. But that is unfortunately not the case. They seem to think that if we could only be brought back to the ox wagon and wooden plow, things would be wonderful."[17]

A rebuttal soon appeared: "An admirer of Roedder's 'Dagens Text' writes in *Nordisk Tidende* for July fourth about the 'slop' that is served on page ten. Now it happens that this is the church page, and it is apparently its contents which, in comparison with Roedder's philosophical viewpoint, are 'slop.' . . . But when such a one casts aspersions on the church and its work, then it is in order to say: 'It is of no use; the church bells will ring long after it has been forgotten that the entire matter ever existed.' Think that over and become wise."[18]

To these fundamentalists the Christian faith represented a closed system in which all truths had been revealed and set down in the Bible. There was little room for additions or amendments. It was a psychological necessity for people who lived by these values to defend them at all costs. This was done in two ways: either by attempting to suppress the opinions of others which would be a threat to any part of the system, or by ignoring such facts or events as in themselves would constitute a threat. The church group in the community was strong enough to use both methods. There was constant pressure on the owner and editors of the newspaper to suppress opinions and news which did not conform to the values of the church group. Direct and veiled threats to boycott the newspaper and to deny it advertising were made, and pressure was brought to bear on the owner to suppress the opinions of writers the group did not like. The newspaper could not publish accounts of suicides, arrests for drunkenness, or anything else which reflected on the personal life and morals of any one in the ministerial profession. It could not accept any liquor advertisements because it would immediately lose the support of the most powerful organized faction of the community; nor were any saloons or taverns allowed to advertise in the newspaper. The result was that the newspaper had to steer a policy course which wound in and out among these ideological shoals. The church group was strongly against anything having to do with alcohol. One of the secular organizations conducted a bazaar for the benefit of one of the Norwegian institutions. In this connection they issued a program with advertising; among the advertisements was one for a saloon. As a result, the institution refused to accept the eight hundred dollars which the organization had collected, saying that it was tainted money.

Intime Forum, a society established in 1935, probably best reflected the spirit of scientific humanism. It presented plays, arranged for discussion groups on art, literature, and science, and invited prominent authors, poets, journalists, and politicians to give lectures on all kinds of subjects. The ideals of Intime Forum were tolerance and broadmindedness, reasonableness, sensitivity to all points of view, and freedom to discuss them. This attitude and these activities were anathema to the fundamentalist Christians who practiced the ascetic life-style demanded by their strict and literal interpretation of the Bible.

When news of the free and open discussions in Intime Forum and the subjects of these discussions got around, the leaders of the Forum were immediately attacked as atheists and radicals. One of them replied in this fashion in the society's tenth anniversary publication: "The Forum's leaders have from time to time been accused of disseminating radical propaganda—of starting a freethinkers' society in the middle of our peaceful community. There is, right in our enlightened century, enough left of the Middle Ages so that 'free thinking' or the use of man's greatest gift is looked upon as an improper activity. This is an old story. It happened in the market place of Athens. And when Galileo Galilei sought to propose his theory that the world was not the center of the universe, there was a dangerous commotion. The confession that the church demanded of Galileo is enlightening reading even today, and should be included in all school books . . .

"Many different points of view have been heard in the Forum, and each time Intime Forum has been pressured by special interests and groups . . . "[19]

*Nordisk Tidende* was watched carefully and nothing that

deviated from the church viewpoint was overlooked. The editor, in a long article, made this incidental remark: "That the Stavanger milieu likewise has created a surplus of frustrated emotions is evidenced by two things: tremendous mission activity and migration."[20] This statement was immediately pounced upon by the church columnist who replied in these words: "There you are—to be interested in spreading the gospel among the heathen at home and abroad is merely one way of demonstrating that one suffers from neuroses and is the helpless victim of a thwarted life . . . As an average emigrant interested in things religious, I haven't the slightest feeling of being thwarted or frustrated. On the contrary, my leaving home was an adventure, a natural expression of my life in God. No, that interpretation of the urge to emigrate and the unfolding of a Christian life will hardly be accepted."[21]

One week "Dagens Text" quoted an article by a pastor which told of a small boy who had looked for fifteen minutes at a book with obscene pictures in it and how, ever since, the book had plagued him terribly. Roedder accused the pastor of exaggeration and then went on to make some comparisons between the contents of the Bible and certain literary works, and to make some remarks on freedom of expression.[22]

He was immediately answered by the church columnist in these words: "Once in a while contemptuous disdain for the Christian way of life finds outlet in some of our own newspapers. Some may think it takes great courage to speak so realistically about filth and freedom of expression. I don't. To class the Bible with the vulgar and obscene literature of the gutter does not denote courage, but rather reveals a perverted sense of the appropriate."[23]

One of the most outspoken attacks on the value system of the church group was made in 1935 by a columnist who expressed his views in this fashion: "I said America is the last citadel [of religious revivals]. There are a few spots left in Europe where this type of revival still shows some spasmodic signs of life. Norway is one of them, especially in southern and western Norway.

"In these regions the so-called 'Pentecostals' are busily 'bringing in the sheaves,' and 'speaking in tongues' appears to be an everyday emotional debauchery. Now and then a community is startled by the commission of a gruesome crime or by a series of sexual irregularities, and not infrequently the doors of the local insane asylums are swung open to admit the victims of delusions, hallucinations, or worse. . . .

"Strictly orthodox Protestant churchmen are . . . hostile to [liberal] doctrines. Why? Because liberalism has a tendency to destroy belief in the ancient traditional religious doctrines handed down by the church from Jewish Bible times. Churchmen do not attack spurious liberals. It is the truly openminded person who in Norway is called *frisinnet* who is the target of their hostility.

"Human society is not static. If it were, a doctrine of any sort, religious or otherwise, might conceivably be true. Some people speak of 'eternal verities.' That is an abstraction and literally means nothing."24

It will be obvious that there was a fundamental and irreconcilable difference between those who believed that certain eternal and universal truths had been fully revealed, and the point of view expressed above. There were clear and decisive cleavages in the community. These differences in value system were reflected in the associational structure.

When values are organized they become social forces within the community. But a community is not composed just of contending forces and groups and their clashing value systems; there must also be cooperation. On what, and in what ways, did the members of this particular community cooperate?

## COOPERATION

There was, of course, much cooperation within the various worlds that have been described; and within the associations formed to further specific values, the members cooperated. But was there any evidence of cooperation on a larger scale that embraced the whole community? Was there something that could unite these divergent points of view?

For the first generation, the principal source of unity arose out of the fact that they were all Norwegians. There was the obvious bond of a common language. But there were other values that they all had in common. They had certain deep feelings for things Norwegian: the Norwegian flag, old songs and music learned in the home, certain fundamental expectations about behavior, and national foods and crafts. The various holidays, national and religious, were celebrated by all even if in different ways. There was a phrase in the colony that seemed to imply much: "with Norway in their hearts." It was a feeling that could hardly be analyzed or described, because it was not verbalized and was a blend of many memories and sentiments. These Norwegians quickly became assimilated. They gave up their language, became American citizens, and adopted American ways of life. They became almost passionately American; but always there was "Norway in their hearts." Such sentiments are well illustrated by excerpts from a speech by a Norwegian: "Deep down there is that which gives us a strong feeling of solidarity—that is, Norway in our hearts.

"On that Nordmanns Forbundet was founded. On the basis that Norway, Norwegian culture, Norwegian heritage were stronger than boundaries—It is as if the Norwegian language, Norwegian national values—melodies from Norway—all that is apparent and all the hidden Norway—satisfies our greatest need, our greatest longing, wherever we roam in the world.

"That which follows us everywhere out there is the light from Norway—not only the light from the country itself, from the glaciers, from the living water—in waterfall, sea, and fjord—the light from sun-spangled foliage and white birches, and from our beautiful Norwegian midsummer . . . but also the light from the Norwegian spirit, as it grew like birches, often from poor soil, from clefts in the crags—the light from Wergeland—Edvard Grieg—Bjørnstjerne Bjørnson—Fridtjof Nansen."[25]

The strong patriotism of the Norwegians has deep historical roots. It must be remembered that Norway did not become completely independent until 1905. Independence came after many centuries of struggle to free itself from domination by or union with other Scandinavian countries. There had been a resurgence of the most intense patriotic feeling beginning in the early nineteenth century. As the old days of greatness were glorified by the poets and writers, Norway set about making itself more completely Norwegian by extirpating "foreign influences." The names of some cities were changed and in a deliberate manner the language was altered to diminish the Danish influence and make the Norwegian language "genuinely" Norwegian. In this way Norwegian self-esteem, which had suffered by being subordinated to Denmark and then to Sweden, was restored.

Norwegian ethnocentrism and strong feeling for the mother country has other psychological roots as well. The nature and religion of Norway may have conspired to create an individual whose social ties are not too highly developed, an individual who often feels lonely and shut out, and who has some difficulty in establishing warm personal relationships.[26] Yet the need for human response and intimate relationship is there. It is possible that all this need, when denied expression in primary relationships by culturally induced inhibitions, is projected onto the nation. In this way history supports the psychological processes of the functioning individual.

The patriotic feeling of the Norwegian community was tremendously intensified by the German occupation of Norway. It was like an electric shock that galvanized all groups to action. Differences were forgotten, and the indifferent were aroused. The circulation of *Nordisk Tidende* rose tremendously in spite of the fact that all immigration had been cut off. All groups organized efforts to help Norway. Norwegian Americans in the United States donated $31,757,000 to help Norway during and after World War II.[27] The fact that the United States and Norway were allies made these undertakings doubly desirable. Even the breach between secular and religious organizations was shakily bridged. Norsk Fylkning (Norwegian Federation) of New York was formed as a joint effort of all Norwegian groups to coordinate help for Norway.

The types of activity that Norsk Fylkning sponsored were in the main lectures and speeches, by Norwegians who had fought the Nazis and who had escaped to tell the tale, and by members of the royal family and government in exile. The programs also included singing and instrumental music.

After the war, there was an unsuccessful attempt to make this organization permanent. The churches sent but two delegates in all, and one of these, in the opinion of the church group, was something of a "black sheep." Only a world war could have brought the religious and secular groups together.

An examination of joint activities over a number of years revealed that such functions were essentially those having to do with patriotism in one form or another. The activities included showing films and slides from Norway, welcoming visiting Norwegian royalty and other prominent Norwegians, and petitioning the city to name a street or park after Leif Erikson.[28]

Conspicuously lacking was cooperation in community affairs. The religious group showed a tremendous spirit of sacrifice when it came to building a church, and the secular societies cooperated in buying and building a hall for their activities. Except for the 17th of May celebration, however, the two factions did not combine on any sustained program that included the whole community. This was understandable, since they were rivals trying to capture minds, loyalty, and souls. Individual members of the two factions had very limited time and money available for activities outside of working hours. Nor did the Norwegian groups within the community participate in programs of civic betterment or neighborhood improvement. One Norwegian who had been active in the civic organizations of the larger community for years said that he had always been the only Norwegian member of such groups. One reason for this lack of involvement may have been that most community needs were met by the larger municipality.

In addition to twenty churches, however, the community supported a hospital, two children's homes, two old people's homes, a day nursery, and a children's camp, as well as some cultural and sport clubs. Many groups contributed to the support of these organizations, but the churches made the greatest effort.

Rygg, in commenting on the history of Norwegian organizations in New York City, indicated the difficulty which Norwegians had in cooperating in larger groups: "It may be said that the numerous Norwegian societies have served useful purposes, but it is nevertheless a fact that the colony has had many more societies than are actually needed. The difficulty that some Norwegians have in getting along together has often led to the duplication of societies of similar aims and purposes. This has resulted in a waste of energy and talent. Fewer, and consequently larger, societies could function better and with more economy and efficiency.[29]

It will be seen that in the main the various factions within the community were able to cooperate on activities that were essentially charitable and patriotic in character. One of the leaders who had for many years attempted to bring groups together said: "Norwegians agree on the value of being Norwegian, but thereafter they seem to be mainly concerned with showing that they are different from other Norwegians."[30]

SUMMARY

It is clear that there were four rather distinct value systems which constituted the dynamics in the social processes of conflict and cooperation within this community: there was the value system of the second generation which was predominantly American, but which contained some Norwegian influences; there was the value system of the "Neo-Vikings"; there was the value system of the church-centered groups; and there was the value system of the group whose basic philosophy was scientific secular humanism. The three main value systems that have contributed to the Norwegian heritage, plus the American pattern, were present as motivators of people's behavior in the community.

The conflict between the first and second generations was essentially the conflict between American values and attitudes and the values and attitudes held by those who were habituated to the cultural pattern of Norway in their youth. The first generation, while it had succeeded in imparting an intellectual appreciation of things Norwegian to its children, had succeeded only partially in establishing Norwegian values as component elements of the value-attitude system of the second generation. This difference was the basis of the conflict between generations. It would seem therefore that the home was not the only factor in shaping values and personalities. The influence of American institutions, particularly the public school, the neighborhood and peer groups, was clearly evident in the result.

The conflict between the "Neo-Vikings" and the Christian outlook on life was perhaps the oldest of all and had been waged for centuries in Norway before the Christian way emerged the victor, yet without completely extirpating Viking influences. Those influences were suppressed and redefined, but continued to live a *sub rosa* existence, always affecting Norwegian behavior.

A tight little world of concepts and values which had been created over centuries of development in Norway interacted as components of the value-attitude systems of the Norwegian-American people. And, as in Norway, the battle lines of the *Kulturkampf* were boldly drawn. In fact, if anything, the struggle was more intense in America than in Norway, because the church that had been established in the early days of the colony had been founded by persons who were imbued with the strong religious fervor and asceticism of nineteenth-century Haugean Lutheranism. The spirit of that church, divorced from the cultural influences of the mother country, had remained essentially the same, while the church in Norway had altered considerably, as had other aspects of the cultural configuration there. The main cultural trend in Norway had been in the direction of the scientific humanistic orientation. This orientation had been lacking in the colony before 1920. There was therefore a wide gap between the value systems of the earlier immigrants and the later ones. This was recognized by one of the leading ministers of the colony who said, "Furthermore, it seems that the majority of immigrants who came over in the decade before the war [1920–1930] have a totally different outlook than the immigrants from earlier times. It cannot be denied that the later groups who had Christian interests are of a different kind than the older groups who in their time founded the Lutheran churches and welfare work in this country."[31]

The relationship of the Brooklyn colony to its parent culture was very apparent, but there was a difference, and an individual just arriving from Norway would observe this difference immediately. In some respects the immigrant culture was the culture of an older Norway with the addition of some new elements. It was as if a section of nineteenth-century Norway had suddenly been detached from the homeland, been isolated, and developed without the evolutionary influences that had continued to shape modern Norway. A woman expressed it this way: "I felt strange at first here in Brooklyn; I had a peculiar feeling as if I had gone up in the attic and rummaged through mother's old things that brought back memories of the old days."[32]

The Norwegian poet Herman Wildenvey visited the colony and wrote a long poem about it; one of the verses goes as follows:

> "I looked about me in the hall.
> It was a most peculiar crew.
> Well, — Brooklyn's children, Norway's all
> Have their special visage new."[33]

In the colony various cultural elements converged that had been separated and that had for decades developed along different lines and under different influences. During this time, differences had been created which resulted in a conflict of cultures within the community. The values of the heritage had persisted because they had met fundamental human social and psychological needs of functioning individuals. Different values became incorporated into individuals' value-attitude systems, and thereby motivated social intercourse. In the processes of conflict and cooperation, values became organized through the formation of associations by the people who held those values and who wanted to combine to protect and sustain them by transforming them into action patterns that would be repeated. These action patterns then became the programs and activities of organizations such as churches, lodges, sport clubs, social, cultural, and patriotic organizations, and saloons.

The American urban environment of the Brooklyn Norwegian colony and the ideological contradictions derived from the Norwegian heritage produced strains and stresses, but the social fabric, though woven from so many cultural skeins, did not break. A viable community was formed and persisted. What made it possible were the bonds of Norwegian consciousness that were stronger than the forces that would tend to divide.

While there is still a Norwegian community in Brooklyn, Knight E. Hoover's research and census data show that there has been some dispersal within Brooklyn and to the outlying areas of metropolitan New York, New Jersey, and Connecticut.[34] Without the benefit of systematic new research on community conflict, but based on a reading of *Nordisk Tidende* and numerous visits to the community, the author's impression is that the lines of cleavage that divided the community have been blurred. The issues that formerly engaged people no longer seem to produce as passionate and bitter debate; ideology may not have vanished, but it has been much weakened.

## Notes

[1]Ted Olsen, "Salute to Norway," in *The Hawk's Way* (New York, 1941), 41–42.

[2]Christen T. Jonassen, *Value Systems and Personality in a Western Civilization: The Norwegians in Europe and America* (Columbus, Ohio, 1983).

[3]Theodore C. Blegen, *Norwegian Migration to America: The American Transition* (Northfield, Minnesota, 1940), 516.

[4]A. N. Rygg, *Norwegians in New York 1825–1925* (Brooklyn, New York, 1941).

[5]Christen T. Jonassen, "The Norwegians in Bay Ridge: A Sociological Study of an Ethnic Group" (Ph.D. dissertation, New York University, 1947).

[6]Rygg, *Norwegians in New York*, 28.

[7]*Nordisk Tidende*, "An X-Ray Picture of a Norwegian American Colony" (Brooklyn, New York, 1941).

[8]*Nordisk Tidende*, May 20, 1946.

[9]*Nordisk Tidende*, January 24, 1935.

[10]*Nordisk Tidende*, June 27, 1946.

[11]Bethelship Norwegian Methodist Church, *Annual Report Book, 1946*, 9, 11.

[12]Bethelship Norwegian Methodist Menighet, *Femti Aars Jubelæet: 1874–1924*. Translated and quoted by Jonassen, "Norwegians in Bay Ridge," 438.

[13]Jonassen, "Norwegians in Bay Ridge," 414.

[14]Jonassen, "Norwegians in Bay Ridge," 416.

[15]*Nordisk Tidende*, December 5, 1946.

[16]*Nordisk Tidende*, February 21, 1946.

[17]*Nordisk Tidende*, July 4, 1946.

[18]*Nordisk Tidende*, August 1, 1946.

[19]Intime Forum, *Tenth Anniversary Number*, 1945, 5.

[20]*Nordisk Tidende*, November 14, 1946. Stavanger is in southwestern Norway, an area which has been called the "Bible Belt" of Norway — a stronghold of religious fundamentalism.

[21]*Nordisk Tidende*, November 21, 1946.

[22]*Nordisk Tidende*, April 10, 1946.

[23]*Nordisk Tidende*, April 17, 1946.

[24]Harry Sundby-Hansen, in *Nordisk Tidende*, January 24, 1935.

[25]Speech at the anniversary of Nordmanns Forbundet, in Wilhelm Morgenstierne, *Et større Norge* (Oslo, 1932), 119, 120. Quoted and translated by Jonassen, "Norwegians in Bay Ridge," 422, 423.

[26]For data supporting this thesis see Jonassen, *Value Systems and Personality* and "Norwegians in Bay Ridge."

[27]A. N. Rygg, *American Relief for Norway* (Brooklyn, New York, 1946), 138–144.

[28]See files of *Nordisk Tidende*, especially before and after the 17th of May.

[29]Rygg, *Norwegians in New York*, 80.

[30]Jonassen, "Norwegians in Bay Ridge," 426.

[31]C. O. Pedersen, in *Nordisk Tidende*, March 21, 1946.

[32]Jonassen, "Norwegians in Bay Ridge," 429.

[33]Herman Wildenvey, "Amerikanske billeder — Bay Ridge," Stanza 62, in *Stjernenes Speil* (Oslo, 1935). Translated by Jonassen.

[34]Knight E. Hoover, "The Ecology of Norwegian Americans in

Metropolitan New York from 1940–1980," in George A. Theodorson, ed., *Urban Patterns: Studies in Human Ecology* (University Park, Pennsylvania, 1982), 202–206; *Sixteenth Census of the United States, 1940: Nativity and Percentage of the White Population*, 80–86; *Twentieth Census of the United States, 1980: Ancestry of Persons*, 581–585.

# 4

# The Haymarket Affair and the Norwegian Immigrant Press

*by Arlow W. Andersen*

On November 11, 1987, a graveside ceremony will undoubtedly take place at Waldheim cemetery in Oak Park, on the western edge of Chicago. There lie the remains of four men whose direct guilt in the Haymarket riot of May 4, 1886, has never been established. They were among those charged with inciting to violence in a bomb-throwing incident which brought death to seven policemen in downtown Chicago. Imprisonment and trial followed, ending with their hanging in the Cook county jail on November 11, 1887. One can only surmise who will be present to observe the centennial of this gruesome historical event. To the majority of their contemporaries the victims were dangerous socialists and anarchists whose punishment was well deserved. Others regarded them as genuine martyrs to the twin causes of reform and justice, seeking to benefit an oppressed working class. Their immediate goal was simply an eight-hour day for all industrial workers.

While the antipodal points of view suggested above do not lend themselves to reconciliation, it is safe to say that the judgment of the twentieth century would be more concerned with the punitive atmosphere and the questionable procedures in the trial than with the social and economic aims of the accused. Radicals in their day, were these dead to rise and

97

look about them they would find comfort in learning that their nineteenth-century vision for the lower ranks of society, including unskilled immigrants, was not completely askew. In fact, their dreams have in large measure been fulfilled.

The labor question was not new in the 1880s. But the rise of the modern factory had created a human robot, paid, to be sure, but nevertheless committed to long hours of tedious work under unpleasant and often hazardous conditions. Fringe benefits were unheard of. Hardly any segment of the western world escaped this dehumanization. Tolstoy painted the picture correctly when he remarked that people he saw on the streets of St. Petersburg seemed to be walking along a wire that drew them unwillingly toward their factory jobs. From the first days of the Christian era, and probably much earlier, the laborer was said to be worthy of his hire. Unfortunately, that worthiness was lost sight of in the impersonal drive for profits.

American labor retaliated by organizing its forces. Among its first nationwide efforts was the founding of the Noble Order of the Knights of Labor, the name itself suggesting both secrecy and grandeur. Its beginning in 1869 received little attention in the Norwegian-American press. A decade later *Bikuben* (The Beehive), the voice of Mormonism for Scandinavian converts in Utah, denounced the yearning for profit but turned its attention more toward allegedly dangerous social and economic philosophies. The editor declared socialism to be "an unmerciful enemy" in European countries. He saw the same red color and the identical destructive pattern in the French Commune of 1871, Russian nihilism, and American railroad strikes. *Bikuben* took seriously the rumors that anarchists were storing ammunition in American cities, and spoke out for gradual reform of working conditions within the law.[1]

The early 1880s brought an unusual sharpening of tension between dissatisfied laborers and adamant employers. Norwegian-American editors and correspondents surveyed the world of manufacturing much as the general public did. Some played the "plague on both your houses" game, scolding the contending parties for ignoring the welfare of the people. Others added that labor's right to organize was not in question, but that unions should not resort to sabotage or drive away "scabs," the non-union strikebreakers. Too bad, they thought, that the Knights of Labor, embarrassed by their large membership — 700,000 in 1886 — and handicapped by the demands of disparate interest groups among them, could not control their rebellious and violence-prone factions. Agitators from France and Germany further aggravated the problem.[2]

A few journalists spoke more positively on behalf of the exploited laborers. Rapid industrial development had produced an unprecedented impulse toward progress, something in which labor would have no share unless capital came to the rescue. Had a larger segment of Norwegians in America been identified with urban manufacturing and processing and with railroad maintenance, perhaps their newspapers would have discussed the sad plight of the working class in greater depth and length. As it was, the majority of their readers were involved in farming, which knew no limitations on working hours and which carried no assurance of a fixed income.[3]

Well-informed Norwegians understood that one of their fellow citizens, of an earlier generation, had championed the workingman's cause in both Norway and America. This was Marcus Thrane, who had provided the original impetus to the rise of labor as an organized force in his native land. In 1850 he drew up a petition which was signed by hundreds and presented hopefully to King Oscar I of the twin kingdoms of Sweden and Norway. In the perspective of the twentieth century, the petition must be deemed reasonable and moderate in its proposals. But the authorities, suspicious of violence, which Thrane had repeatedly warned his followers against, moved in and arrested him. He spent the next eight years in prison.

The second half of Thrane's life was lived out in America. Through the medium of two Chicago newspapers,

*Marcus Thrane's Norske Amerikaner* in 1866 and *Dagslyset* (Dawn), a philosophical-religious monthly from 1869 to 1878, the exile from Norway supported a new radical reform movement then coming upon the American scene. He likened the party to the Social Democratic organization in Europe. In 1878, still in Chicago, he and Louis Pio, a Danish-American socialist, edited *Den Nye Tid* (The New Times). Thrane's declining years, until his death in 1890, were spent rather uneventfully in the home of his son Arthur, a physician in Eau Claire, Wisconsin.[4]

Norwegian-American responses to Thrane's death were tolerant in tone but lacking in appreciation. None associated him with conspicuous service to society. All condemned him for his freethinking agnosticism. They conceded his importance to the labor movement in Norway but thought him too superficial to be great.[5]

Concerning the Chicago Haymarket violence of 1886, the Norwegian immigrant press appraised it, for the most part, from the cautious perspective of the propertied classes. Readers learned of a confrontation between policemen and strikers at the McCormick Harvester Company plant on May 3 and of the socialist-inspired protest meeting of the following evening at Haymarket Square. There the fateful and mysterious bomb was thrown and the seven policemen killed. Suspects were rounded up, known socialist leaders in particular, whether they had attended or participated in the meeting or not. During the ensuing weeks the metropolitan and national press covered the trial of the alleged murderers. Jury verdicts were finally announced in August. Eight men were declared guilty of murder, primarily because of their socialistic-anarchistic philosophies. Seven of them were sentenced to death. Governor Richard Oglesby of Illinois commuted the sentences of two of the doomed men, namely Samuel Fielden and Michael Schwab. Louis Lingg committed suicide in his cell. Eventually four men were hanged: August Spies, George Engel, Albert Parsons, and Adolph Fischer.[6]

American popular opinion saw the bombing as the work

of a motley crew of radicals infesting Chicago. Immediately there arose a cry for vengeance, with no thought of suspending judgment until the facts in the case could be determined. News accounts were sensationalized. The *Chicago Tribune*, the leading voice, left no doubt of its position. Because of a "hellish deed" at Haymarket Square the ground was covered with dead and mutilated police officers. The anarchists, "led by the wiry-whiskered foreigners, grew bolder and made repeated attempts to renew the attack," a description hardly supported by other evidence. The "windbag orators" themselves slunk away. This, in part, was the *Tribune*'s version of the night of May 4.

Foreign-born newsmen in America resented the implication that all the immigrants in this country had been hounded out of Europe and that they were all habitual lawbreakers. Like the vast majority of Americans, however, they registered indignation, if not hostility, toward the weapon-wielding participants in labor strikes. No doubt the condemnation of the Haymarket prisoners in Norwegian-American newspapers came easier by virtue of the circumstance that no Scandinavian name emerged in the search for the bomb thrower. Overall, they registered disgust or horror at the killings. *Budstikken* (The Messenger) of Minneapolis said little, the editor choosing merely to write a column on the rise of un-American socialism among Germans, Poles, and Bohemians. *Skandinaven* of Chicago appears to have deliberately avoided mention of the clash of May 4. It had kind words, however, for Grand Master Workman Terence V. Powderly of the Knights of Labor, who was urging moderation among his unruly and heterogeneous membership. When the dust had settled, *Skandinaven* addressed two columns to employers, suggesting that most troubles derived from misunderstandings, and that employers, in their own interest, would do well to offer reasonable and acceptable terms to their employees. Let workers have a say in the conditions of their employment, as John A. Johnson of Madison, Wisconsin, was doing in his machine-tool industry. *Decorah-Posten*, though less outspoken, deplored the vandalism (*pøbeltøier*) in

Chicago. It feared that the struggle for an eight-hour day would be lost because of the acts of anarchists "chased out of Europe."[7]

Other journals merely echoed the factual reports of the American dailies. Only *Budstikken* opposed the death penalty. The condemned men had not been proved guilty, it argued. The newspaper also sympathized with the Knights of Labor, who were caught in a dilemma. On the one hand, they denounced the philosophy of anarchism, with which critics identified the accused. On the other hand, the Knights pleaded for justice for the men under trial. This attitude placed the Noble Order in a position of seeming to implore mercy for men who showed no mercy themselves. *Budstikken* raised doubts concerning the fairness of the jury system. Judgment by peers was a good thing, it conceded, but impartiality was often impossible. Bribery, ignorance, public pressure, and prejudgments formed on the basis of early reports on the case might result in unjust decisions. Norwegian-American journals otherwise made no objection to the judicial proceedings and findings. Many believed that the courts and judges had correctly upheld law and order. Sentiment for life sentences rather than death weakened even more after the sensational discovery of bombs in the cell of Louis Lingg, one of the condemned men. Now nothing but the death penalty would do.[8]

Compassion tempered judgment somewhat when the wire services brought word of the hangings. *Skandinaven* had maintained a guarded silence, but now editor Peter Hendrickson, in an editorial entitled "Justice is Done," called the executions "a significant event in the nation's history." Let there be no hatred or bitterness, he wrote, but rather sympathy for the bereaved families; perhaps the home and the church had failed to influence these rebellious persons. In the spirit of the adage, "Show me the landscape and I will show you the man," Hendrickson seemed to portray the victims as products of bitter experience and cruel environment. *Decorah-Posten*, through an anonymous Chicago correspondent, sensed that most Chicagoans deplored the executions, feeling that justice might have been better served without the taking of human lives. Albert Parsons, one of the doomed four, was thought to have been less guilty than the others. All had faced death with dignity. But if the radical wing of the labor movement was thus severely prosecuted, might not would-be anarchists retaliate with violence in years to come? Hallvard Hande of Chicago's *Norden* (The North) also voiced this concern. He found it ominous that 15,000 mourners had joined the funeral procession and many more lined the streets. Other editors responded variously. One said that August Spies, a known anarchist and a highly intelligent man, was most guilty and that Governor Richard Oglesby of Illinois had had no choice, inasmuch as state law demanded death in murder cases. Another writer declared that Norwegians and anarchists were in basic disagreement: The freedom and unity preserved in the Civil War had to be maintained. *Nordvesten* (The Northwest) of St. Paul, and *Fædrelandet og Emigranten* (The Fatherland and the Emigrant) of La Crosse reported the details of the hangings but made no further comments.[9]

Though the immigrant press in general addressed itself specifically to the Haymarket experience, there were some newspapers that looked at the events in the light of the social gospel, which preceded the Christian Socialism of the 1890s. *Budstikken*, consistently humanitarian in its outlook, came out in favor of the eight-hour day as a measure that would insure a more relaxed and a more intelligent citizenry. It expressed regret when the railroad brotherhoods decided not to cooperate with Powderly and the Knights in any further demands. *Reform*, in Eau Claire, praised Powderly for his steady and wise labor leadership and not least for his stand on temperance, quoting from a speech delivered in Chicago in 1889. Four years later editor Ole Br. Olson regretted Powderly's resignation, calling the Grand Master Workman one of the great men of the time. Apparently Powderly held too many reins in his hands; his horses were taking off in all directions. As Chicago's *Amerika* indicated, many of the Knights were strong in demands but weak in work incentives.

The fight for the eight-hour day, however, was not completely lost. In 1892 Congress passed an eight-hour bill covering government employees in the District of Columbia. The Norwegian-American congressman Nils P. Haugen, formerly railroad commissioner for the state of Wisconsin, succeeded in getting the measure amended so as to include "drivers and conductors on streetcar lines, and employees in certain corporations doing business with the government, or in the public interest." In passing this bill, Congress probably spoke for the vast majority of Americans in a nation then witnessing rapid and substantial industrial growth.[10]

Among those deeply concerned on ethical and judicial grounds over the Haymarket hangings was the new governor of Illinois, John Peter Altgeld, elected in 1892. His Civil War experience as a volunteer infantryman and his demonstrated sense of a fairness notwithstanding, Norwegian-American editors accused him of liberal views and anarchistic sympathies after he pardoned the three remaining Haymarket prisoners. As a leading spokesman for the Democratic party he was destined to incur the wrath of Scandinavian Republicans. Nicolai Grevstad, the new editor of *Skandinaven*, led the way, charging that the German-born governor would some day be ashamed of the speech he deliverd to the state Democratic convention in the spring of 1892. In it Altgeld was said to have attacked the Republican leadership as threatening American institutions. Grevstad concluded that the governor had yielded to a political urge to foment German-American hatred of the Yankees.[11]

Undoubtedly Altgeld was aware of his potential strength in the class-dominated society of Chicago, where economic giants like Marshall Field, Gustavus F. Swift, and George Pullman prevailed in finance and government. Altgeld knew his political ground. He knew that the population of Chicago, the great metropolis within his administrative domain, was sixty-eight percent of foreign stock. These were the people who rendered aid in his election as a German immigrant to the highest office in the state.

No Norwegian-American newspapers acclaimed Altgeld's pardoning of Samuel Fielden, Michael Schwab, and Oscar Neebe on June 26, 1893. Grevstad of *Skandinaven*, craving a wider audience, responded in English, as if to sound a note of protest to the citizens of Chicago and of the entire state and country. He cited the governor's action as "anarchy at the helm." He saw it not as pardon, but as an act of compassion suggesting that the prisoners had not been given a fair trial. This distinction Grevstad understood, as a student and admirer of the American judicial system. But the electorate as a whole hardly comprehended the distinction. The governor was telling the nation that the prisoners had been unjustly condemned. At a ceremony at Waldheim cemetery, where a monument to the men hanged in 1887 was unveiled, the governor, in a long speech, extolled the deceased as martyrs. This was too much for Grevstad. "On behalf of the Scandinavians," he wrote, "we emphatically brand Governor Altgeld's message as a menace to law and order."[12]

*Amerika, Nordvesten*, and *Budstikken*, while speaking for themselves, agreed in the main with *Skandinaven*. To reject the judge's decision was one thing, to pardon was another. Men who openly advocated the use of dynamite in support of their political philosophy deserved no leniency simply because of good behavior. The governor was suggesting that anarchy and innocence were reconcilable. *Budstikken* questioned not so much the governor's action as his reasoning. The editor of this normally Democratic newspaper, and hence one likely to defend a fellow Democrat, would have preferred a simple statement without a lengthy review of the issues in the trial. Altgeld's implication of injustice in the heated atmosphere of the courtroom back in 1886 seemed to him unwise.[13]

If Governor Altgeld was criticized in 1893, Mayor Carter H. Harrison of Chicago had earlier been the target of many darts in the popular tumult which erupted after the mysterious bombing in 1886. *Norden* correctly reported that the American press, led by owner Joseph Medill of the *Chicago Tribune*, charged Harrison with having coddled socialists, even in the city government. Yet Harrison fared better than

Altgeld in the aftermath. Chicagoans reelected him repeatedly. *Amerika* felt that the people trusted the Democratic mayor despite his known propensity for collaborating with political gangs. Even Republicans voted for him. *Amerika* wished that both political machines would vanish. *Budstikken* seemed to go along with others in at least tolerating the worldly-wise Mayor Harrison.[14]

Harrison's murder on October 28, 1893, shocked the public and brought condolences, even praise, from all quarters. A disappointed office-seeker had gained entrance to the mayor's Ashland Boulevard home and shot him on the spot. Harrison had addressed an assembly of visiting mayors that day at the Columbian Exposition, or World's Fair. *Norden* remarked that there was more sorrow in Chicago at the murder than there was joy over the memory of Columbus's discovery of America. The editor described the exposition as a lasting monument to the mayor. *Amerika* headlined its eulogy "Our Carter is Dead." Yet Carter Harrison, it was said, fell victim to the lawlessness that characterized his administration. Succumbing to the low ideals of the people around him, he looked through his fingers at violations of law by saloon-keepers and gambling operators.[15]

Other journals spoke in the same vein. *Decorah-Posten* acknowledged Harrison's popularity and absolved him of demagoguery. Grevstad of *Skandinaven* claimed that even foreign countries would feel Harrison's loss. He called him "preeminently a whole-souled man," strong, vigorous, impressive, and gifted. This was high tribute coming from one of the staunchest Republicans among Norwegian Americans. The publisher of *Scandia* in Duluth-Superior, who clearly had socialist leanings, had once denounced Harrison. Now he declared, in a three-column editorial, that Chicago would never experience a greater sorrow. *Nordvesten* proclaimed that the murder of this public official was a blot on the record of American civilization, coming as it did at an exposition where many official representatives from all over the world were present. How long must the nation wait for civil service reform? First Garfield, and now Harrison, both excellent men, had fallen to the guns of office-seekers.[16]

Knute Nelson, then governor of Minnesota and later United States senator, withheld any public comment upon learning of Carter Harrison's violent death. No doubt he remembered his words of five years earlier, in 1888, spoken on the floor of the House of Representatives. On that occasion he defended foreign-born Americans, who would be the losers under the terms of a proposed new land law. Using his opportunity, he voiced his displeasure at Harrison's coddling of "a few crazy anarchists in Chicago" prior to the Haymarket explosion. At that time, he declared, "Chicago had something worse than the anarchists themselves. It had Carter Harrison (laughter and applause), who had nursed them for years here" and "got them to believe that they had come to this country to do anything under the sun except pay attention and be respectful to the flag of the United States. . . . We had better incorporate into the land laws that men like Carter Harrison should have no business in this country." In 1893, when eulogies were in order, Nelson held his peace.[17]

The Haymarket affair revived fears of violence and generated reappraisals, pro and con, of alien ideologies. Wiser heads came to understand that socialists wore coats of many colors, not all deep red. As a concept, socialism defied definition because of the diversity of kind and degree of social change intended and the methods to be employed. It ranged widely from radical to moderate, from atheistic to Christian, and from anarchistic to reformist working within the constitution. Criticism of socialism, however, was directed mainly toward the Marxist philosophy of class struggle, ultimate victory of the proletariat, obliteration of national boundaries, and a world at peace which had no room for patriotism, let alone nationalism. Most Norwegian analysts in America shied away from Marxism and of course had no kind words for anarchism. The assassination of President Sadi Carnot of France and Tsar Alexander III of Russia by anarchist hands in 1894 tended to make this predominantly European ideology more than a simple bogeyman. By 1903 Congress enacted a measure which banned alien anarchists from entering the United States and prohibited their naturalization.

Of the newspapers presently under review, only *Scandia* offered a clear defense of socialism around 1890, between the time of the Haymarket disturbance and the death of Carter Harrison. *Scandia* debated socialism with *Nordvesten*, claiming that the latter did not understand this new social doctrine. *Nordvesten*, it is true, sided with judges who denied citizenship to socialists, suspecting danger to American institutions. *Nordvesten* also took *Amerika* to task, conceding that socialism was acceptable in theory but that in practice it threatened both state and church. *Budstikken* leaned in *Scandia's* direction, citing the arbitrariness of the Chicago police. The editor's animosity toward *Skandinaven* may have colored his stand. Normally Democratic, *Budstikken* charged the generally Republican daily newspaper in Chicago with being two-faced, trying to satisfy both political parties, pretending to speak for agriculture and labor while favoring great monopolies, and pleading for temperance while not averse to running saloon advertisements.[18]

The press found it difficult to distinguish between anarchism and socialism, if indeed it made serious attempts to do so. *Syd Dakota Ekko* (South Dakota Echo) attributed anarchistic outbursts to poverty and portrayed anarchism as mainly a European phenomenon. *Folkebladet* (The People's Newspaper) of Minneapolis balked at the idea of honoring the four "anarchists" who paid with their lives. The editor held that such radicals were either Germans or Jews, Albert Parsons being an exception. When a German Jew from Russia praised Michael Schwab and a Farmers' Alliance leader made a martyr of Parsons at a Minneapolis meeting, *Folkebladet* wondered how far this adoration could go. Wasn't Ignatius Donnelly enough?, editor A. M. Arntzen asked, referring to Minnesota's leading exponent of populism. With an eye on this new people's party, *Syd Dakota Ekko* appealed to labor not to draw class lines.[19]

The Haymarket affair coincided with important labor

developments in Norway. It was at that time that a Social Democratic organization, a labor party, and a permanent party organ, *Social-Demokraten*, came into being. While Norway experienced nothing comparable to the rise of big business in the United States, the Norwegian press as a whole observed with concern the reform trend across the water. For the most part newspapermen in Norway were well informed about the Haymarket affair. They seemed to view it from the position of the peaceful American workingman, business manager, or government official. Their views paralleled in most cases those of the anti-socialist press in America; this cannot be attributable solely to imitation. Like their American counterparts, they were obviously ignorant of the identity and motivation of the bomb-thrower. Could it be, as Governor Altgeld of Illinois was later to suggest, that Captain John Bonfield of the Chicago police department had antagonized certain strikers and onlookers at the McCormick works with brutal clubbing and that one of the offended workers had decided to retaliate on his own against the police?[20]

The specific events of the Haymarket affair are relatively easy to record. Causes and consequences, however, remain more elusive. It is clear that the American people were outraged and that the Knights of Labor, although opposed to strikes, suffered a terminal blow. Skilled workers withdrew from the organization en masse. The Knights soon ceased to exert any significant influence in labor-management relations. The American Federation of Labor, with its union of unions, all skilled workers, fared better, though it suffered a temporary setback in the Homestead strike against the Carnegie steel mills in 1892. Few Americans, whether native or foreign-born, looked far beneath the surface of social and economic circumstances. For the vast majority, execution because of radical ideas and execution for murder were not inconsistent. Given the emotional pitch of the time, circumstantial evidence was enough to justify extreme punishment. If aliens were involved, and especially if they promulgated disturbing ideas, retribution seemed even more justifiable.

The Haymarket affair raised many troubling questions.

The issue of freedom of speech was involved. How far should public speaking be allowed without becoming license to advocate overthrow of existing institutions? A nation grounded in revolution found itself perplexed. When, if ever, should direct action take precedence over political avenues to change? How could a "new world" proletariat succeed against bourgeois opposition, represented by the moguls of finance and their protective guardians, the police and the courts? When could a repressed working class expect to be free from the domination of a laissez-faire economic system which seemed to rest upon an inhumane theory of the survival of the fittest? All of this made the search for the bomb-thrower of May 4, 1886, a matter of less importance.

Norwegian-American journalists devoted their attention mainly to the men being tried for the murder of the Chicago policemen, not to the elusive killer whose identity may never be known. As a rule, they were not bent on punishment. They sought no scapegoats. They showed signs of both justice and mercy, of the eye-for-an-eye principle on the one hand and a measure of Christian forbearance on the other. Some wondered whether employers had done their part to improve the lot of the working man. Others inquired whether the police had provoked the tragic Haymarket incident. Still others doubted that guilt had been proved in the courtroom. Opinions varied on the appropriateness of the punishment. Would the sensational deaths of the four condemned men only create martyrs useful to the cause of violent radicalism? Immigrant editors felt for the families of the doomed socialists but showed little sympathy for the prisoners who were pardoned. In this respect their views differed little from American opinion in general.

Notes

[1]Henri Troyat, *Tolstoy* (New York, 1967), 76; *Bikuben*, June 6, 1878.
[2]*Fædrelandet og Emigranten*, March 20, 1883; *Skandinaven*, June 17, 1885, and March 31, 1886; *Amerika*, May 20, 1885.

[3]*Folkebladet*, March 3 and May 5, 1886; *Norden*, April 27, 1886; *Budstikken*, May 4, 1886.

[4]Halvdan Koht, *Marcus Thrane. Til hundreaarsdagen, oktober 14* (Kristiania, 1917), 31–50; Aksel Zachariassen, *Fra Marcus Thrane til Martin Tranmæl* (Oslo, 1962), 43–44. In 1949 the Social Democratic government of Norway arranged to have the earthly remains of Thrane removed, with appropriate ceremonies, to Vor Frelsers Gravlund (Our Savior's cemetery) in Oslo, the final resting place of many of Norway's immortals.

[5]*Nordvesten*, May 8, 1890; *Amerika*, May 7, 1890; *Decorah-Posten*, May 7, 1890; Johannes B. Wist, "Pressen efter borgerkrigen," in *Norsk-amerikanernes festskrift 1914* (Decorah, Iowa, 1914), 92–93.

[6]Henry David, *The History of the Haymarket Affair* (2nd ed., New York, 1958) is the most thorough and comprehensive treatment of the subject. The first edition was published in 1936.

[7]*Budstikken*, June 1, 1886; *Skandinaven*, May 19 and June 9, 1886; *Decorah-Posten*, May 12, 1886; *Nordvesten*, May 13, 1886; *Norden*, May 11, 1886; *Amerika*, May 12, 1886; *Fædrelandet og Emigranten*, May 11 and June 1, 1886.

[8]*Budstikken*, November 5, 1886, and May 4, 1887; *Norden*, August 24, 1886; *Amerika*, December 1, 1886, and November 9, 1887; *Decorah-Posten*, November 9, 1887. According to the Norwegian-American writer Hjalmar Hjorth Boyesen, the Chicago press during the trial "complimented the Scandinavians of the West on their law-abiding spirit, and the counsel for the defense emphasized the compliment by requesting that no Scandinavian should be accepted on the jury." See "The Scandinavians in the United States," in *The North American Review*, 155 (November, 1892), 526–535. It is possible that Boyesen overstated the case.

[9]*Skandinaven*, November 16, 1887; *Decorah-Posten*, November 16 and 23, 1887; *Minneapolis Daglig Tidende*, November 10 and 12, 1887; *Amerika*, November 23, 1887; *Nordvesten*, November 10 and 17, 1887; *Norden*, November 18 and December 6, 1887; *Fædrelandet og Emigranten*, November 16, 1887.

[10]*Budstikken*, July 10, 1889, and September 3, 1890. This newspaper (April 30, 1890) expressed some scepticism over the designation of May 1 as International Labor Day, with the eight-hour day as the immediate objective. It was possibly editor R. S. N. Sartz who cautioned labor against moving too fast. *Reform*, October 15, 1889, and December 12, 1893; *Amerika*, November 20, 1889; *Congressional Record*, 52nd Congress, First Session (1892), 5730–5736.

[11]*Skandinaven*, May 4, 1892.

[12]*Skandinaven*, July 5, 1893. The monument was dedicated on June 25, 1893.

[13]*Amerika*, July 5, 1893; *Nordvesten*, July 6, 1893; *Budstikken*, July 5, 1893. Sigvart Sørensen edited *Budstikken* from 1891 to 1894. When Altgeld declared in December, 1893, that he would not be a candidate for the United States Senate, Sørensen called it an example of sour grapes, stating

that Altgeld would never have been chosen. He had lost the nomination in 1884. For a brief account of Altgeld see "John Peter Altgeld (1847–1902): Man of Conscience," in Cecyle Neidle, *Great Immigrants* (New York, 1973), 43–66.

[14]*Norden*, May 25, 1886; *Amerika*, April 12, 1893; *Budstikken*, April 5, 1893.

[15]*Norden*, November 4, 1893; *Amerika*, November 1, 1893.

[16]*Decorah-Posten*, October 31, 1893; *Skandinaven*, November 1, 1893; *Scandia*, November 3, 1893; *Nordvesten*, November 2, 1893; *Reform*, October 31, 1893; *Syd Dakota Ekko*, November 8, 1893, where editor Gabriel Bie Ravndal appears to have "echoed" Wist's remarks in *Nordvesten*: no more "to the victors belong the spoils"; *Fædrelandet og Emigranten*, April 9, 1888.

[17]*Congressional Record*, 50th Congress, First Session (1888), 2460. Apparently only *Fædrelandet og Emigranten* (April 8, 1888) took note of Knute Nelson's remarks on the occasion. Editor Ferdinand Husher, in approval of Nelson's contribution, called attention to the Democratic as well as the Republican applause after the speech.

[18]*Scandia*, November 13, 1891; *Nordvesten*, October 29 and November 19, 1891; *Budstikken*, March 28, 1888, and January 23, 1889.

[19]*Bikuben*, April 26, 1894; *Folkebladet*, November 11, 1891; *Syd Dakota Ekko*, January 11, 1893.

[20]Henry M. Christman, ed., *The Mind and Spirit of John Peter Altgeld: Selected Writings and Addresses* (Urbana, Illinois, 1960), 94.

# 5

## "I Live Well, But . . .":
## Letters from Norwegians in Industrial America

*by John R. Jenswold*

The brown heirloom daguerreotype of the frontier farm family of the mid-nineteenth century is beginning to give way, in the light of recent research, to the starker black and white portrait of the turn-of-the century immigrant.[1] The new picture bears the stamp of the bustling city. It is the image of a solitary young man. He is dressed for work and holds a lunchpail in his left hand, his tools in his right. In the background is the suggestion of a busy dock, a factory floor, or a shipyard.

His experience differed from that of his compatriots who had settled the Illinois and Wisconsin countryside in the 1840s and 1850s. The earlier immigrants had tended to cluster together in "communities of neighbors of like origins." The rural settlers worked, played, and worshipped with a small group of neighbors who were themselves immigrants from Norway, even from the same district in Norway. Their compact settlements were preserves of Norwegian language and culture. Isolated in newly settled frontier land, these subsistence farmers were able to live their daily lives with few contacts with Yankees and other outsiders.[2]

In contrast, the new Norwegian immigrant of the city encountered non-Norwegians daily. His enclave may have been no larger than his room in a boardinghouse. Outside his

113

door were a variety of people, languages, and cultures. Down the hall may have lived an Italian, a Swede, a Finn, and a Canadian. On the street he passed shops with signs bearing unNorwegian names — an Italian grocer, an Austrian cobbler, a Jewish tailor. The workday was punctuated by the sound of strange languages. He may have been supervised by a Yankee foreman and received his pay from a British clerk. On Sunday, his day off, he may have attended church, visited friends from Norway, or sung in a Norwegian chorus. Only then was he among his own people, speaking his native language. For most of his American experience, he was a stranger in a land of other strangers.

The new Norwegian immigrants were but a small contingent of the great migration of workers from all parts of Europe who contributed to the industrialization of America. While overshadowed in raw numbers by those coming from eastern and southern Europe, the flow of immigrants from Norway and other northern and western lands did not merely continue but increased. Three-quarters of a million Norwegians left for America between the end of the Civil War and the beginning of the Great Depression, dwarfing the better-documented wave of 71,000 who emigrated in the rural migration of 1846–1865. Emigration from Norway and other parts of Europe followed American economic cycles. It accelerated in times of prosperity, such as 1882, when 28,804 Norwegians left in the migration's peak year. It lagged when depression and war dimmed the opportunities promised by American industry.[3]

The new immigrants' identity as workers is established by the group's demographics. While the majority of the earlier group had migrated in families, the later Norwegians usually came to America alone. Most were men, 60 percent of those who came between 1880 and 1930. The proportion of male emigrants rose in periods of heavy emigration, when the appeal of industrial opportunities was strong, and fell when general emigration declined. Most of these immigrants were between the ages of 15 and 29 — younger than those who had arrived in the first wave. Between 1866 and 1915 the proportion of men in that age group increased from 40 percent to 78 percent, while among the women those in that same working-age group increased from 35 percent to 70 percent.[4]

A quiet revolution had changed the face of Norwegian emigration, making the newcomers, in the words of Einar Haugen, "children of a new age in Norway." They were members of a mid-century "baby boom" that more than replenished the population the country had lost to the earlier emigration. Coming of age in the second half of the century, they were witnesses to the vast changes an incomplete industrialization had brought to everyday Norwegian life. They had seen new machinery change forever the old work processes in the mills, on the farms, and in the forests and fisheries. The streams and rivers of fairy-tale Norway were harnessed to power plants. Rail lines and telegraph wires crossed the mountains to link the countryside with the factories and markets of the towns.[5]

Rural Norway sent to the towns not only its crops and livestock, but its people as well. While boosting production, the new mechanization created a surplus of farm workers and craftsmen. For the remainder of the century, many of those displaced abandoned the traditional life of farming to move to the cities and towns. The country became increasingly urban: from fewer than 20 percent of the population in 1865, over a third were living in the towns and cities by the turn of the century. And the towns, themselves no havens for persons with traditional skills, became but a stage in a longer journey—emigration to the United States. Increasingly, the Norwegians brought some urban experience with them to America. Nearly one-third of those who emigrated between 1880 and 1915 came from towns, as compared with one-tenth in the period before the Civil War. Even if many of them had come from the countryside originally, they arrived in the New World not totally unfamiliar with urban life.[6]

While Norwegians continued to settle on American farms—with relatives in the Midwest or on new farms in the Great Plains and the Pacific Northwest—a growing number were lured to the cities. As Norwegians Rolf Kåre Østrem and Peter Rinnan state with compelling logic, "Persons with urban skills and experience would more naturally migrate to American cities."[7] Norwegians began to be found in urban occupations. In the 1880s, the number of Norwegian men working in manufacturing tripled, while those in the trades and urban service jobs also increased dramatically. Similarly, the number of employed women (excluding farm wives) tripled during the 1880s, the majority of them migrating to cities and towns to work in trades, transportation, and domestic service.[8]

These immigrant workers were the pioneers of a new kind of Norwegian community in America—the urban *koloni*. As Norwegian America became less rural after 1880, ethnic neighborhoods began to appear in several cities. Chicago served as the first major urban center for Norwegians, to be rivaled by Minneapolis and Seattle as the main destinations for Norwegian immigrants in the 1890s. These three cities became the cultural centers of their respective regions: Chicago for Norwegians in the Great Lakes states, Minneapolis for those in the Upper Midwest and Great Plains, and Seattle for both new arrivals and transplanted midwesterners in the Pacific Northwest. After the turn of the century, greater numbers of Norwegians made it no farther into the new land than New York City. There they found residence and work among their compatriots in Brooklyn, the emerging center of Norwegian culture on the Atlantic coast. The percentage of Norwegians residing in four major urban centers—Brooklyn, Chicago, Minneapolis, and Seattle—grew from 6 percent in 1880 to 20 percent in 1920.[9]

In these four cities, the later immigrants joined descendants of the rural pioneers who were leaving the Norwegian enclaves of the Midwest to seek work in industry. Visible elements of ethnic community life appeared among the urban Norwegians—churches and their subsidiary charitable and social associations, fraternal and athletic clubs, and singing societies, as well as Norwegian-language newspapers and ethnic business enterprises. Less comprehensive colonies appeared in such American cities as Boston, Philadelphia, and San Francisco. By 1930, most Norwegian Americans, like most Americans in general, were classified as "urban."[10] Within a century, Norwegians had found their way from the countryside to the city.

A large number of Norwegians, however, cannot be found in the records of the colonies' population or institutions. An uncounted number of Norwegians—and other Europeans—roamed through the cities in search of work. Many sought seasonal employment in factories and mills on the eastern seaboard before returning home. Their search led them through industrial cities—Chicago, Detroit, San Francisco, and, on the east coast, Brooklyn, Philadelphia, Boston, and the ports of New Jersey.[11]

Like other immigrants of the era (and "guest workers" in present-day Europe), these Norwegians were temporary members of the American work force. According to Norwegian government records, one-quarter of all those who emigrated to America between 1881 and 1920 returned home between 1891 and 1940. The percentage rose during recessions and depressions.[12] Such persons had not made a permanent commitment to America. They were uncertain how long the American industrial boom would last. Some had simply given up on their dream of America and returned home. Others had never intended to stay in the first place. Married workingmen left Norway determined to earn and save for a few years before reuniting their families—on either side of the Atlantic. Young men who would have been apprenticed to craftsmen or hired out to farmers in an earlier time were sent to supplement their family's income by working in American factories. Young women sought positions as housekeepers, intending to build a dowry. They had left determined to work in America only for a summer or for a year or two.

These birds of passage tend to escape the historian's vision. They present two major problems: First, as residents of two countries and people of two cultures, they have often been unclaimed by either American or Norwegian ethnic historians and genealogists. Second, like other working persons, they tend to be underdocumented. A footloose carpenter is not as likely as a successful industrialist or a prolific journalist to leave a diary or a collection of letters treasured by descendants and by archives.

Traditionally, immigrants' letters have been invaluable tools in reconstructing the world they lived in. Scandinavians' "America letters" had the effect, Theodore Blegen noted, of "a vast advertising movement," attracting immigrants in the first half of the nineteenth century.[13] Passed from hand to hand and home to home in a Norwegian community, or read aloud at family gatherings, the accounts of Norwegians' adventures in a new world "were undoubtedly the decisive influence in ripening many a decision to emigrate."[14]

More often than not, the early America letters were desperate attempts of permanent immigrants to keep in contact with neighbors and relatives whom they might never see again. The first dispatch home would contain a lengthy description of the once-in-a-lifetime trip across the Atlantic to an uncertain future. Reading further, those at home learned of the immigrants' first feelings about setting foot in the new homeland, the legal procedures of entry, and the initial, and usually unpleasant, encounter with the city. The first stage ended with an account of the long trek across the vast continent to the new farm in Wisconsin or Minnesota.

Subsequent letters described the first year in America — the search for shelter, the difficult winter on the prairie, and the coming of the first spring. The immigrant would attempt to describe new kinds of implements, crops, and livestock to people who had never seen them. He might write about the region and its climate, the neighboring farmlands, and the closest town. The immigrants' first steps toward American citizenship were recounted along with news from the new homeland, including political and economic events. The reports to Norway ended with requests to be remembered to friends and family left behind. They promised vaguely to return to visit after becoming more prosperous, and exhorted others to emigrate.

In time, the letters became annual reports of major events in the American experience, and then they came less often until one correspondent finally stopped writing altogether. In some cases, the exchange was ended by death. In others, the separate lives they lived in America and Norway drew the letter writers away from the common feelings and experiences they had shared before one of them had emigrated.

The letters Kristian Kristoffersen posted from Chicago to his friend Frants Michaelsen between 1885 and 1891 followed this pattern.[15] Like the initial letters from the rural emigrants, Kristoffersen's first letter, in December, 1885, detailed his experiences after leaving his native Buskerud. He described the trip from Kristiania to Liverpool and across the Atlantic to New York. The inconvenience of the immigration formalities at Castle Garden was contrasted with the exhilaration of setting foot in his new homeland.

During his first year in Chicago, Kristoffersen reported proudly on his American adventures, balancing enthusiasm for his new home with nostalgia for the old. He left no doubt that he would become a permanent resident. He told of finding work in terms that could be considered an encouragement to emigrate. For the past six weeks he had been one of 250 men working in a piano factory. It was hard work, but good pay—ten hours a day for a dollar a day. Despite his good job, Kristoffersen found everything—even the necessities of life—very expensive. But this frustration could not dim the glamour of Chicago. The city was a wonderland "so big that we see little of it." At the end of each letter, his thoughts returned to Norway. He inquired about Michaelsen's family and their mutual friends. He closed by insisting that his "dear friend in Old Norway" write soon.

After a few months, Kristoffersen became more deeply immersed in his new environment. In August, 1886, he wrote lengthy and breathless commentary on American events—the Haymarket Affair and forest fires in Wisconsin—in a way that assumed that these events were well reported in the Norwegian press. His work remained steady and satisfying, but prices were still high. Nonetheless, he confided, he planned to splurge and go boating on Lake Michigan on Sunday, his day off. Labor violence, the factory routine, and idyllic leisure left little time to feel homesick for Norway.

After a year, Kristoffersen began to write of returning to Norway to visit. He told Michaelsen that his homecoming would not be the homing flight of a bird of passage. Nor would it be the embarrassed return of a prodigal son. It would be the homecoming of a successful immigrant. He would return "as an American, not as a Norwegian." Like one newly betrothed, his enthusiasm broke through an affected coyness as he reported that he had just visited the courthouse to take out citizenship papers. Being American has many practical benefits, he informed Michaelsen solemnly. With the beginning of the new year of 1887, his first-year papers filed, he subtly changed his signature. "K. Kristoffersen" of Buskerud had become "C. Christophersen" of Chicago, Illinois, U.S.A.

In the summer of 1891, Christophersen took up his pen again to invite his Norwegian friend and his wife to the World's Columbian Exposition of 1893. The fair, he promised, would display wonders the two Norwegian boys would never have thought possible. He offered the Michaelsens free lodging "if I'm alive and healthy." He recorded his address and suggested that Michaelsen write if he had the inclination, ink, and paper. Beneath the signature, C. Christophersen scrawled, "I hope you remember the name."

With this poignant plea to be remembered, the collected correspondence ends. The boyhood friends became two men facing middle age in separate lives on different continents. Their shared experiences had dimmed as, with commitment to permanent American residence and citizenship, K. Kristoffersen of Buskerud vanished into the bustling milieu of turn-of-the century Chicago.

The Kristoffersen-Michaelsen letters differ greatly from a group of urban America letters discovered at Grimstad in

Norway. The accidental finding of these letters underscores the difficulty in documenting the experience of most immigrants. In the fall of 1981, a worker repairing an old building in Grimstad, East Agder, uncovered a sack of mail hidden behind an attic beam. The cache contained sixty-seven letters postmarked from various American cities in March and April of 1896 and addressed to persons in the area. After several months of public debate and controversy, Norwegian officials declared that the Grimstad letters were public property, as national historical materials whose value exceeded the interests of the descendants of the letters' intended recipients.[16] Indeed, these letters from Norwegian immigrant workers provide a rare glimpse into the world of the later Norwegian immigrant.

Fate, in the form of two young postal employees who stole the letters in the 1890s, delivered these America letters to historians in the 1980s. Mail theft was a common fear among correspondents through the period of immigration. The abrupt end of a correspondence raised the suspicion that letters had been stolen from the mail on one side of the ocean or the other. One suspects that "mail theft" sometimes provided a convenient alibi for curtailing unwanted correspondence. The presence of large amounts of cash in the letters provided the thieves with a motive and the recipients with a fear. Ironically, the writer of one of the purloined letters suspected mischief on the part of the "mail boys." "I would not put anything in the letters after you said 'Stop!' " she wrote, "but at that time we had already sent a letter with four dollars enclosed."[17]

Such references help define the letter writers as birds of passage, temporary workers who sent a portion of their earnings home in cash. In part, their willingness to send cash through the mail reflects the immaturity of the Norwegian-American banking system. While banks that were "Norwegian" or "Scandinavian" in name if not in management appeared in Chicago and Minneapolis, as well as smaller midwestern cities, Norwegians on the east coast had few alternatives to Yankee bankers. Brooklyn's *Nordisk Tidende* noted periodically the reluctance of the immigrants to patronize American banks. The newspaper warned its readers of the dangers of hoarding cash or sending it through the mail, and advised them to open savings accounts and send non-transferable money orders to Norway.[18] The newspaper praised the opening of the Hamilton Bank in the heart of the Norwegian colony in 1892, noting the large number of Norwegian names on the accounts register. An "American Norwegian Envoy Bank," established in New York in the following decade, also won *Nordisk Tidende*'s approval, although the newspaper noted darkly that most of the depositors were Swedish.[19] A more satisfactory ethnic arrangement was found when Edwin O. Lee opened a "savings bank division" in his popular store and ticket agency. Among other services, Lee offered "Scandinavian Money Orders" for the immigrants to send money safely. One such money order — $33 for a memorial fund for a deceased worker — was among the few enclosures the mail thieves left in the Grimstad letter sack.

Despite their nearness to New York, the emerging banking center of the world, most itinerant workers lacked the confidence or the stability of residence to patronize banks, be they run by Yankees or fellow immigrants. They eschewed non-transferable certificates for American currency, preferring its convenience or, perhaps, its symbolism. The value of American currency was apparent: it represented a hard-earned wage that was parted with only at great sacrifice.

Money — the motive for both emigration and mail theft — was the most common theme of the letters. Many writers promised future shipments of cash and apologized for not sending more. One young man pledged to his family to send money "in three or four weeks. It has already cost a lot to travel so far," he wrote, "and I have no money to give you or I would give you some." A man advised his "dear wife and little daughter" to "be glad if I can earn a little so we can get our debts paid." In the meantime, he pointed out, "I must live and have good health until next summer, so that we can soon be free of debt." "It is about time for me to send home money again," Anna Jensen wrote her parents, but she could not send any until the second of April. Then, she advised them to deposit the money in the bank, even if they are "in need." Her family was not to think her "hardhearted" for her frugality. These promises and apologies reflect the frustrations of people living at the subsistence level during the depression of the 1890s.

At that level, work and the search for work were at the center of life. The new immigrants found that the industrial economy and their position in it affected all aspects of their experience. "When I have work, I am in a better humor," J. Håland wrote from Booklyn, "and time goes faster." Poverty was a common concern and a startling reality between jobs. Theodor Gundersen, apologizing to his mother for not writing, claimed that he lacked the five cents needed to post a letter. Like other immigrants, he sought to understand his position in the fluctuating economy during the depression when job security was rare, and during the rough winter of 1895-- 1896 when unemployment rose and wages fell. Optimists predicted improvements in the spring. "Here times are still bad," Jacob Olsen Fevig wrote home in April, "but things will soon get better when summer sets in."

Working and surviving in the new environment seemed to demand a tougher attitude than the immigrants had been used to at home. Those with steady employment accepted their wages stoically but complained of high prices. After paying for his own tools and paying $4 a week for board, one man calculated, his job at the docks left him with only 50 cents a day.

Work in American factories was more regulated than in Norway, the immigrants reported. Hours were long and voluntary time-off was not common. Holidays were fewer in the more secular country. J. Håland complained that he had to work not only on Maundy Thursday and Good Friday, but on Easter Monday as well. "Today is Easter Monday," another immigrant wrote his family from Westline, Pennsylvania, "and I think I would rather be home now."

Sundays offered some relief. The immigrants reserved

their day of rest for simple pleasures and nostalgia. On Sundays, J. Håland wrote, he could sit contentedly with a pot of coffee and a bit of tobacco at his side to write letters. Others ventured out to explore the new land, to take in a concert or a circus, or the city's parks and museums. Norwegians in New Jersey and New York traveled to Brooklyn to seek friends from home, or to socialize in the cafes and taverns. The day might end with a small party in a home. It is not surprising that many of the Grimstad letters were written on Sundays.

Through their letters, many immigrants tried to manage their affairs in Norway. Intending to return, they were determined to keep their farms and households running, their families and loved ones faithful, and their children obedient during their absence. In one letter, a man expressed concern for the family farm, directed renovations, and advised on fire insurance. In another, a husband gave his wife permission to buy a loom and a rocking chair. A young woman wrote her parents to protest their decision to take her younger sister out of school. "She needs another year of school," she begged. Her own education, she told them, "stays in my head and I have often wished I could go to school again." Nils Danielsen advised his ill wife to seek medical treatment in Kristiania. Another man tried to prevent his daughter from leaving home for Kristiania. He was certain, he wrote her, that she had badgered her mother into allowing her to go. "Isn't Grimstad good enough for you anymore?" he scolded. "I have few children, and I worry about you in such a big city as Kristiania," he wrote—from Brooklyn.

The letter writers sought not only to influence events at home, but to retain ties of family and friendship by reporting on others in America. Kristine Olsen greeted her family for Anders, who is greatly respected in his job, and from Danjel Olvesen, who has found work at last. B. G. Aanonsen sent greetings from his co-worker Aanon and from Mathias, who "drives around town selling potatoes for someone from Kristiansand." Reports of neighbors' successes and failures ended frequently with pleas to greet a host of named persons in Norway.

This common desire to maintain control of events and persons from overseas reflects a general frustration with poor communications. Throughout the period, Norwegian-American newspapers printed regular columns of names of immigrants from whom little had been heard. The immigrants had similar worries about persons at home who had become silent. "I have been over to Brooklyn every day and asked after letters from you," one writer lamented, "but nothing." A young immigrant appealed in desperation to his girlfriend from whom he had heard nothing in two months. He was tired of waiting, he wrote her from Philadelphia. This letter would be his last, he vowed, if he did not hear from her in the next few days. Another young man, Carl Christiansen, confessed to his correspondent that "it has been a long time since I heard anything from you, so I thought you were dead." His letter was written in Philadelphia but mailed from Boston—a reflection of the effects of mobility on communication.

In addition to their frustrations over money, work, and lack of letters, the immigrants expressed their homesickness freely. "I have now been over here in this fabled land a long time" one wrote from Boston, "but my thoughts are on that little island where I was happiest." A young woman urged her best friend to recall their school days. Although Johan Andersen feared that he had been forgotten at home, it would be nice to return. "O, if only I were there today," he wrote. "I should have gone home earlier." A young woman described her loneliness on her eighteenth birthday. At home, it would have been a great event, she lamented, but she felt alone in Chicago.

Although reunion was the permanent solution to the problem of loneliness, the decision to stay in America or to return home was by no means simple. A man in Elizabeth, New Jersey, wrote that he could not possibly afford to stop working. Things were going so badly that he would be lucky to save anything at all. Maybe he would return home "next summer." A young woman admitted enjoying herself in America, but confessed "it would be good to see Norway again." Such comments reflect the sentiments of people leading split lives.

One solution to the problem was to encourage others to emigrate, to rebuild the worker's family and friendships in America. "I hear that Ida and Galugna will come over in May," one wrote, adding, "so you should come too." Writers filled letters with detailed practical advice. In his last letter to his wife prior to her departure, B. J. Aanonsen advised her to sell everything in their Norwegian household except the children's schoolbooks, her clothes, bedding, and some family photographs which she was to bring to their new home in America. He reminded her to take some refreshments and an unbreakable chamber pot on the journey, "for the children's sake." Their four children's hair should be cut short, he advised, so that they do not attract attention on the streets of New York. When she arrives in America, she will enter Ellis Island, "a big building the likes of which you have never seen." "Don't be shy," he advised her, "act as if you were at home." She was to sign her name as Andersen, as Yankees cannot handle the name of Birgette Aanonsen. She should stay at the immigration station until he or a substitute came to meet her. "I certainly look forward to the day when I shall see you again after four years of separation," he concluded.

Another Brooklyn man advised his brother on the difficulties of finding work during the American depression. As an added challenge, the young man was advised, "You must learn early to drink beer, for that is the main thing in this country." Another man sent a brother a ticket with the stern advice not to tell anyone that he had a job waiting for him, such an admission might identify him as a contract laborer, imported at the expense of native workers. Although an immigrant had to prove that he would not become a public charge, prepaid tickets and contracts for unskilled jobs made prior to emigration were outlawed by the contract labor law of 1885. A careless remark, the letter writer warned, could send the brother back to Norway.

The other solution to the problem of the split life—return to Norway—was described by Kristine Olsen in a letter to her sister. Her husband's ill health required them to recross the Atlantic. The hardest part of turning their back on America seems to have been the necessity of selling all of their household goods, including a new icebox.

In such candid accounts of their everyday experiences and emotions, the immigrant letter writers described the new country. Most letters reveal aspects of American society and culture by implication. Stories of loneliness, alienation, and nostalgia reflect the Norwegians' collision with a confusing and unsettling new environment. Some letter writers commented more directly on American society. A nurse bragged of socializing with "the best people of Staten Island" at a large wedding. "Seven hundred guests were invited!" she reported breathlessly. "They have the whole celebration in a church, not in the home!" she marvelled, adding, "It is really grand to be invited to such a place because there are only rich people there." She ascribed her successful penetration of the prosperous class to the fact that "I am so well liked." Another young woman revealed another way to American success. Beneath the letterhead of the Bryant and Stratton Business College, she demonstrated that she had learned to type fifty words a minute. In addition to studying bookkeeping, she worked from nine to five every day except Saturday. Her experience presaged the increasing availability of clerical jobs for women.

The commentary on America provided in these letters may be less explicit but it is no less powerful or valuable than that in the earlier immigrant letters. In his pioneering study of that group, Theodore Blegen identified three strengths of the America letters as historical sources. First, he noted, the letters provide details of the immigrant experience. Second, they reveal the reactions of the immigrant mind to the new environment, and third, they illustrate the types of influence brought to bear on the mind of the prospective emigrant in Norway.[20]

The letters of the later Norwegain immigrants, such as those found at Grimstad, reflect no less vividly the identity and concerns of their writers. Together, these brief notes between persons who expected to see each other again soon furnish a cross section of the continuous translatlantic communication. Unlike the earlier, painstakingly written letters of record, the Grimstad letters are rich in details of the everyday lives of ordinary Norwegians in urban America at an important historical moment. They are among the very few sources scholars have with which to begin developing the portrait of the new Norwegian immigrant, making human figures appear from the rough outlines suggested by statistics and faded memories.

## Notes

[1]Ingrid Semmingsen, *Norway to America: A History of the Migration* (Minneapolis, 1978), and Odd S. Lovoll, *The Promise of America* (Minneapolis, 1984), are two recent general histories that include treatment of the urban industrial immigrants. Recent research on the group was included in the symposium, "Scandinavians and Other Immigrants in Urban America," held at St. Olaf College, Northfield, Minnesota, in October, 1984.

[2]Peter A. Munch, "Segregation and Assimilation of Norwegian Settlements in Wisconsin," in *Norwegian-American Studies and Records*, 18 (Northfield, Minnesota, 1954), 102–140; Carlton C. Qualey, "A Typical Norwegian Settlement: Spring Grove, Minnesota," in *Norwegian-American Studies and Records*, 9 (1936), 54–66; Jon Gjerde, "The Effect of Community on Migration: Three Minnesota Townships, 1885–1905," in *Journal of Historical Geography*, 5 (1979), 403–422.

[3]Arnfinn Engen, ed., *Utvandringa. Det store oppbrotet* (Oslo, 1978), 36; *Utvandringsstatistikk* (Kristiania, 1921). On the relationship between economic trends and general immigration to the United States, see Harry Jerome, *Migration and Business Cycles* (New York, 1926).

[4]Ingrid Semmingsen, "Norwegian Emigration to America during the Nineteenth Century," in *Norwegian-American Studies and Records*, 11 (1940), 78–80. See *Ekteskap, fødsler, og vandringer*, published by the Norwegian Central Bureau of Statistics (Oslo, 1975).

[5]Semmingsen, *Norway to America*, 106 and following pages.

[6]Ingrid Semmingsen, "Family Emigration from Bergen, 1874–92: Some Preliminary Results of a Statistical Study," in *Americana-Norvegica*, 3 (1971), 38–63.

[7]Rolf Kåre Østrem and Peter Rinnan, "Utvandring fra Kristiania,

1880–1917. En studie i urban utvandring" (cand. philol. thesis, University of Oslo, 1979), 217.

[8]Edward P. Hutchinson, *Immigrants and their Children, 1850–1950* (New York, 1956), 135, 150–151; *Eleventh Census of the United States, 1890,* 2:484–508.

[9]*Fourteenth Census of the United States, 1920,* 2:926–929, 959–962; *Fifteenth Census of the United States, 1930,* 2:213, 232.

[10]*Fifteenth Census,* 232.

[11]A summary of several studies of geographical mobility by Stephan Thernstrom, in *The Other Bostonians: Poverty and Progress in the American Metropolis, 1880–1970* (Cambridge, Massachusetts, 1973), 220–225, reveals that roughly half of the studied population could not be located in the same city ten years later. Thernstrom postulates that they joined the "floating proletariat."

[12]*Ekteskap, fødsler og vandringer,* 218.

[13]Compilations and analyses include: Theodore C. Blegen, *Land of Their Choice: The Immigrants Write Home* (Minneapolis, 1955); Per Jevne, ed., *Brevet hjem; En samling brev fra norske utvandrere* (Trondheim, 1975); H. Arnold Barton, ed., *Letters from the Promised Land: Swedes in America, 1840–1914* (Minneapolis, 1975). Translations of many early America letters have appeared in volumes of *Norwegian-American Studies.*

[14]Theodore Blegen, *Norwegian Migration to America, 1825–1860* (Northfield, Minnesota, 1931), 196, 212.

[15]The collected Kristoffersen-Michaelsen letters are to be found in the America-letter file of the Norwegian Institute of Historical Documents (Norsk Historisk Kjeldeskrift-Institutt) in Oslo, and in the archives of the Norwegian-American Historical Association.

[16]News releases and correspondence relating to "Brevfunnet i Grimstad," 1982, are located at the Norsk Historisk Kjeldeskrift-Institutt. Additional information comes from discussions with Steinar Kjærheim, director of the Institute. See also Ingrid Semmingsen, "A Unique Collection of America–Letters in Norway" in *Swedish-American Historical Quarterly,* 35 (July, 1984), 316–321.

[17]This and subsequent quotations are from the "Grimstadbrevene" collection of sixty-seven America letters dated February 2 – May 1, 1896, East Agder Archives, Arendal.

[18]*Nordisk Tidende,* March 18, 1915.

[19]*Nordisk Tidende,* May 13, 1892, February 18, 1909.

[20]Blegen, *Norwegian Migration,* 213.

# 6

# Minneapolis Picture Album, 1870–1935: Images of Norwegians in the City*

*by Deborah L. Miller*

The selection of images presented here is meant to convey a sense of the many possibilities of photographic research for urban ethnic history. But the photographs are the starting point. That is the difference between using pictures as illustrations for assertions already derived from verbal sources and using them as sources themselves along with more traditional materials. The author does not subscribe to the easy idea that a photograph is worth 1,000 words. Picture research carries with it the responsibility and the opportunity for investigating verbal sources, both written and oral, as well. Such research produces facts and stories stimulated or evoked by the picture that even a close "reading" of the image alone would never yield.

Once the researcher begins looking at photographs, they often become quite alluring. The apparent "truth" of a historical image differs considerably from that of a document, but it is important to be as skeptical of pictures as of other

*The author acknowledges with gratitude the assistance of those people who made pictures available from their private collections: Nina Draxten, Hilda and Ole Kringstad, Rolf and Joyce Wunder. She also wishes to thank Bonnie Wilson, Tracey Baker, and Marcia Anderson of the Minnesota Historical Society, the Sons of Norway's Liv Dahl, and freelance writer Dave Wood for their enthusiastic assistance.

sources. Like words, photographs can manipulate and distort the past and convey misinformation. The absence of material may be as telling as its presence, though the reasons for the absence are often complex. There may be few pictures of city people at work, for example, for a number of reasons: because photographers did not choose to take pictures of those activities; because people did not save pictures of those activities; because people have not donated such pictures to the repositories that now hold photographs of Norwegian Minneapolis. Each of these possible reasons in turn suggests several possible answers to the question: "why not?" Photographers may not have taken many pictures of city people working because many city people worked inside, where lighting conditions made photography difficult in its early years. Professional photographers took pictures that they were hired to take, or that they thought people would want to buy; people working may not have fit into either category. Most amateurs took family pictures, expressing pride in possessions, commemorating family outings and major events in family life. Some subjects seemed to cry out to be photographed by professional and amateur alike: massive ethnic celebrations and small gatherings to celebrate Norway's Constitution Day (May 17) or Midsummer, synodical annual meetings or reunions of *bygdelag* members.

The compiler of this essay found, to her surprise, that relatively few pictures of Norwegian Minneapolis have found their way into repositories in the Upper Midwest or in Norway. Research at the Minnesota Historical Society, the Minneapolis Public Library's Minneapolis History Collection, the Norwegian-American Historical Association Archives, Northfield, Minnesota, and Vesterheim: the Norwegian-American Museum in Decorah, Iowa, turned up far fewer images than expected. Research in Norwegian collections, even the large ones in Hamar (the Emigration Museum) and Stavanger (the District Archives), yielded almost nothing. All of which probably means only that most photographs documenting the Norwegian experience in Minneapolis are still in private hands.

The fact that more photographs in this essay document the Norwegian-American celebrations of 1914 (the centennial of the Norwegian constitution) and 1925 (the centennial of the arrival in America of the first Norwegian emigrant ship, the *Restauration*) than young women working as domestic servants or men laboring in the flour mills means only that more pictures exist of the former activities than of the latter. Although one might wish for more pictures of people doing the family laundry or making barrels, the importance of all the photographs from 1914 and 1925 should not be minimized. They reveal a great deal about Norwegian-American identity in Minneapolis in the first quarter of the twentieth century. Studio portraits, too, contribute to the self-image of Minneapolis Norwegians, and portraits, though not many are included in this essay, are even more numerous than celebration photographs. The pictures that follow may reveal many aspects of the ethnic identity of Minneapolis Norwegian Americans.

A last caveat: Photographs of Norwegian Americans are not unique in their ability to contribute to the history of the group; parallel research could be done on Swedes, Poles, Italians, Chinese, blacks, and many other groups. Yankees, too, gathered their families to pose in front of their houses and pictured themselves at 4th of July picnics. In that sense, this essay uses Norwegians as an example. Nor are urban photographs the only ones that have much to tell about immigrant life. A similar essay on rural Norwegian Americans would raise comparable questions and reveal other kinds of information about material culture and intra- and intergroup relationships. The point is to begin incorporating photographic research into general investigations of ethnic life. As the following pictures and their captions will attempt to show, it can both broaden and enliven the study of the past.

# SKANDINAVISK

## REPUBLIKANSK

# Massemöde

— i —

# Pence Operahus

## Mandag, 26de October 1874.

## Kl. 8 Aften.

## Alle Skandinaver,

uden Hensyn til politiske Anskuelser, ere inviterede.

A. H. Edsten.    G. F. Johnsen.    C. M. Reese.    S. E. Listoe.    And. Tharalson.
A. Slotten.    Chas. Brown.    John Thompson.    L. A. Austin.    A. Walstad.
P. Engberg.    C. G. Vanstrum.    E. M. Titterud.    J. E. Gjedde.    George H. Johnson.
Paul Johnson.    Alfred Söderström.    John Johnson.    J. Landberg.

The Pence Opera House at Hennepin Avenue and 2nd Street, shown here in about 1875, was not a Scandinavian-owned or operated establishment, but it catered to the events of many groups, some of them ethnic, in the growing city. The poster announces a Scandinavian Republican mass meeting there the evening of October 26, 1874, shortly before the photo was taken. All Scandinavians, regardless of political persuasion, were invited to attend this meeting by the men whose names appear at the bottom of the broadside. Swedish as well as Norwegian names appear, suggesting organized interaction among Minneapolis Scandinavians during this period.

*Minnesota Historical Society*

Ole and Kari Draxten arrived in Minneapolis from Selbu in Trøndelag in 1867. Their granddaughter, who owns the originals of these photographs, also provided information about their content. In 1870 Ole, a trained carpenter, built the houses shown in this photograph at 2nd Street North and 18th Avenue, near what is now West Broadway. The one in the center was for his growing family; the others, parts of which can be seen along 18th Avenue behind the Draxten home, were for fellow immigrants, many of them Trønders like the Draxtens. In addition to building houses, Ole worked for Caleb Dorr on the log booms on the nearby Mississippi River. The photograph was taken in the early 1880s; it shows Kari and two of the Draxten children, Olina, born 1875, and Christian, born 1879. Not pictured was son Bersvend, born 1866, one of the founders of the Sons of Norway and its first president. He is seated next to his mother in the family portrait taken by the prolific Scandinavian-American photographer A. Larson in his Washington Avenue studio some ten years later. The pictures suggest a number of questions that further research might answer, on topics ranging from average family size of urban Norwegian immigrants during the late nineteenth century to immigrant material culture. Does the house display any evidence of Norwegian building techniques or stylistic elements? What does the clothing in these pictures tell about the status or fashionability of their wearers? One might ask on what occasions such a family would make a trip to the photographer's studio? Did they plan to send copies of these photos back to friends and relatives in Norway? The photograph of the houses might lead one to ask if Trønders settled together in other Minneapolis neighborhoods.

*Both in Minnesota Historical Society*

Two of the few known Minneapolis photographs taken by the noted Norwegian–American photographer Andrew Dahl of De Forest, Wisconsin, are these stereo views of the 1875 annual meeting of the Lutheran Norwegian Synod.* The group of men pictured at top are the representatives of various Norwegian Synod churches in the Upper Midwest to the annual meeting; at bottom, where the board sidewalk is plainly visible, small boys peer out the church windows at the camera as a more select group of Synod ministers poses for posterity. A photograph of the Sunday school of Our Saviour's Church, at 7th Street South and 14th Avenue, in the summer of 1887 includes many men and women teachers along with the children. The women, all well dressed and hatted, display tightly corseted waistlines. The boys in the back row are hamming it up for the camera; one has his (or someone else's) hat on a stick, which he holds aloft; three others are taking advantage of the banner to call attention to themselves.

*The stereo format of the Dahl photographs suggests that the photographer hoped to sell many of these pictures as souvenirs of the occasion.

*Dahl photos, Norwegian-American Historical Association; Sunday school, Vesterheim: the Norwegian-American Museum*

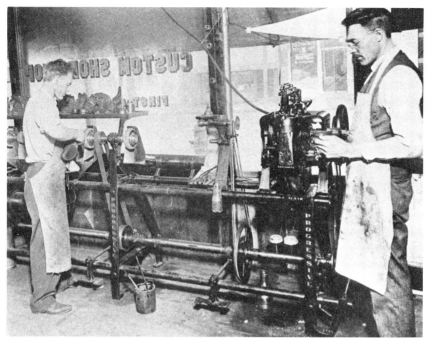

Pictures of people at work are not easy to find. Norwegian immigrant Hans Barlow is photographed here driving a horse-drawn streetcar on the Plymouth and Bloomington Avenue line in 1887; the unidentified conductor stands at the rear. There could hardly have been many distractions in the traffic that year; neither of the horses is wearing blinders. A Hans P. Barlow is listed in the 1889 Minneapolis City Directory living at 521 23rd Avenue South. The other photograph shows Norwegians at work in the shoe business. Ole Karlsgodt, the shoemaker on the right, arrived in Minneapolis from Valdres about 1911. Some years later, according to his daughter, he opened his own shop in north Minneapolis, where he did both shoe repair and custom shoe work. The latter involved making shoes to order and altering ready-made shoes to fit. This photo was probably taken not at the Karlsgodt shoe shop but at an earlier place of employment where Ole worked during the 1910s. City directories show him at various shoe shops and at one harnessmaker's during that period. This is an unusual picture because it shows people actually at work, rather than posed in or near their place of employment. Historians of technology could probably date the photograph from the footpedal-operated machinery.

*Streetcar photo Minnesota Historical Society; shoe photo Hilda Kringstad*

Pictures of Norwegian Americans in old-country costumes, often with flags, are one of the most obvious displays of ethnicity for American consumption. A Cedar Avenue photographer posed these women in front of a huge Norwegian flag during the 17th of May celebration in 1888. Women and children are most often pictured in costume, as are folkdancers. Members of Minneapolis' Valdres Samband were enthusiastic folk dancers who met at each other's houses, rolled up the rugs, and danced. In the mid-1930s the group posed, with the women—all but one—in Hardanger dress and the men, even the fiddler, in suits. The woman on the right in the front row was not a dancer; the difference in her costume signals her different role in the group. The musician held his Hardanger fiddle so that its craftsmanship can be properly appreciated.

*Both Minnesota Historical Society*

AUGSBURG SEMINARY, MINNEAPOLIS, MINN.

Two of the city's major Norwegian institutions were named for a place associated with Lutheranism in Germany: Augsburg. This impressive group of men, displaying a wide assortment of the facial hair fashions of their era, encircle a picture of the school where they taught — Augsburg Seminary — in the 1890s. The president and the secretary have pride of place: top center at left is Georg Sverdrup and at right, Sven Oftedal. The substantial brick building is Old Main, built on the corner of 7th Street and 21st Avenue South in 1872 and 1875 and demolished immediately after World War II. The Augsburg Publishing House, begun in a room at Augsburg Seminary, settled into its own building near the Minneapolis City Hall in 1908. There it declared itself to be "sort of a center for Norse-American culture," as well as "the largest printing plant and book business ever built up by *Norse Americans*" and the headquarters of the Norwegian Lutheran Church in America.* The advertisement in the 1918 Minneapolis city directory emphasized its church-related publications, which include the famous Christmas annuals.

*Quotations are from the Norse-American Centennial Number of the *Augsburg Publishing House Bulletin*, June, 1925.

*Minnesota Historical Society; Augsburg College Archives*

Two major Minneapolis hospitals had their roots in the fund-raising
and humanitarian work of Norwegian-American women. Deaconess
Hospital (now Fairview-Deaconess) was the outgrowth of the Norwegian Lutheran Deaconess Institute. Deaconesses were unmarried
Lutheran women who were trained to care for the ill and needy.
Like nuns, they wore a distinctive garb; unlike nuns, they often left
deaconess work for marriage. The first hospital was in a house at
2731 Hennepin Avenue, but the institution soon settled at 1427 East
23rd Street, in the middle of Scandinavian south Minneapolis. Here
deaconesses and patients were posed carefully by photographer A.
Larson. In 1905 other Norwegian Lutherans, planning a hospital for
north Minneapolis, were led by various circumstances to build
Thomas Hospital for tuberculosis patients near Riverside Park in
south Minneapolis. In 1916, after fund raising by women's
auxiliaries in many congregations, the full-service Fairview Hospital
opened nearby. The photograph by Sever P. Eggan, probably taken
in 1910, shows some of the fund-raising efforts.

*Minnesota Historical Society; Norwegian-American Historical Association*

⊲FJELDE SISTERS.⊳
DECORATIVE ART NEEDLE WORK.
STAMPING.

Society Banners and Emblems          Call and Examine our Work
        a Specialty.                        and Designs.

ART PARLORS
408 NICOLLET AVENUE.    ROOM 3.    MINNEAPOLIS, MINN.

The artistic activities of Minneapolis Norwegians have been less studied than those of the Chicago Norwegian community, but the Fjelde family from Ålesund looms large in any assessment of Norwegian-American art. Jakob Fjelde, the sculptor who created the famous Minnehaha and Hiawatha statue at Minnehaha Falls, as well as the Ole Bull statue pictured later in this essay, had two sisters who were award-winning textile artists. In the group portrait, probably taken in Minneapolis about 1890, the Fjelde siblings (clockwise from upper left) Herman, Pauline, Jakob, and Thomane, pose with an unidentified older woman who may be their mother. The fact that each person in the photograph is holding a newspaper, a book, or some other reading material may be an assertion of intellectual interests by the family or by the photographer. Pauline Fjelde created the tapestry of Hiawatha and Minnehaha seen hanging here in her eclectically furnished home at 4715 15th Avenue South in about 1924. The room at the back of the picture contains her loom; windows there provided good north light for her weaving. The rooms are decorated with Victorian furniture, along with some Scandinavian arts and crafts pieces. A small business card in a scrapbook owned by Thomane Fjelde Hansen's descendants shows that the sisters worked on commission in their own "art parlors" for a time.

*Minnesota Historical Society photographs; card from Rolf and Joyce Wunder*

Norwegian-American photographer Sever P. Eggan took this com-
posite photograph of the officers, all Norwegian, of the Minnesota
Total Abstinence Association. The undated print in the Minnesota
Historical Society has a printed sticker on the back that says (in
Norwegian): "With heartfelt greetings and best wishes for the progress of abstinence work. Yours for the cause, Gustave Eide." Women
were also active workers for the cause of abstinence, or temperance.
They figure prominently in the bunting-decked four-horse float
assembled by the Norwegian Good Templars, another active
temperance organization, for a parade in the centennial celebration of
1914. In this Skage Brothers photograph, Norwegian and American
flags and Norwegian costumes proclaim ethnic affiliation proudly.
The group was an affiliate of the International Order of Good
Templars, which had many non-ethnic members as well.

*Both Minnesota Historical Society*

Romsdalslaget of Twin Cities. April 21, 1929.

Group photographs are frequently found, not only for Norwegians but for other ethnic groups, occupational groups, etc. Here (left) a local committee greets visitors from Valdres outside a flag-bedecked Ark Lodge Hall at 31st Street and 1st Avenue South. Christopher Heen and his violin lent a festive air to the photo, which certainly depicts a gathering of old friends. The relaxed poses, jacketless men, and affectionate touching reflect warmth and informality. The photograph is from 1915. Almost thirty years later Romsdalslaget of the Twin Cities, a *bygdelag*, or homeland regional association, gathered for a picture at the Citizens' Club, a kind of settlement house near Franklin Avenue and Minnehaha. American heroes look down on them from above the doorway, but the arrangement of the American and Norwegian flags echoes the earlier picture.

*Norwegian-American Historical Association; Minnesota Historical Society*

Old photographs from the library of the Sons of Norway's international headquarters help to tell the very Minneapolis-centered story of that organization. Not all the Sons of Norway's early lodges were organized in larger towns, but Minneapolis was the place where it all started. Founder Bersvend Draxten organized the first lodge with fellow Trønders and a few others from north Minneapolis, but the idea spread quickly to Norwegians from all over Norway who lived in many places in the United States and Canada. Most early lodge pictures were taken of members posed in their lodge halls or in photographers' studios rather than on parade. This early-20th-century marching group (top left) may be Nordlyset No. 13 lodge, which was organized in 1903 and dissolved in the 1940s, since another photo, taken in their Minneapolis lodge hall, shows the same Viking on their lodge banner. Oslo No. 2 lodge members (perhaps officers) posed in an undated photograph (bottom left) with American and Norwegian flags. This picture provides a reminder that secret lodges were a widespread phenomenon in American society in the late nineteenth and early twentieth centuries; some had ethnic connections, but many did not. Most Sons of Norway pictures the author has seen show men dressed either in suits, decorated with ribbons or sashes, or in more military-looking uniforms. This group, with their fez headgear and exotic robes for the highest ranking officers, look more like Shriners than Sons of Norway.

*Both photographs, Sons of Norway*

A view of the Seven Corners, a center of the southside
Scandinavian neighborhood, in 1910. The photograph,
looking down Washington Avenue and dominated by the
Southern Theater, presents a picture of street life before the
automobile. Other identifiable businesses include a laundry,
a shoe repair shop, the Interurban Pool Room, and a
saloon; streetcar tracks and people used the muddy street.

*Minnesota Historical Society*

Many photographs showing the public face of Norwegian-American ethnicity in Minneapolis come from the centennial celebrations of 1914 and 1925. The festivities reflected the nature of the events they commemorated. In 1914, an event of great national importance to Norwegians was being celebrated in the homeland as well as in America; eleven years later, a Norwegian-American event, which was understandably of less significance to Norwegians back home, was the focus of the pageantry. The earlier event advocated the continuation of Norwegian language and traditions; the latter, coming after World War I had dealt a heavy blow to ethnic subcultures throughout the state, had a stronger American focus. In 1925 Norwegian Americans threw themselves into an All-American celebration complete with the President of the United States, Calvin Coolidge, and first lady Grace Coolidge.

INN, MAY 17 1914.                    PHOTO BY SKAGE.

The picture above shows Kristianialaget, emigrants from Oslo dressed as the men of Eidsvoll, the drafters of the 1814 constitution. The banner at front right proclaims the royal motto, adopted in 1905, *Alt for Norge* (Everything for Norway). This picture was not taken in Minneapolis, but at the fairgrounds in St. Paul, where participants went after the Minneapolis parade. The Dayton's float of a Viking ship suggests that Minneapolis may have been Norwegianizing even as its Norwegians were Americanizing, especially considering that the Dayton family was not of Norwegian descent.

*Both Minnesota Historical Society*

Norwegian- and English-language newspapers gave enormous
coverage to the 1925 events. The Minneapolis *Morning Tribune*
quoted chairman Gisle Bothne's ambitious hopes for the celebration:
"The past will be clarified, the present intensified, and the future
magnified. Tens of thousands of the present generation will have
visualized the life of the early Norse pioneers, how they labored and
sacrificed that we might gain wisdom and happiness and material
comfort." The re-enactment of mythic events of the Norwegian and
Norwegian-American past was one of the most picturesque aspects
of the 1925 festivities. The grounds of the Dunwoody Institute saw
two Vikings — or parodies of same — battle with swords (top left),
and the Lincoln pageant lionized the hero of the homesteaders in a
fascinating series of images (bottom left) with Civil War and other
overtones. The Coolidges, seen here (above) in the first car,
conveyed the acceptance of Norwegians as good Americans to all
those in attendance, Norwegian and otherwise.

*All Minnesota Historical Society*

During the late 1920s and the 1930s many 17th of May celebrations began at Jakob Fjelde's statue of Ole Bull in Loring Park. Norwegian male choruses, costumed women and children, flags, speeches, and the placing of wreaths seem to have been popular elements of the event, which was always enhanced by the budding trees of spring. It was this era about which historian Carl Chrislock once wrote: "Many participants in May 17th observances celebrated without having a clear idea of what they were celebrating, and as often as not, festival orators failed to enlighten them." Here a group of nattily dressed singers doffed their hats to sing "Ja vi elsker," the Norwegian national anthem, under the direction of S. Walton in 1929.

# 7

## Washington Posten: A Window on a Norwegian- American Urban Community*

*by Odd S. Lovoll*

In 1938 Frank Oleson of Trondheim, Norway, described how he had happened to start a Norwegian-language newspaper in Seattle. "Early in 1888," Oleson wrote, "I was employed as a distribution clerk at the post office in Seattle. . . . The entire staff consisted of four persons in addition to five letter carriers. As a clerk at the post office, I discovered that many bundles of *Decorah-Posten, Skandinaven, Budstikken,* and other Norwegian-American newspapers were being sent to subscribers here. They were not only for people in Seattle, but many were addressed to post offices in the surrounding area for which Seattle served as a distribution point. This circumstance gave me and my brother Richard, who also worked in the post office, the idea of publishing a Norwegian newspaper in Seattle. I was at that time twenty-six years old and my brother two years younger. We had no experience whatsoever in the publishing business and even less experience in editorial work," Oleson concluded.[1]

Seattle in 1888 still gave the impression of being a pi-

*This article is based in part on a paper read at the Conference on Scandinavian Immigration, Settlement, and Acculturation, at the University of Wisconsin, Madison, August 27-30, 1984. The paper was titled "The Norwegian-American Press: Its Twofold Role in the American Transition."

oneer town; its institutions were yet to be developed. The traditional date of Seattle's founding is November, 1851, when the first group of white settlers landed at Alki Point in west Seattle. The city established itself, however, to the east of Alki Point, where Elliott Bay, an arm of Puget Sound, provided an excellent harbor. Seattle was bounded by bodies of water, on the west by Puget Sound and on the east by Lake Washington. Wooded hills and slopes characterized the area, and in the distance mountains—the most imposing being Mount Rainier—provided a magnificent scene. The rugged beauty of the region might easily remind a Norwegian of the homeland.[2]

By 1890 Seattle's population had grown to almost 43,000. On June 6 of the previous year much of the city's downtown had been destroyed by fire. Rather than hampering growth, the disaster served as a spur to rebuilding and new development, so that the number of inhabitants nearly doubled in the next decade, to about 81,000 in 1900. Seattle gradually took on a Scandinavian flavor, although before 1890 the Nordic population in the city was not numerically significant. Of the citizens of Seattle in 1890, 3,335 had been born in Denmark, Sweden, or Norway—the Norwegian-born accounting for more than 40 percent of the total Scandinavian group. In addition there was a sizable second generation: in the Norwegian group it surpassed the parent generation by a few hundred.[3]

Communications eastward improved greatly with the completion of the Northern Pacific railroad line to Seattle in 1883. It carried people and goods, and it provided efficient postal service, which also, as has already been suggested, made ethnic newspapers accessible to Norwegians on the west coast. The number of Norwegians grew substantially from the 1890s, a large percentage moving out from the Middle West, and they naturally continued to subscribe to newspapers they were familiar with. "Wherever Norwegians go, *Decorah-Posten* follows" was a popular slogan. Other Norwegians moved to the region directly from Norway, arriving in Seattle by rail. By 1920 people of Norwegian birth or descent formed an urban colony of 17,628. They represented a little more than a quarter of the Norwegian population in the state of Washington.[4]

"It had not really occurred to me how many Norwegians there were here until we began to celebrate May 17," Oleson wrote. The first celebration of the homeland's constitution day took place in 1889, and on that same day Oleson launched *Washington Posten*.[5] In time it became the Norwegian voice in the Pacific Northwest. *Washington Posten* addressed itself directly to the local Norwegian population and could thus serve its needs and interests better than the larger Norwegian-language journals published in the Middle West, although, as Oleson related, the link to these newspapers was direct. "We had not had time to get newspapers from Norway," Oleson wrote, "so items from the homeland were taken from newspapers farther east which in turn had taken them from the Norwegian newspapers." *Washington Posten* thus quite literally represented an extension of the immigrant press into the Pacific Northwest.[6]

The Norwegian-American press was well established when *Washington Posten* emerged as one of the 243 newspapers that were begun between 1877 and 1896, the period of the greatest expansion in the number of immigrant journals. A special Norwegian immigrant press had been initiated in July, 1847, when *Nordlyset* (Northern Lights), edited by the talented and versatile James D. Reymert, appeared in the Muskego settlement in Racine county, Wisconsin. This press had a remarkable vitality and tenacity. At least 400 Norwegian-language newspapers have been published in the United States up to the present time, an impressive fact even though, to be sure, one-third of the newspapers lasted less than a year. The most successful ones, however, such as *Skandinaven* in Chicago and *Decorah-Posten* in Iowa, had much larger circulations than the major newspapers published in Norway. Around the turn of the century the semiweekly *Decorah-Posten* found its way into 37,000 homes, and *Skandinaven* was the largest Norwegian-language newspaper in the world, with about 50,000 subscribers to its semiweekly edition. Nearly half that many copies were distributed of its daily edition. *Minneapolis Tidende* also approached these circulation figures and was published in a weekly and a daily edition. Other successful Norwegian-American journals had circulations ranging from about 5,000 to 10,000. These become truly significant statistics when compared to the spread of newspapers in Norway. That country's largest daily, *Aftenposten* (The Evening Post), was at the same time printed in an edition of only 14,000; its distribution increased, however, in the present century, so that in the 1960s it passed 170,000.[7] Still, the growth of newspapers in nineteenth-century Norway and the rapid expansion in American mass communication in the same period may not be directly comparable phenomena. America was "the land of newspapers," as the pioneer editor of *Skandinaven*, Knud Langeland, described it. Newspapers appeared in small and large communities throughout America, gave essential information, and in the new land had a basic community-building function. The impressive circulation figures for immigrant journals attest to their vital importance in the ethnic community, as well as to their affordability.[8]

The immigrant newspapers served as urban community mediums and local news sheets, or they strove to become national Norwegian-American organs. They were all in the tradition of the penny press, written for, and frequently about, the common man. The penny daily, written in an entertaining and simple style, with its attention to local news coverage and its use of foreign correspondents, emerged in the mid-1830s. The newspapers were hawked on the streets by newsboys and sold for a penny. In Norway, also, periodicals intended for the ordinary person appeared, but the penny press was not a part of that country's journalism in the nineteenth century. In 1870 the annual subscription rate to a Norwegian daily equaled ten days wages for a male industrial worker, and although this figure sank to six days in 1880 and three-and-a-half days in 1890, the high subscription price throughout the last century limited total newspaper circulation.[9]

The weekly *Washington Posten* was offered to potential

subscribers for $1.50 annually, "frit tilsendt" — "sent free"; the rate was later reduced to $1.00. A weekly could obviously be sold cheaper than a daily, and the majority of immigrant journals were issued on a weekly basis, making them more affordable. Besides, people in Seattle had more money for newspapers. Wages in Seattle were above the national average, and they became even more inflated with the increased demand for labor after the fire of 1889, so that unskilled workers enjoyed a daily wage of $2.00 to $2.30 and skilled workers $4.00 to $6.00. These favorable circumstances did not automatically assure success for a publication venture, a fact *Washington Posten*'s publishers soon learned. In order to succeed, the newspaper had to gain the confidence and support of readers and advertisers; several Norwegian and other Scandinavian journalistic enterprises in the 1890s competed for the favor of the immigrant community. *Washington Posten* had 411 prepaid subscribers when it began publication; the American business community, according to Oleson, especially welcomed it as a means of reaching potential Norwegian-American customers. At first it carried an excessive amount of advertising, causing people to complain.[10]

Oleson himself left the newspaper venture in September, 1890; by that time it was in grave financial difficulties. Part of the problem was inexperience and mismanagement, and the fact that from early that year a newly formed company, Scandinavian Publishing Company, owned *Washington Posten* and published it along with Swedish and Norwegian journals in both Seattle and Tacoma. The inevitable competition for advertising revenue among the newspapers published by the same company caused a decline in advertising by American businessmen, who tended to limit themselves to only one of the newspapers. *Washington Posten* lost revenue. The Scandinavian business community was also divided in its loyalty. Scandinavian Publishing Company was owned by a group of Scandinavian businessmen who had thought to capture the advertising market within the Scandinavian community. The intrusion into this community by and its dependence on American commercial interests indicate an obvious symbiotic relationship. The purchasing power of the Scandinavian community was considerable, while at the same time American businesses injected money into immigrant community ventures.[11]

The depression beginning in 1893 further weakened the base for the newspaper. The Scandinavian Publishing Company was dissolved in 1892; that year *Washington Posten*'s circulation fell to only 1,345 copies. During the next several years it went from owner to owner, its existence precarious and its future less than promising. On September 24, 1896, A. J. Thuland announced in *Washington Posten* that he had purchased the newspaper and gave the following critical assessment: "As I take over the publication of the newspaper, which for several years has been in the hands of various leaseholders whose interest was momentary, I express the hope that my own personal concern for securing the success of the newspaper will continue to make *Washington Posten* a welcome guest in the thousands of Norwegian homes out here."[12]

Thuland had emigrated in 1884, at the age of thirteen, from Vestfossen in Buskerud. He struggled to keep *Washington Posten* alive, but it was not a paying proposition, although its circulation increased steadily, to about 2,400 in 1899. This and later figures might, however, be somewhat inflated as they are the ones reported by the publisher, who for purposes of gaining advertising revenue might easily overstate the newspaper's actual distribution. In any case, in 1902 Thuland sold *Washington Posten* and it again commenced on a succession of changes in ownership and editorial leadership. Then, in November, 1905, Gunnar Lund took over as publisher and editor. It was from that time that *Washington Posten* gradually attained its position of influence and power in the Pacific Northwest. Lund was born in Stavanger, Norway, on August 30, 1865. After having completed some secondary education, he emigrated in 1889 to the west coast of America. There he had to be satisfied with common labor on railroad construction and in the sawmills. In 1893 he moved to Chicago, taught English in night-school classes for Norwegian newcomers, and started his own business. Returning to Seattle, he continued to make a living in the business world, but when *Washington Posten* was offered for sale in 1905, as his wife Marie Vognild Lund later recalled, the temptation to pursue intellectual interests as a Norwegian-American newspaperman moved him into journalism. Lund invested the family's savings in the venture. He undoubtedly possessed business acumen, he had good relations with the Scandinavian commercial community, and he benefited from a surge of nationalism among Norwegian Americans following the dissolution of the Swedish-Norwegian union. Probably the greatest factor in his success was the big influx of Norwegian immigrants in the years prior to World War I. And *Washington Posten* prospered under Lund's guidance, giving him social status and a comfortable living. Circulation rose from 2,900 in 1905 to 8,000 in 1915, and peaked in the 1920s at about 15,000; revenue from advertising, as was the case for successful urban newspapers in general, provided a handsome income.[13]

Lund ran the newspaper business until his death in 1941. The most important person in *Washington Posten* in the next few years was O. L. Ejde, who assumed ownership in 1943. Ejde had emigrated from Orkdal in South Trøndelag in 1910 as a young man of twenty-one. He had worked on *Washington Posten* since 1913, save for a brief absence in the 1920s, and from 1941 he had had sole editorial responsibility. In June, 1959, he sold *Washington Posten* to Henning C. Boe, a Norwegian typographer and newspaperman, who in 1961 decided to give the newspaper a broader geographical appeal by changing the name to *Western Viking*. It was then printed in less than 4,000 copies. In this essay the role and character of *Washington Posten* will be considered up to that time—a period of seventy-two years.[14]

The democratic tone common to immigrant newspapers was evident in the columns of *Washington Posten*. Readers maintained a lively contact with the newspaper. It became a friend, and people wrote to *Washington Posten* to relate personal experiences, request information, express opinions, or reach friends. In 1925, for instance, a subscriber who had moved back to Norway wrote: "As we would like very much to greet friends and acquaintances in Bellingham and wherever else they might be on the coast, I cannot think of a better way than using *Washington Posten*, as most of them read it." Or someone might begin in the following fashion, as a contributor did in 1926: "Dear Editor, As I send my subscription money, I would like to add a couple of words which if you have a little space and do not consider them too trivial you can put in your paper." And the publisher felt obliged to do just that, even when, as in this case, it was a lengthy letter dealing with several issues, but mainly an argument for preserving "good Norwegian." Newspapers in America became the province of the common man. Readers of the immigrant journals had a proprietary attitude, at times to such an extent that the editor in 1953 reminded people that subscribing to *Washington Posten* did not guarantee that they could "get in the paper." But the situation—the interest in the ordinary person and the closeness between reader and publisher—is important to bear in mind when considering the function of ethnic newspapers.[15]

In many communities the editor and the publisher of an immigrant journal were prominent cultural and social leaders, active in clubs and organizations and in arranging public festivals. The offices of a newspaper might become an important center. When *Washington Posten* moved to new quarters in 1961, Editor Ejde nostalgically noted that "in and out of this office since 1917 have wandered most of the thousands of Norwegians who live in Seattle, in other towns and cities in Washington, and in neighboring states." For nearly fifty years the old offices of *Washington Posten*, on the ninth floor of the Seaboard Building on Fourth and Pike in Seattle, were a fixed point of orientation in the lives of Norwegians on the coast. The newspaper as a prime mover in upholding a separate ethnic community life was a familiar and reassuring weekly guest in the homes of its many readers.[16]

A large percentage of the Norwegians moving from

Norway to the Pacific coast hailed from North Norway or the coastal districts in West Norway. The topographical, physical, and climatic similarities between those regions and the Pacific Northwest attracted them to that part of America. An exuberant testimony from a former resident of the west coast, one O. H. Skotheim, then living in Albert Lea, Minnesota, was inserted in *Washington Posten* for August 17, 1906: "People generally have a deep longing for our wonderland around Puget Sound. A land that is free from blizzards, tornadoes, hail in the middle of summer, and booming thunder with murderous lightning has a special appeal for people here in the east. And our wonderful west coast is out there, with its multitude of resources, its constant betwitching power for the imaginative and industrious, its alluring beauty for the nature lover, and its promises of a brighter and richer future than any other part of America has offered any generation that has ever lived." It might be claimed that a Norwegian coastal culture was transferred to the west coast of America. Not only was the landscape reminiscent of home, but there were also familiar modes of livelihood in shipping, fishing, and lumbering which added to the region's appeal.[17]

People reading *Washington Posten*'s coverage of events and circumstances in Seattle could almost imagine they were in Norway. A sense of living in a Norwegian coastal city was created, an illusion of being in Tromsø, Ålesund, or Stavanger, or one of the other port cities of the homeland. Topics and concerns were similar. And in reality, the move from rural Norway, where many of the immigrants came from, to one of these Norwegian cities might not have differed much except in distance from the move to Seattle. Both represented a move from a rural to an urban environment. The comparison is appropriate and intriguing.

*Washington Posten* carried such regular features as *Nyheder fra Kysten* (News from the Coast), *Fra Havnen* (From the Harbor), *Bynytt* (City News), or *Seattle-Nytt*. Under these general headings one might find news items about the launching of a new halibut schooner, the departure of the halibut fleet for the Alaskan fishing waters in spring, and individual catches upon its return. There were reports and advertisements about employment possibilities. In 1917, for instance, Nordby Fisheries Supply Company advertised for men for the cod fishing season in the Bering Sea. And in 1906 the local employment office sought fifty newcomers to work in lumber operations or on railroad construction. If one adds the notices indicating activity in the building trades and, for women, the many appeals for "capable maids," not uncommonly inserted by non-Scandinavians, most of the major economic pursuits of Norwegians in Seattle have been listed.[18]

"The advertisements of the priest, the doctor, and the lawyer appear as soon as the immigrant community attains any size," wrote sociologist Robert E. Park in *The Immigrant Press and Its Control* (1922). *Washington Posten* soon after its appearance in 1889 listed "Our Lawyers" and "Our Doctors," as well as other Norwegian professionals, and encouraged its readers to patronize these countrymen. In early 1892 the Scandinavian-American Bank, owned and operated by persons in the Scandinavian business community, opened its doors to serve the Nordic population in Seattle. At the personal level the newspaper gave intimate glimpses of life among the immigrants. In 1917 a Norwegian bachelor advertised for a Scandinavian woman between the ages of seventeen and thirty who would consider marriage; in the same issue of *Washington Posten* the editor congratulated Mr. S. J. Hannevig and his wife at 2853 West 69th Street on the birth of a baby daughter. A more disturbing insight was given in 1890 when *Washington Posten* reported the suicide by hanging of one Christ Johnson. The community focus of the newspaper was obvious.[19]

Charitable concern encouraged social functions. An active hospital society arranged annual picnics and bazaars to raise funds, and in 1923 this society opened a Norwegian hospital in Seattle "where the sick boy's message will be understood and sent back home to an old mother." An appeal was made to ethnic solidarity in this and numerous other community projects. It is indicative of the role of ethnic newspaper publishers that Gunnar Lund, the editor and publisher of *Washington Posten*, served as chairman of the hospital society.

Many of the needs of the poor, ill, and aged members of the Norwegian community were met by religious groups. Yet historians have identified a certain religious indifference among Norwegian Americans on the west coast. Far fewer Norwegians than in the Middle West sought a church home. This circumstance may have had several causes. It might even point up a general regional condition. A new society was taking shape, and opportunity for material advancement attracted people to the region from Europe and from other parts of the United States. Their arrival coincided with a period of increasing secularization and a consequent decrease in religious fervor. Perhaps temporal interests were fueled by a certain anti-clericalism, at least in the Norwegian group. And those who came were in large part, as is the case in most new societies, young men not ready to settle down and establish permanent commitments to church and community. As recently as 1940 the percentage of men among Norwegians in Seattle was 60.1. Newcomers arriving after the turn of the century frequently intended to return to the homeland and their sojourn in America was thus seen as temporary. Under such conditions organized religious life was bound to suffer. Furthermore, they tended to enter non-farming occupations in an urban center with many competing interests. A pronounced lukewarmness to religion is evident. *Washington Posten*, to be sure, opened its columns to religious denominations, whether Lutheran, Baptist, or Methodist, and to evangelical missionary efforts, but secular interests were better represented. Norwegian newspapers in the Middle West, with their large readerships of churchgoing rural people, gave considerably more attention to religion.[20]

*Washington Posten* wrote mainly for an urban Norwegian-American population with many non-churchly interests. These interests produced a lively ethnic organizational and social life. *Washington Posten* regularly carried advertisements and announcements for Scandinavian dances, lodge meetings, amateur theater productions, workingmen's societies, Norwegian coffee houses and restaurants, and stores that sold ethnic foods. *Washington Posten* played a significant role in transforming what to begin with had been merely ethnic neighborhoods into a Norwegian community, and in making Norwegian Americans, wherever they resided within the city, feel a part of and participate in the life of this community. It was not necessary to reside in an ethnic neighborhood to join Norwegian-American organizations or to found societies of compatriots; and *Washington Posten* also made its influence felt among Norwegian Americans in other towns and communities on the west coast. Still, Norwegians in Seattle tended to be more residentially segregated than most other ethnic groups. Ballard in the northwestern part of the city, which was annexed in 1907, had the greatest concentration. Of the foreign-born in Seattle in 1940 the Norwegians were the second largest group after the Canadians, and about one-fourth of them resided in Ballard. As the Norwegian community in Seattle changed with time, so did the appearance and content of *Washington Posten*.[21]

Analyses of the foreign-language press have generally been based on its function. That is also a concern of the present essay, although the discussion will move beyond the limiting question of whether the press, along with other immigrant institutions, retarded assimilation or represented the first step toward it. Marion Marzolf in her study of the Danish-American press suggests that these two functions — as preserver of ethnic cultures and as Americanizer — do not conflict. The twin roles were played out simultaneously. Even more significantly, they represented neither a clannish segregation nor a passive acquiescence in the inevitability of assimilation, but rather a dynamic interplay with the larger society based on ethnic social and cultural resources. The press consequently became a primary expression of the resilience of ethnic cultures, their interaction rather than assimilation with American society, and their influence on the cultural, social, and political fabric of the American social order.[22]

Any more restricted view obscures the active participation of immigrants in the shaping of industrial and urban America. In the traditional scholarly debate, ethnic institutions of all kinds have in general been seen as lessening a sense of dislocation in new and strange surroundings, and they have therefore primarily been thought of as aiding in the process of adjustment and assimilation. Robert Park, for example, described the ethnic press as an instrument of Americanization, but qualified this view by maintaining that the extent of the Americanizing influence depended on the contents of the individual journals. These publications could if they so chose explain the American environment in a familiar language. Thus, Park did not regard immigrant institutions per se as a step toward Americanization. In his study of the German-American press Carl Wittke expressed the idea that the ethnic press tended to retard assimilation, but he also described how the immigrant press eased the immigrants into American society. "The immigrant press, besides preserving old memories, opens the gate to new experiences and boundless hopes," Wittke stated. A major function of the immigrant press, he maintained, was to assure contact between the old country and the new, "which is so important in the early years of residence in a strange land, if serious maladjustment and mental and emotional conflicts are to be avoided." In Wittke's view it was essential to preserve ethnic cultural values and identification with an ethnic past in a transitional period. The press, according to Wittke, facilitated Americanization while it also encouraged nationalism.[23] Wittke's ambiguous conclusion suggests the limits of this approach.

There is, in fact, no definitive study of subscribers to ethnic newspapers: educational background, length of time in America, first or second generation, and so on. In his study, *The Relation of the Swedish-American Newspaper to the Assimilation of Swedish Immigrants* (1935), Albert F. Schersten merely showed that readers of Swedish-American newspapers were in general less assimilated than non-readers, but he did not demonstrate a causal relationship. His investigation revealed little about the tendency of readers or non-readers to become

Americanized, only that, as one would expect, people who felt closer to the homeland's culture were more likely to read an ethnic newspaper than those who had moved farther into American society. Norwegian-American statistics likewise indicate that it was the rural, and least assimilated, Norwegian Americans who subscribed to Norwegian-language publications. In 1906, for instance, only 53 percent of the Norwegian-American population was rural, yet 76 percent of the press circulation was in rural communities. Such statistics reveal little about the actual Americanizing impact of immigrant newspapers.[24]

How then did the publishers of immigrant journals see their role? The answer to this question is much clearer. Although few newspapermen actually discussed the issue, through their editorial policies they consistently strove to provide their readers with news and information that would facilitate adjustment to American society. For example, *Washington Posten* took great pains to instruct its readers in how to become American citizens, printing in several installments the questions and answers on American history and government that ought to be memorized for the naturalization proceedings. *Emigranten*, the most important immigrant journal before the Civil War, in its first issue, published in Inmansville, Wisconsin, on January 23, 1852, had addressed itself directly to "Our American Friends" in English to reassure them that the main purpose of *Emigranten* was "to emancipate ourselves from the degrading bondage of ignorance, regarding your institutions and customs, regarding the privileges and duties devolving upon us with the rights of citizenship extended to us." The goal was thus to Americanize Norwegian immigrants through the medium of a Norwegian-language newspaper.[25]

With the emergence of *Skandinaven* in 1866 there came into being a newspaper that to a greater degree than *Emigranten* addressed itself to the ordinary immigrant, in conviction as well as in subject matter and linguistic style. It is significant that it was published in a large urban center; it was distributed far and wide among Norwegian Americans throughout the country. A smaller daily edition served the Chicago Norwegians. In the same manner as *Washington Posten* did in Seattle, it knit Norwegians who belonged to churches, fraternal societies, and other kinds of social and cultural groups together into a unit. The national semiweekly edition of *Skandinaven* with its wide circulation from coast to coast encouraged a sense of a national Norwegian-American community.

Americanization, according to *Webster's Third New International Dictionary*, is "instruction of foreigners in the English language, in United States history and government, and in other studies to prepare them for life in the United States, or familiarize them with United States culture, institutions, and ideals." It is this traditional definition of cultural assimilation that most people have in mind when describing what Americanization implies. *Emigranten*, for example, embarked upon the publication of a translation into Norwegian of a general history of the United States. Other journals in time gave instruction in English and advice on how to enter civic life, or they provided information on many practical aspects of life in America, from purchasing land to cooking American foods. Certainly, if judged by content, immigrant newspapers thought of themselves as agents of Americanization.

The term "Americanization" as thus defined is, however, limiting, since it tends to place the immigrants in a passive role, rather than seeing them as actors in a larger drama of cultural change and transformation. In order to have relevance to the actual situation the term must be further refined. The environment the immigrants entered was not merely American but urban. Cities were growing in America and in Norway, as well as elsewhere. Historian Frank Thistlethwaite views the entire saga of migration in the nineteenth century as a part of a worldwide process of urbanization, whether regional or international in character. Americanization might therefore more properly be equated with urbanization. "To the country people of the Norwegian fjords a fellow countryman on his way to embark was already an 'American,' and even after the second World War 'Americani-

zation' was a synonym for 'urbanization' in an immigrant
Norwegian community which was attempting to preserve its
Lutheran integrity in rural Wisconsin," writes Thistlethwaite.[26] Mass emigration occurred during the period of the
urban revolution, when a factory culture was enveloping all
of Europe and transforming America into an industrial giant.
Patterns of behavior and life-styles spread from the cities and
modified the traditional rural existence. "The history of the
latter part of the nineteenth century," writes the historian
Carl Degler, "can be written in terms of the gradual spread
of urban life until it pervaded the uttermost crannies of society."[27] Immigrant peasants had to adapt their folk society to
the modern world—back in Norway a similar process was
taking place. In America the ethnic press became a primary
guide to an urban way of life.

The Norwegian-American press was well represented in
towns and villages, but most of these journals fall into the
category Park described as provincial. They were filled with
local gossip and local news items and their circulation was
small. It is significant that only *one* major Norwegian-
language newspaper was published in a small town. This was
*Decorah-Posten*, founded in Decorah, Iowa, in 1874, which
existed for nearly one hundred years. Its success and long life
are indeed a reflection of the rural preeminence of Norwegians in America. The newspaper was oriented toward a rural
and established immigrant tradition. But all other major
Norwegian-American newspapers were urban mediums, including *Nordisk Tidende*, founded in Brooklyn in 1891, *Skandinaven*, from 1866, and *Minneapolis Tidende*, founded in 1887.
These, as well as *Washington Posten*, became primary instru-
ments in urbanizing Norwegian immigrant peasants. Ethnic
newspapers, states Morris Janowitz in his *The Community
Press in an Urban Setting* (1952), "mediate the impersonalized
aspects of urban life for a wide portion of the population."[28]

Thus, when speaking of the Americanizing influence of
the ethnic press, what is actually being considered is its role
in preparing immigrants to live in a rapidly changing urban
environment. Subscription to a Norwegian-language news-

paper might lead to interest in Norwegian cultural values, and thus to joining a male chorus or a reading society. The like-minded could meet in social settings, whether formalized through organization or not; and all could participate in public celebrations based on old-country memories and historical events. These were urban activities, and they were also to a marked degree ethnic. They promoted group cohesion and Norwegian cultural expression. The columns of *Washington Posten* indicate that many of the social activities might even be based on regional loyalties—attachment to a specific rural community in Norway. Yet the societies that were formed based on these loyalties, such as Sunnmørslaget (Society of Sunnmørings), were urban organizations, which met to perpetuate the memories and traditions of home. Norwegian folk life thus survived in new surroundings.[29]

One may follow the process of growth and adjustment of the Norwegian community in Seattle simply by studying the advertisement and announcement sections of *Washington Posten*. There are clearly definable stages in the life of the community. It emerged during the last two decades of the nineteenth century, reflected in advertisements for real estate sales, notices for workingmen's societies, employment opportunities, appeals from charitable organizations, and announcements of public festivals. There were numerous notices of secular and religious activities. By the 1890s there were, in fact, no needs, either for professional services or for daily living, that the immigrant community itself could not satisfy. In the 1920s greater prosperity is evident in advertisements for homes in the suburbs, national advertising for automobiles, and not to be forgotten, the regular advertisements claiming, in Norwegian, that there is no friend like a Camel cigarette. Norwegians were entering the consumer society of the post-World War I era.

*Washington Posten* was closely connected to the community and its development. But the impact of the urban press went beyond the local community. The newspaper carried local news items from Norwegian communities throughout the state and beyond. It helped to spread an urban way of life

far outside the boundaries of Seattle. "Long before radio and
the movies," writes Bernard A. Weisberger in *The American
Newspaperman* (1961), "the newspaper played a part in infus-
ing the countryside with urban attitudes and habits, dulling
the edge of conflict between the two worlds but preparing
the inevitable triumph of the city." The ethnic journals took
part in this process. The communities these newspapers
served did not, however, surrender to the new environment,
but adjusted to it and interacted with it. It was in such a context that the immigrant press functioned and played out its
dual role.[30]

Perhaps the two areas where the immigrants most visibly interacted with the American environment and influenced
American institutions were the work place and the political
arena. Occupational patterns, as has been suggested earlier,
reflected old-world experience in fishing, lumbering, the
building trades, and beyond the city in farming and mining.
Employment considerations might also motivate involvement in American politics; places of employment had to be
protected, supported and on occasion regulated through legislative action. In 1896, for instance, *Washington Posten* appealed in English to the state legislature to curb the greed of
the canning factory operators, who, it insisted, practiced
wholesale extermination of fish through maintaining fish
traps. The common fisherman needed to be protected from
this practice.[31]

From the start *Washington Posten* limited its news coverage mostly to happenings and events within the Norwegian-
American community, with a strong local emphasis, and to
news items from the homeland. This practice became even
more evident in the latter history of *Washington Posten*; the
newspaper became more ethnic in its reporting, focusing ever
more narrowly on affairs of special interest to a dwindling
readership.[32] Only during such dramatic events as the union
crisis between Sweden and Norway in 1905 and the trau-
matic upheavals during the periods of the two world wars
did *Washington Posten* regularly report world news on its front
page. On its editorial page there were, however—at least un-

til the end of the 1930s—opinions on political issues: local, national, and international.

The publisher of *Washington Posten* might reap personal benefits from rallying compatriots around a specific cause or political candidate. And there was by no means a political consensus among Norwegian Americans. Obvious political and social cleavages existed. Kenneth O. Bjork in his *West of the Great Divide* (1958) found Norwegians on the west coast to be less dogmatic in political persuasion and generally more liberal than Norwegians residing in the Upper Midwest, although they were influenced by the same partisan drives. Bjork treats only the early period of Norwegian settlement, and it might be argued that conservative leanings became more evident as the immigrant community matured, at least as they were expressed in *Washington Posten*. During its initial five or six years *Washington Posten*, save for a short-lived attempt by the immigrant commercial elite to move it into the conservative camp, held to liberal Democratic or Populist views. From the summer of 1890 until early in 1893 the liberal Peter Røthe from Hardanger edited the newspaper; he later stated that his editorial policy had been a struggle between "conservatism and progress, between corruption and honesty, between trolls and humans."[33]

In 1896 Populists and Democrats gained political control of the state, while nationally the Republicans were the victors. The depression years of the 1890s stimulated liberal and radical thinking and the many Norwegian workers and small farmers on the coast frequently sided with the liberal forces. But *Washington Posten* deplored the liberal political victory locally, having moved into the Republican fold when Thuland purchased the newspaper in September of 1896. Thuland was well connected in the Republican party and had the support of Norwegian businessmen in Seattle; the hope of the conservatives had been to win the immigrant vote in general. Editorially Thuland comforted himself with the thought that the Republicans had fought manfully against the enemy.[34]

Nationalistic pride tended, however, to blur political distinctions, so that ethnic origin—Norwegian or at least

Scandinavian—frequently became a determining factor in gaining *Washington Posten*'s support. And whenever the welfare and honor of the immigrant community was at stake, the newspaper acted with dispatch to come to its defense. Local concerns dominated. In 1900 *Washington Posten* cooperated in organizing the Scandinavian Republican League to get Scandinavian candidates on the Republican ticket for King county, where Seattle lay. That year they were not successful in finding Scandinavian candidates for county offices. Scandinavians had, however, long served in the state legislature. As early as January, 1891, *Washington Posten* listed the names of three Scandinavian members of that legislative body, all of them Republican.[35]

Gunnar Lund continued *Washington Posten*'s affiliation with the Republican party, and in 1905 when he took over the newspaper, a number of Norwegians and other Scandinavians were running for both local and state offices. In 1912, however, the newspaper's support went to the Progressive party, but in doing so, *Washington Posten* reminded its readers that the foremost concern should be to elect Scandinavians, if they were otherwise able men. Because, as *Washington Posten* noted editorially, "one can safely assume that Nordic men through their upbringing are Progressive regardless of the ticket on which they appear." The prevailing progressive spirit and movement for reform were subjugated under ethnic self-assertion. *Washington Posten* argued the question of Scandinavian representation to the point of wanting to set up a quota system which assured fair Scandinavian input in city and county affairs. Considering what Scandinavians had done to develop the region, *Washington Posten* was convinced that other nationalities would see the justice of such an arrangement.[36]

After its return to the Republican party in 1914, *Washington Posten* continued to insist on a greater Scandinavian political say. In the Norwegian community there was considerable evidence of a growing political maturity and ethnic independence. In 1928, for instance, the Republican *Washington Posten* abandoned the Republican candidate for governor,

Roland H. Hartley, whom it had supported in two previous elections. *Washington Posten* portrayed the governor as being incompetent; besides, he had insulted the Norwegian community and offended their national sentiments. *Washington Posten* reminded its readers that the governor had been invited to be present at the large Norse-American Centennial festival in Seattle in 1925, but had not even had the grace to respond to the invitation. When asked why, he had answered arrogantly: "Well, I didn't owe those Swedes anything."[37]

In the national election that year, on the other hand, *Washington Posten* vigorously supported the Republican presidential candidate Herbert Hoover while attacking the Democratic candidacy of Alfred E. Smith. Editorially the newspaper joined in the racist and biased attacks on Smith, "who is a representative of those elements in our population who more or less consciously oppose the Anglo-Saxon point of view which has governed this country." "This view," *Washington Posten* declared, "is by and large the same as the Nordic view." A more self-confident and prosperous Norwegian community was, if judged by the opinion expressed in *Washington Posten*, obviously identifying itself closely with a Protestant Anglo-Saxon tradition. As members of the community moved into middle-class America, they put a distance between themselves and more recent immigrant groups from southern and eastern Europe, the element Smith was seen as representing. Hoover won the favor of *Washington Posten* also in the next contest in 1932, but the newspaper editorially predicted defeat, contending that the American people were looking for a scapegoat for the grave economic situation. By the next presidential election, however, *Washington Posten* had embraced the Democratic cause and Franklin Delano Roosevelt's New Deal program. It thereby followed the change in political allegiance of many immigrant journals and a movement of Norwegian-American voters into the Democratic party, which in 1936 assumed political control of Washington state.[38]

*Washington Posten* maintained a Norwegian voice in the Pacific Northwest. Its impact in the immigrant community and on the region of course diminished as immigration from Norway slowed and American-born generations moved away from the old-country heritage. The most vivid impressions of a developing immigrant community and its relations with the host society emerge in the four or five initial decades of its existence. A correct reading of *Washington Posten* shows the newspaper as an active agent in the process of immigrant adjustment; this adjustment was based on a national Norwegian heritage, rural folkways, and experiences from the homeland. Using these resources the immigrants ultimately helped to give form to an increasingly industrial and urban nation. The nature, phases, and dynamics of this process as it pertains to a regional urban community of Norwegian immigrants may be seen in the many volumes of *Washington Posten*.

## Notes

[1]*Washington Posten*, May 13, 1938.

[2]For a popularly written history of Seattle, see Roger Sale, *Seattle Past to Present* (Seattle, 1976).

[3]Sale, *Seattle Past to Present*, 51; Patsy Adams Hegstad, "Scandinavian Settlement in Seattle, 'Queen City of the Puget Sound,'" in *Norwegian-American Studies*, 30 (Northfield, Minnesota, 1985), 57.

[4]Jorgen Dahlie, "Old World Paths in the New: Scandinavians Find Familiar Home in Washington," in *Pacific Northwest Quarterly*, April, 1970, 65–71; Odd S. Lovoll, "*Decorah-Posten*: The Story of an Immigrant Newspaper," in *Norwegian-American Studies*, 27 (Northfield, 1977), 94; Lovoll, *The Promise of America: A History of the Norwegian-American People* (Minneapolis, 1984), 156.

[5]*Washington Posten*, May 13, 1938; *Trønderlagets aarbok 1940–1941* (n.p., 1941), 57–61.

[6]*Washington Posten*, May 13, 1938.

[7]Lovoll, "*Decorah-Posten*," 93–94; Jean Skogerboe Hansen, "*Skandinaven* and the John Anderson Publishing Company," in *Norwegian-American Studies*, 28 (Northfield, 1979), 35–68; Svennik Høyer, *Norsk presse mellom 1865 og 1965. Strukturutvikling og politiske mønstre* (Oslo, n.d.), 24–25; Chr. A. R. Christensen, "Fra 'Tiden' i 1814 til vår tids presse," in Johan T. Ruud, ed., *Dette er Norge 1814–1964* (Oslo, 1964), 383; O. M. Norlie,

*Norwegian-American Papers, 1847*–1946 (Northfield, Minnesota, 1946), 33–34.

[8]Lovoll, *The Promise of America*, 117–133.

[9]Høyer, *Norsk presse*, 24–25; Frank Luther Mott, *American Journalism: A History of Newspapers in the United States through 260 Years, 1690 to 1950* (rev. ed., New York, 1950), 228–241.

[10]*Washington Posten*, May 17, 1889, May 13, 1938; Hegstad, "Scandinavian Settlement," 59.

[11]*Washington Posten*, May 13, 1938.

[12]*Washington Posten*, September 24, 1896; N. W. Ayer & Sons, *American Newspaper Annual* (Philadelphia, 1892), 766.

[13]*Decorah-Posten*, October 21, 1943; *Sønner av Norge*, January, 1941; *Trønderlagets aarbok, 1940–1941*, 59; Ayer, *American Newspaper Annual* (1899), 843, (1905), 891, (1915), 1009, (1929), 1131.

[14]*Washington Posten*, July 6, 1945, March 26, May 22, June 6, 1959, May 12, 1961; Ayer, *Directory of Newspapers and Periodicals* (Philadelphia, 1961), 1072. Henning C. Boe continues as publisher and editor of *Western Viking*, which is one of the very last representatives of a once flourishing Norwegian-American press.

[15]*Washington Posten*, December 25, 1925, October 1, 1926, April 3, 1953.

[16]*Washington Posten*, May 26, 1961.

[17]*Washington Posten*, August 17, 1906.

[18]*Washington Posten*, April 27, 1906, March 16, 1917. See files of *Washington Posten* in the archives of the Norwegian-American Historical Association, Northfield, Minnesota, and at the Luther College Library, Decorah, Iowa.

[19]Robert E. Park, *The Immigrant Press and Its Control* (New York, 1922), 121; *Washington Posten*, July 19, 1890, May 16, 1917.

[20]*Washington Posten*, March 23, 1928; Calvin F. Schmid, *Social Trends in Seattle* (Seattle, 1944), 111.

[21]Schmid, *Social Trends in Seattle*, 99, 111.

[22]Marion Tuttle Marzolf, *The Danish-Language Press in America* (New York, 1979), 3–19, 217–221.

[23]Park, *The Immigrant Press*, 49–88; Carl Wittke, *The German-Language Press in America* (Lexington, Kentucky, 1957), 1–8.

[24]Albert F. Schersten, *The Relation of the Swedish-American Newspaper to the Assimilation of Swedish Immigrants* (Rock Island, Illinois, 1935); Park, *The Immigrant Press*, 323.

[25]*Washington Posten*, series beginning January 29, 1926; Lovoll, *The Promise of America*, 71.

[26]Frank Thistlethwaite, "Migration from Europe Overseas in the Nineteenth and Twentieth Centuries," in *XIe Congrès International des Sciences Historiques*, Rapport V (Uppsala, 1960), 53.

[27]Carl N. Degler, *Out of Our Past: The Forces That Shaped Modern America* (rev. ed., New York, 1970), 314.

[28]Morris Janowitz, *The Community Press in an Urban Setting* (Glencoe, Illinois, 1952), 29.

[29]For a history of the movement, see Odd Sverre Lovoll, *A Folk Epic: The Bygdelag in America* (Boston, 1975).

[30]Bernard A. Weisberger, *The American Newspaperman* (Chicago, 1961), 149.

[31]*Washington Posten*, November 12, 1896.

[32]It is generally true that ethnic newspapers as they address a gradually smaller group of readers become more limited in focus, concentrating on events and personal relationships within this group.

[33]Kenneth O. Bjork, *West of the Great Divide: Norwegian Migration to the Pacific Coast, 1847–1893* (Northfield, Minnesota, 1958), 601–621.

[34]*Washington Posten*, October 8, November 5, 1896.

[35]*Washington Posten*, January 22, 1891, August 10, 1900.

[36]*Washington Posten*, September 20, November 1, 1912.

[37]*Washington Posten*, September 7, 1928.

[38]*Washington Posten*, June 22, July 6, November 2, 1928, November 4, 1932, October 30, 1936.

# 8

# *Skandinaven* and the Beginnings of Professional Publishing

## *by Orm Øverland*

Only a minority of the Norwegians who came to the Midwest in the middle of the nineteenth century settled in urban areas, and the first publishing ventures of the 1840s and 1850s, *Nordlyset, Democraten*, and Den skandinaviske Presseforening (The Scandinavian Press Association), the first publisher of the weekly *Emigranten*, the monthly *Kirkelig Maanedstidende*, and a dozen or so reprints of religious books, were all based in rural settlements. To Knud Langeland, the pioneer editor, the rural base was one reason for the failure of the early ventures.[1] Even though *Emigranten* moved its press to Madison in 1857 and fairly successful presses were soon established in small towns like La Crosse, Wisconsin, and Decorah, Iowa, urban publishing on a large scale did not begin until the founding of the newspaper *Skandinaven* in Chicago in 1866 by the three partners John Anderson, Knud Langeland, and Iver Lawson. *Skandinaven* not only became one of the most influential and successful Norwegian-American newspapers but also soon developed a publishing business that became the largest venture of its kind in "Vesterheimen," the name Norwegian Americans, taking their cue from Rasmus B. Anderson, fondly gave to *their* America.[2] This essay will trace the beginnings of professional publishing among the Norwegian Americans and show how the growth of the book business in Chicago and the prominence of *Skandinaven* served to foster a Norwegian-American literature.

The lack of urban centers, however, was not the only obstacle experienced by the early editors and publishers: editorial laments on the lack of literary interests among the settlers and pleas for increased support from their fellow immigrants were frequent in *Nordlyset* and *Democraten* and continued to appear in *Emigranten* and later newspapers. In the first issue of *Emigranten* for 1858 the editor, Carl Solberg, reflected on the problems of publishing for the Norewegian immigrants and on the many difficulties "unknown to a newspaper in Europe": "While there is in Wisconsin a Norwegian population of about 70,000, and Minnesota has one of perhaps half that size, and northern Illinois and northern Iowa have a considerable Norwegian population, the Norwegian newspapers published in this country have hardly more than 3,000 subscribers."[3] The main reason for this deplorable lack of support, for Solberg as for his colleagues, was the narrow reading habits of the average immigrant: "We wish that we could convey a clear notion of the usefulness of reading and of expanding the boundaries for intellectual entertainment beyond the area to which it has been limited with so large a portion of the Norwegian rural population: the Bible, the Hymnbook, and the [Pontoppidan] Explanation [to Luther's Catechism]."

In spite of such jeremiads from editors and publishers, however, and in spite of the small and scattered potential market, enterprising businessmen began to see a profit in the book trade by the late 1850s. One indicator of the growth of the book trade among Norwegian Americans in this decade is Bertel W. Suckow's bookbinding business, first in Beloit and then in Madison when *Emigranten* moved its press there in 1857.[4] Suckow bound and sold books for the Scandinavian Press Association, but an advertisement that ran in 1855 and 1856 suggests that he had an expanding business binding books and journals for private customers as well. By June 17, 1857, another bookbinder and onetime partner of Suckow,

Christian Sahlquist, was advertising his Norwegian book-bindery and sale of Norwegian books in Portage, Wisconsin. That the sale of books to Norwegian immigrants was considered a worthwhile business is also brought out by an advertisement for another bookstore in Beloit with the un-Norwegian name of Wright, Merrill & Co., which claimed to have a large stock of Norwegian books and promised future imports.[5] A considerable volume of business for the Scandinavian Press Association is also suggested by a notice in 1858 elaborating on the different procedures that could be used for mail orders. When Elias Stangeland advertised his edition of Luther's Homilies for sale on July 31 of that year, eleven outlets were listed, all in Wisconsin. The following year T. M. Holst, who for a short time had run Suckow's bookbinding business in Madison, was established as the first Norwegian bookseller in Chicago. He may have found the competition too strong in Madison, where at least five firms were selling Norwegian books, one of them established by Knud J. Fleischer.

The book trade among Norwegian immigrants continued to proliferate in the 1860s. Many of those who appear at various times as sellers of books were merely agents for a few titles, while others were able to establish firms with a relatively large stock and a stable business. In 1861, for instance, Ole Monsen in Madison, still working as a printer for *Emigranten*, began advertising his bookstore, followed the next year by Anders Gulliksen in Decorah, Iowa, and C. Amundsen & Co. in Winona, Minnesota. The first advertisement in *Emigranten* (January 9, 1865) for B. Tobias Olsen's *Noget om den christelige børneopdragelse og undervisning* (On the Christian Upbringing and Education of Children) lists sixteen places where it can be bought, and by February 6 it lists thirty-four such places, all in Wisconsin, Iowa, and Minnesota. Even though a good number of these addresses are simply clergymen or parochial-school teachers who served as agents, the number still speaks not only of the availability of books but of the possibilities authors had for distribution of their works. By the mid 1860s there are also advertisements for several booksellers in Chicago; the founding of *Skandinaven* in 1866 marked the beginning of that city's dominance in the Norwegian book trade.

The Norwegian immigrant population was scattered throughout the midwestern states, and the location of a bookstore mattered less than the frequency of advertising in the few Norwegian-American newspapers. Since so small a proportion of the potential book buyers ever came close to the store, announcements of books in stock had the function of window displays and most of the trade was by mail order.[6] Not only the increasing volume but the changing nature of the book trade is evident from the variety of books listed for sale.

In a large advertisement for "Fleischers Boghandel" in *Emigranten* for July 11, 1859, most of the list consists of devotional books and school texts, but under the subhead "Children's Books etc." some fiction is listed, for instance Bjørnson's *Synnøve Solbakken*, which had been serialized in *Emigranten* earlier that year. When Ole Monsen began running announcements for his "Norsk Boghandel" in 1861, titles on history, some moralistic fiction, and three books by Eilert Sundt, the pioneering Norwegian sociologist, appeared in addition to the two dominant categories of religious books and school texts. By 1864 his list of 101 titles has 54 devotional and theological works, while the second largest category is fiction, with 18 titles, closely followed by school texts with 14.[7] The trend toward a more diversified stock is evident two years later in the advertisements for Anders Gulliksen's "Norsk Boghandel i Decorah," where his list is divided into the following categories: "Homilies and Devotional Books," "School Texts and Children's Books," "History and Geography," "Hymnals," "Language," "Handbooks," "Novels and Stories," "Books of Various Content," and "The Latest Poems." The first of these categories is still the largest with about one-fourth of the titles, but it is apparent that immigrants could by now acquire a fairly varied and balanced collection of books in their old language as their new country gradually gave them the material conditions that made such acquisition possible.[8] Most of the books available for sale among the immigrants at this time were still imported from Norway or Denmark, but the proportion of those produced in America was increasing. While the church-related publishing initiated by the Scandinavian Press Association continued to grow and prosper, the new development of the 1860s was the gradual emergence of professional commercial publishing, the forerunners of the large-scale urban businesses of John Anderson, I. T. Relling, and Christian Rasmussen, as well as the many other publishing firms active by the end of the nineteenth century.

The two main competitors in the book trade of the 1860s were Anders Gulliksen in Decorah and Ole Monsen in Madison. Both tried their hand at publishing, but here Monsen clearly had an advantage over his competitor since he was employed by *Emigranten* as printer and could make good use of this connection for the production, marketing, and distribution of his books. Monsen had the successful businessman's sense of what will sell and also the sense of humor that gives an edge in advertising. His first venture in publishing, of which no copies are known to exist, was a broadside or pamphlet announced in *Emigranten* on May 1, 1865: *En ny og rørende sang om krigens slutning og Præsident Lincolns mord af den forvorpne skuespiller Wilkes Booth* (A New and Moving Song on the End of the War and the Murder of President Lincoln by the Corrupt Actor Wilkes Booth). The editor dutifully supported his colleague with a review in an adjacent column, calling it "one of the best ballads we have ever seen" and predicting that the publisher would do a good business. Monsen continued to publish in the popular vein and brought out a translation of the German juvenile *Genoveva of Brabant* by Christoph von Schmid and other light reading. His greatest success was no doubt the popular autobiography of the famous robber and escape artist of early nineteenth-century Norway, Gjest Baardsen. This book was to become a staple of Norwegian-American commercial publishing. It is frequently mentioned in Norwegian-American fiction as the only secular book regularly found among the devotional books in the homesteader's cabin.[9]

Monsen was the first commercial publisher of any note, with at least eight titles in 1866 and 1867, while Anders Gulliksen in Decorah, his main competitor, was primarily a bookseller, publishing only one book with his own imprint. In spite of the brief spell of success of an Ole Monsen, however, it was still too early in the development of a Norwegian-American literary culture to sustain a publishing business over a long period of time. Booksellers are heard from and disappear, often after only a year or so in business. Publishers appear with a single book, and there are notices asking for subscribers to works that are never heard from again. Thus in 1866 Ole E. Trøan made his first appearance as a publisher in Chicago with a translated book about the infamous Andersonville prison. After a few months he published a songbook, *Den norske Amerikaner*, and then apparently overreached himself. At least nothing seems to have come of the last two projects he announced, an English volume of *Thrilling Stories of the Great Rebellion* and *Gjest Baardsens levnedsløb*.[10] The many attempts to establish a book-publishing business as well as the many single book projects in the 1860s suggest that though the market was not yet sufficiently developed for publishing on a large scale, the potential Norwegian-American public appeared both affluent and literate enough to encourage a good number of ventures where an important motive seems to have been profit. While most book publishing in the previous decade was prompted by the need to make central texts for religious instruction and devotion available to the immigrants in their own language, the more secular, but equally idealistic, motive of keeping the mother tongue alive and promoting Norwegian culture among the immigrants began to take prominence in the 1860s.

This ideal was an abiding concern with Knud Langeland, the first editor and initially a co-publisher of *Skandinaven*, throughout his long and distinguished career. In his first editorial for *Skandinaven*, June 1, 1866, he made clear that he "regarded it as a sacred duty for the Scandinavians in America to do all in their power to support and maintain the language of their fathers and their Scandinavian literature." John Anderson, a printer by trade, was the senior partner and driving force in the management of *Skandinaven*. He was surely in agreement with Langeland's views on language preservation and the value of maintaining a Norwegian culture in America, but for him printing and publishing in Norwegian was first and foremost a profitable business. Although Anderson soon began to print books on his press, in addition to the job printing that was always a significant part of the total volume of his business, he was cautious, and had printed or published only a few books by the end of the 1860s.

The foundation for the kind of publishing *Skandinaven* and the John Anderson Publishing Co. were to thrive on during the following decades was laid when two of the partners, Langeland and Lawson, for unknown reasons broke with Anderson in 1872. They established a competing newspaper and publishing company, *Amerika*, with the active support of a new partner, John A. Johnson, a successful businessman with strong cultural commitments. Their interest in Norwegian book publishing may be seen in the ambitious project they launched as soon as their newspaper began to appear: a volume of Norwegian folk tales and stories edited by Rasmus Bjørn Anderson, the Wisconsin-born professor of Scandinavian languages at the University of Wisconsin.[11] Although *Amerika* had merged with *Skandinaven* by the time the book was ready for marketing as *Julegave* (Christmas Gift), it nevertheless bore the imprint " 'Amerika's' Forlag."

The editor's preface makes clear that Rasmus B. Anderson regarded the modest volume as an important event in the development of Norwegian-American publishing: "When I have visited Norwegian families in the cities and in the country I have almost always found a lack of Norwegian books, and especially books that contain light reading for children and young people. If we are to maintain the Norwegian language in this country we will have to supply our bookshelves with some of our fatherland's literature and try to awaken the taste and interest for the mother tongue in our children." Anderson was optimistic because of the rapid growth of the book trade in recent years: "Ten years ago we hardly had a single Norwegian bookstore in America. Now there is a considerable Norwegian book trade in Chicago, Decorah, LaCrosse, etc., and some Norwegian libraries have had considerable growth." The number of newspapers, church periodicals, and literary magazines had also increased. Nevertheless, he continued, "of Norwegian books that are not specifically religious almost none have been published in this country with the exception of feuilletons in the Norwegian newspapers, and even these may be counted on one hand.

"Is it not time that we begin to publish historical works, collections of stories, poetry, and folk tales? I think it is. The Germans in America have already published the literature of their country with good results, and even though the Norwegian public is small compared to the German one, I still believe it is a worthwhile experiment."

The publishers had not been so convinced to begin with. Langeland wrote to the impatient author in English on October 18, assuring him that "We have commenced work on the Book," but expressing his doubts about the venture: "I am afraid the Eventyr [fairy-tales] are too old and worn to sell, but Johnson thinks otherwise." Johnson, however, seems to have had his doubts as well. "You are correct about that Julegave book — it's a bad business," wrote Victor F. Lawson to Johnson on January 24, 1873, "we have sent quite a number by mail in single copies [to agents], but it is noticeable that *no one sends for a second copy*."[12] They were far too pessimistic, however, and sales picked up unexpectedly. Some weeks later Lawson was writing, "Has Prof. Anderson any 'Julegave' books on hand? . . . Think we shall have to have some more bound soon," and in the correspondence that spring the need for more copies was frequently mentioned. So little faith had the publishers had in this venture, however, that they had not even bothered to advertise the book until they suddenly discovered that there might be a market for it after all. The first *Skandinaven* advertisement for *Julegave* was not until February 11, 1873, after unexpected sales had infused the publishers with optimism. It promised "Liberal discounts for agents, and since the book is ensured a quick turnover those who want to sell it will have a good profit. Agents wanted in all settlements." The volume became one of *Skandinaven*'s many popular successes, and it remained in print for about thirty years, with the eighth and last edition published in 1900.

While it was with a sense of mission rather than any expectation of great profit that the proprietors of *Amerika* agreed to publish *Julegave*, they showed great reluctance in taking on their second book publication even though it was in the well-tried field of theological dispute: the proceedings of a "Free Conference" of representatives of several Norwegian-American churches.[13] Lawson, writing to Johnson on the last day of the conference, claimed he was ignorant of the whole affair and reported that Langeland wanted no responsibility for the publication. Their hearts were evidently not in this project and they doubted that it would serve any business purpose. But they soon found that this was the kind of literary fare Norwegian Americans still wanted. One of their agents, a schoolteacher in Wisconsin, ordered 20 copies of *Julegave* but requested 200 copies of the report on the church meeting. The ratio of one to ten suggests that though the collection of folktales was the first of its kind to appear in America, a volume of 128 closely printed double-column pages of theological dispute was potentially far more popular.

Few books of this kind were to be published by *Skandinaven*, however. Two other volumes published later that year are indicative of the kind of literary fare that was to dominate their list all the way up through the 1920s: popular fiction, often in translation, and generally printed from the plates used for prior serialization in the newspaper. The two translated novels published in 1873 were Henrik Schmidt, *Bondehøvdingen. Historisk fortælling fra reformasjonstiden* (The Peasant Chieftain. A Historical Tale from the Time of the Reformation), and D. James, *Abyssiniens Perle* (The Pearl of Abyssinia). An editorial note in *Skandinaven* for October 14, when the serialization of the former was concluded, suggests that Langeland's liberalism was influencing the selection of fiction for the newspaper: the theme of the novel is "a strengthening of love for the people's liberty and independence and a humane government on the one hand, and a detestation for all despotism and oppression on the other. At least that was our intention in publishing it." Although the increasing number of titles suggests a growing market, it was still too early to make a good business of this kind of publishing in 1873. Writing about the historical novel by the German Schmidt, Lawson observed in a letter to Johnson, December 6, 1873, that "Bondehøvdingen don't seem to set the Scand. West on fire. We have sold 3 copies."

By this time two other firms in Chicago were doing a fairly prosperous business in books imported from Scandinavia: I. T. Rellig and Fritz Frantzen, for a time close neighbors on Milwaukee Avenue. They were followed in 1874 by a similar Scandinavian bookstore operated by Christian Rasmussen and Christian Jørgensen, who in 1876 merged temporarily with Fritz Frantzen.[14] Frantzen, a Dane, had started rather modestly in the late 1860s with a tobacco and stationery shop. In the summer of 1868 one of the several Norwegian bookstores and rental libraries in Chicago, F. Herfordt, went out of business and its stock of 700 volumes was auctioned.[15] Although some of the stock seems to have been bought by the major competitor, M. N. Olsen,[16] Frantzen also made use of this opportunity to branch out in a new business. Later that fall he began to advertise his "Rental Library. Several hundred volumes of fiction and literary works."

The main initiative in book trade on a large scale in Chicago, however, had come from I. T. Relling. On arriving in the United States from Norway in 1866 he had first been employed as a clerk in Winona, Minnesota, where there was a Norwegian bookstore at that time. Soon he moved to Chicago and an editorial position with *Skandinaven*. Returning to Norway in 1869 Relling contacted publishers in Christiania and Copenhagen and was encouraged to go back to Chicago

and establish a bookstore there.[17] Frantzen's plans may merely have matured at the same time or he may have been goaded
by the example of Relling; at least both now began large-
scale advertising in the Norwegian-American press in the
summer and fall of 1870, Relling stressing his contacts with
Scandinavian publishers, Frantzen claiming to be the "only
American member of the Book Sellers' Association at home"
and thus able to get books from Norway and Denmark at the
lowest prices.

The advertising of Relling and Frantzen became increasingly competitive and the claims of one were immediately
taken up by the other. Reading societies were obviously important for their businesses, and both laid claim to being
dominant in this trade. When Relling, for instance, on January 4, 1874, boasted of his excellent service to reading societies, claiming that almost all that had been started in the past
three years had bought their books from him, Frantzen answered with a large advertisement on January 29 making
similar claims and asking rhetorically: "Why do we get almost daily orders from reading societies?"[18] In the early
1870s their business was almost exclusively with books published in Europe, and both claimed that they had the best
connections with large firms in the Scandinavian capitals and
reported on the beneficial effects of their journeys there. An
escalation of their advertising war reveals that the volume of
their business in imported books was quite large. In
*Fædrelandet og Emigranten* for February 26, 1874, Relling concludes with the following: "Since we see that Mr. Fritz Frantzen writes copies of our advertisements, we would like to
submit that according to the books of the Customs House in
Chicago I. T. Relling & Co. have paid $2,077.49 in duty for
books imported from November 15, 1872, to November 15,
1873. Fritz Frantzen [has paid] $165.12. We will now see if
he will copy this advertisement as well." Frantzen, however,
was not so easily defeated. On March 19 he came up with the
following conclusion to his advertisement: "As proof that the
book trade has made considerable progress in this country I

submit that in the past year I have paid about $1,600 in gold in duties for books in Detroit, New York, and Chicago. I cannot state what other booksellers have paid since the Customs House rules strictly forbid the giving of such information to others."

In the decade after the Civil War the increased volume of the book trade among Norwegian immigrants had made it possible to establish several substantial businesses in Chicago alone. In 1874 *Skandinaven* ran a series on Scandinavian businesses in Chicago written by David Monrad Schøyen. The installment for February 24 dealt with bookbinders and printers as well as booksellers, and about the latter Schøyen wrote: "Until a few years ago the sale of Scandinavian books in Chicago was limited to religious books and the most commonly used school books, and at the most there were in addition to these a few entertaining storybooks of the most popular kind. The first important step toward a book business that could satisfy present-day requirements came when I. T. Relling opened his store in the fall of 1870. He and F. Frantzen now have bookstores with assorted stocks that probably cannot be found outside of Christiania, Copenhagen, and Stockholm, and they do not merely supply Chicago with books but have customers all over the Northwest. Their large businesses are both telling and encouraging proof of the fact that a taste for literature and thus for culture is growing among those of our nationality. Some other Norwegians and Danes have smaller bookselling businesses, often in connection with other trade. The North Side has three Swedish bookstores. Several rental libraries are established in connection with these bookstores."

In Chicago and other cities, as well as in small towns with a concentration of Norwegian immigrants, bookstores flourished for several decades. If immigrants did not have one close at hand, the Norwegian-American newspapers to which they subscribed advertised bookstores that based much of their trade on mail orders. Although these booksellers did not primarily distribute books by Norwegian-American writers, the mere existence of a well-organized commercial distribution of Norwegian books in America was one of several factors encouraging aspiring writers to produce books of their own.

*Skandinaven* established a bookstore division (Skandinavens Boghandel) in 1876, though they had imported books for retail before this formal reorganization. The main impetus behind their interest in the book trade, however, was to find a profitable use for the excess capacity of their modern printing press as well as ways to strengthen their growing newspaper, which by the mid 1870s had weekly, tri-weekly, and daily editions as well as a special European one for distribution in Norway and, to a lesser extent, in Denmark. In October, 1873, *Skandinaven* began the publication of *Husbibliothek. Et Tidsskrift for underholdende Læsning* (The Home Library: A Journal for Entertaining Reading), making Scandinavian novels, stories, and poems available at very low prices. The monthly issues could be bound in handy booksize volumes and the idea propounded in the advertising was that a subscription would make it possible for the immigrants to build up a library of a kind unavailable to most of them in the old country. *Husbibliothek* was an immediate success. Not only did *Skandinaven* make this claim in their December advertising campaign, but the publishers were privately congratulating themselves. Victor Lawson, who, on January 25, 1873, had written rather cautiously to Johnson that "it is a new feature in Scandinavian papers and I think we shall get our money back *in time*," was quite pleased with the results of the first two months on December 6: "Husbibliothek will bear some 'brag,' even '*much*,'—I think. We have now 900 subscribers—fully 700 have paid 1 year in advance."

Until 1896, when it became a supplement to *Skandinaven*, *Husbibliothek* was an independent publication, only indirectly supporting the various editions of the newspaper. In 1874, however, the publishers began to plan another venture that was more intimately linked to circulation-building. On March 24 a notice appeared offering a new two-volume history of the United States as a premium to all of the 13,000 subscribers who paid for one year in advance. This eventually became the three volumes of David Monrad Schøyen's *Amerikas Forenede Staters historie* (1874, 1875, 1876, and many later reprints). Apparently most subscribers fulfilled the terms set. The publishers had launched a major marketing campaign and written a form letter to local public officials all over the large region covered by the newspaper, requesting "the names and addresses of as many Norwegians and Danes (not Swedes) in your town (and others outside of the town if known to you) as you can give. We propose to send to each one of these names a specimen copy of our newspaper, and a full announcement of our history. As this work will be the first of its kind ever issued, its value is at once apparent, and as it can be had, in connection with our paper, WITHOUT COST, it is evident that you are really conferring a favor upon the Scandinavians in your town in thus assisting us in bringing the announcement before them."[19] They suggested that the tax roll or poll list be used and promised "to recipro-cate this favor" at any time. Their sales campaign seems to have paid off. On February 21, 1876, Victor Lawson wrote to Johnson about the logistics of getting out about 10,000 copies of the second volume of the history and the need to set a deadline to qualify for the premium. This figure would have been a very respectable first printing for any American book in the mid-1870s, but it is quite remarkable considering the size of the Norwegian reading public at a time when the total Norwegian-American population can be estimated at about 150,000.[20]

As book publishing could be used to increase newspaper circulation, so could the newspaper be used both to advertise a book and to publish favorable reviews. This practical com-bination of a printing business, the publication of newspa-pers, journals, and books, and bookselling proved so success-ful that those Chicago booksellers who could, followed suit. Thus I. T. Relling in 1874 expanded his bookselling business to publish the weekly newspaper *Norden*, where reviews of books available from his bookstore were a prominent feature. Increasingly he also published books.[21] Christian Rasmussen, a Dane who was a printer by trade like *Skandinaven*'s John Anderson, came in 1874 to Chicago where he became a partner in a bookstore, acquired a printing press, and in 1877 established his own publishing house for journals as well as books. After ten fairly successful years he moved his business to Minneapolis, probably to get out from the shadow of John Anderson. At the time of incorporation in Minneapolis in 1887 his capital was $40,000 and after a few years the firm employed about fifty people.[22]

One reason publishing could prosper among the Norwegian immigrants in America in the face of competition from the far more experienced presses in Norway and Denmark was the cost factor. The competitive price of Norwegian-American books was from the very beginning an important theme in their marketing. Thus a review of Knud Henderson's *Koralbog* (Hymnal) in *Emigranten* (January 25, 1866) observed that while the price was $1.00, an imported book of the same kind would cost at least $2.00. The high cost of imported books was not due merely to transportation and handling. Increasingly, the tariff, which imposed high import duties on books of all kinds, protected the growth of Norwegian-American publishing. On the other hand it probably had an adverse effect on the conditions offered Norwegian-American writers, since the publishers could draw upon all the writers in the Scandinavian countries for cheap reprints. Discussing the negative effects of the protective tariff as well as the lack of international copyright in a review of the American edition of a British Bible concordance in *Budstikken* (Minneapolis) for February 15, 1881, Erik L. Petersen points out that this not only made all European books unnecessarily expensive, but it tended to encourage pirating and deprived authors of their income. His examples of price differences between London and New York editions of the same books also illustrate the practices as well as the working conditions of Norwegian-American publishers. The American bookseller, in Petersen's hypothetical example, would select a promising book without any honorarium paid to the author, "stereotype it and publish it on poor paper and in small print, and sell . . . the book that in London cost $10 for 50 cents bound in cloth." For some specific titles Petersen gives the prices as $12.50 and $8.00 in London as compared to the New York prices of $2.50 and 40 cents.[23]

How this situation affected *Skandinaven*'s publishing practices may be seen in a letter from Lawson to Johnson (December 6, 1873) where he considers the possibility of improving the poor sales of *Bondehøvdingen*: "The reason we put the price at $1.50 was because for amount of reading matter it is cheap compared to the imported Norweg. books. Shall we reduce to 1.00?" Production costs were apparently so negligible, especially since *Skandinaven* only made use of the free capacity of their own press for their early books, that they did not figure significantly in price-setting. The main concern was to keep the price well below that of comparable imported books. Apparently they would still be making a profit after reducing the price by a third! With local competition in publishing, however, discussions of prices had to take other factors into account. When Johnson wrote to Lawson on May 8 the following year about the marketing of Jules Verne's *Journey to the Center of the Earth*, he seemed to remember that the book "was 90c at Rellings stitched, but that is *too much*. I think 75c is all it will bear. The sales will be mostly with the paper cover. I would run that, get 500 bound and push it at 75c. I suppose it would pay pretty well at 50cts, but that would give dealers no margin. Allow dealers 30%. I think we can print books if we can strike the right kind to advantage. If we can get the money back on them in a reasonably short time, the increase of stock will give us something to draw upon after a time." By the mid 1870s Norwegian book publishing and selling in America had become both a professional and a competitive business.

Actual sales figures for this period are seldom available, since the archives of these publishers have not been preserved. In a letter to R. B. Anderson, July 28, 1880, Louis Pio, who had arrived from Denmark three years earlier, presented a list of his literary accomplishments in America. Several of the books he had edited or translated had been published by the Chicago Methodist publisher Christian Treider and the sales figures for two of these were given as 1,500 and 1,000 copies. He further claimed that his privately published *Den lille amerikaner* (F. W. Günther's bestseller *The Little American*) had sold 6,000 copies and a similarly published history of Chicago (*Chicagos historie og beskrivelse*) 2,500. The figure he gave for *Fuldstændig lovbog for hvermand* (Everyman's Complete Legal Handbook, published by C. Rasmussen in 1879), 1,500 copies sold, may also throw light on the business volume of *Skandinaven*, since they had published a competing volume by David Monrad Schøyen, *Lovbog for hvermand* (Everyman's Legal Handbook) in 1878. That book seems to have been the more successful of the two since it was reprinted four times by 1884, one reason no doubt being that it had only 320 pages compared to Pio's more ambitious 608 and thus would have been cheaper.

The increasing importance of the book trade for newspaper publishers is evident in *Skandinaven* for October 20, 1874, where the front page takes on a new look with two full columns of book announcements. An editorial note on the same page claims that "The books advertised here are entertaining, educational, and in other respects useful, and are all deserving of a place in the bookcase of any intelligent man. We would like to admonish our readers that in this country, where one does not count every penny as we were used to doing in Norway, it will be wise for parents to supply their family with good books in order to make the home a pleasant place for the young, among whom there will always be some who acquire a love for books, and you will discover that money spent on books carries interest." Only four of the eight advertised books were actually published by *Skandinaven*, and two of these were reprints of books originally published in Scandinavia. The remaining six books, however, were all in their different ways Norwegian-American products. Two of these were written in English (Hjalmar Hjorth Boyesen's *Gunnar* and Rasmus B. Anderson's *America Not Discovered by Columbus*) and the other four were the first volume of Schøyen's United States history, Henderson's *Koralbog*, O. M. Peterson's *100 timer i engelsk* (100 Lessons in English), and Anderson's *Julegave*. In the same issue, Anderson, using his pen name "Frithjof," had a review of Boyesen's *Gunnar*, hailing it as the first novel written in English by a Norwegian author. Two weeks later (November 3) Anderson reviewed Peterson's textbook and commented on what he saw as a literary awakening among the Norwegians in America: "So it seems that not only are we Norwegians in this country gradually becoming self-sufficient as far as our literary products are concerned, but that we are also beginning to deserve the respect of our motherland. . . . I would appreciate having more Norwegian-American books to review in the near future."

Anderson was at this time seeing such a book through the press himself, his own *Den norske maalsag* (The Norwegian Language Question), published by *Skandinaven* some months later.[24] This was a book on the development of the new Norwegian written language (*landsmaal*) based on Norwegian rural dialects, and the volume included a story in that language by Kristofer Janson, a prominent Norwegian writer soon to become Norwegian correspondent for *Skandinaven*. Two reviewers used the publication of *Den norske maalsag* as the occasion to note that an important change was taking place in Norwegian-American culture and that the mere existence of Anderson's book was a sign of what was happening.

*Skandinaven* always had favorable reviews of their own books, so the positive comments on the book itself by "B.T." on May 18 are not as interesting as his introductory reflections on the current status of Norwegian-American literature: "It is common knowledge that Norwegian-American literature, as far as books are concerned, has until recently been sparse and insignificant and mainly limited to a few religious books, while there has been virtually no original material and the translations and adaptations have often been terrible. We have all the more reason for satisfaction now that a more active interest in both better and more wholesome reading may be observed among our people. . . .

"The reasons this development has been so slow up to now should be obvious to all who have studied the growth of our people over here. We have lacked the intellectual as well as the material resources—the first necessary for the writing of a readable book, the other for its publication. For even though there may have been intellectual powers hidden away in some corner, our material conditions have been such that books have been kept from publication . . . and the barrier has been so great that it must many a time have broken the courage of those who may have had the ability to produce fairly good books." The reviewer speculates in romantic terms on the "sparks" that glow in the masses, some of which may burst into flame, and on the signs of an awakening among the Norwegians in America. Books are beginning to appear, "and the publishers of *Skandinaven* deserve our gratitude for their recent initiative in book publishing, through which they have opened the door to an independent Norwegian-American literature."

The second reviewer, in the Minneapolis newspaper *Budstikken* (May 25, 1875), also felt duty-bound to make the public aware that the publishers of *Skandinaven* were increasingly taking on the role of book publishers. His observations on the conditions for a Norwegian-American literature were much the same as those made in the Chicago newspaper the week before: "For natural reasons the writing of books by Norwegians in America has been very rare. The immigrants who had the knowledge and the gifts for such work were few, and those few were so poor that they had to rely on manual labor in order to sustain life. . . . Now the situation is somewhat different; there are now more Norwegians whose education and genius may be measured with a European yardstick and who may wish to try their hand at literature if only a favorable occasion were offered. It is with this in mind that we lead your attention to the publishers of 'Skandinaven'; they are men with great financial resources and they also seem to be inspired by the greatest will to further all that can be to the honor and usefulness of our nationality. Men who wish to appear as authors could now perhaps have hopes of a helping publisher's hand in Chicago."[25] Two would-be novelists had already acted on such hopes. Tellef Grundysen, a cotter's son from Telemark, had sent the manuscript of *Fra begge sider af havet* (On Both Sides of the Ocean) from Fillmore county, Minnesota, to *Skandinaven* for publication in the newspaper or *Husbibliothek*. Lawson had realized the potential interest of an original Norwegian-American novel and sent it on to Rasmus B. Anderson in Madison on May 20, asking his "opinion as to advisability of publishing it." Bernt Askevold, an ambitious young immigrant in Decorah, Iowa, had actually already signed a publishing contract with *Skandinaven* for the novel he had recently completed.

R. B. Anderson, although always surrounded by controversies, largely of his own making, held a position of prominence in the Vesterheim of the 1870s that should not be underestimated. As professor of Scandinavian languages at the University of Wisconsin he was the only member of the Norwegian-American group, outside the conservative Norwegian Synod, with fully respectable academic credentials. More important, however, was the fact that although he identified himself with the immigrant group, he was a born and bred American from Koshkonong, Wisconsin. When Bernt Askevold, a teacher who had immigrated in 1873 and was employed by B. Anundsen as editor of *Decorah-Posten* from its beginning in 1874, completed his first novel, it was natural for him to send it to Professor Anderson in Madison for approval. Anderson, who was indefatigable in his support of aspiring (and admiring) talent recommended the novel to John A. Johnson, still an active partner in *Skandinaven*. The partners discussed the project with Anderson breathing down their necks, and Lawson had to assure him that they were working on the matter.[26] The reply came to Bernt Askevold in the form of a complete contract dated May 15, 1875, and the conditions offered the author of the first American novel written in Norwegian and published in book form were as follows: "With reference to discussions with Prof. Anderson on the publication of your book we can inform you that the book, nicely printed and set up and bound in cloth, must sell at $1. We will, if we print the book, have an edition of about 1,000 copies. When 400 copies at $1 are sold our expenses will be about covered, counting the unbound 600 copies. So if you can get 400 subscribers for the book at $1, we will print it and pay you 10% of the sale price of all copies sold in addition to the 400, but nothing for the 400, so that if 1,000 are sold at $1 per copy you will receive $60. A financial report to be made each year or, if you prefer, twice a year. When 400 have subscribed printing will begin and be completed as soon as time and other business permit. You may advertise free of charge in *Skandinaven* for six months, not using more than 3 inches of a column each week, excepting reviews etc. You to receive the subscriptions, but will send us all correspondence with a list before printing begins. The advertisement to explain that no money is required before the book is completed. When the book is printed you shall have 30 copies free of charge for distribution or sale as you decide.

"The copyright is ours.

"If you find these conditions satisfactory please sign this letter as 'accepted' in your own hand and send us a copy. It will then be a valid contract . . . .

> Sincerely,
> Johnson, Anderson & Lawson"[27]

These conditions may appear stringent, but they were essentially the same as those offered R. B. Anderson himself for *Den norske maalsag*, and he, too, had advertised for subscriptions in *Skandinaven* in the fall of 1874. Askevold responded immediately to Johnson's offer of a contract, buoyed by the interest and support of all whom he had approached. His employer, B. Anundsen, the Decorah publisher and printer, let him run the subscription advertisements in his name, thus giving his stamp of approval to the project as well as a dependable address for the subscription campaign. Scarcely two weeks after Askevold had received the contract, the first announcement inviting subscribers interested in receiving the forthcoming novel, *Hun Ragnhild eller billeder fra Søndfjord. En fortælling* (Ragnhild or Scenes from Søndfjord: A Novel), to send their name and address, but no money, to B. Anundsen appeared in *Skandinaven* (June 1, 1875). What followed must have dampened the spirits of the young novelist.

When invited to subscribe to the first Norwegian-American novel the public did not seem to be overly impressed by the historical import of the occasion; at least they did not find that this publishing venture merited their financial support. After two and a half months of advertising Askevold made an appeal to the readers of *Skandinaven* ("Til 'Skandinavens' Læsere," August 17, 1875) in which he presented the book and assured them that it did not contain "gossip" but was "an entertaining and interesting story of life in Norway." After revealing that publication had been recommended by the many competent people who had read the manuscript, he explained that his contract with the publishers of *Skandinaven* required a list of 400 subscribers. Two weeks later R. B. Anderson made a similar appeal: "Will not the Norwegian people in America take part in encouraging and supporting a Norwegian-American literature?" More specifically, Anderson appealed to the clergy, claiming that they had a special responsibility for the promotion of Norwegian-American literature, but observing that of the 100 subscribers to Askevold's novel to date only two were clergymen.[28] When Anderson wrote again on October 5, forty-four more names had been added to the list (three of them clergymen), but this was still far below the initial optimistic expectations. The advertisements continued in *Skandinaven* for more than a year, with the last one appearing August 22, 1876. By then the conditions of the contract were finally met, and the publication of the novel was announced on October 17.

The notice was prominently placed and quoted a lengthy passage from the novel; it was repeated several times, but not after November 21, when the newspaper published an article by Askevold in support of the Norwegian parochial schools in opposition to the strong stance taken by *Skandinaven* in favor of public education. The book was not even mentioned in the alphabetical listing later that month of books available from *Skandinaven*. Neither was the book ever properly reviewed; it was merely given a brief notice in the literary supplement to *Skandinaven* for December 5. Such was the difficult birth of the first Norwegian-American novel in book form.

Even when it flourished, the publishing and retailing of Norwegian-American books was a successful business in relative terms only. Neither Anderson's *Den norske maalsag,* which had seemed to augur the birth of a Norwegian-American literature, nor his other books appear to have had impressive sales. At least Lawson wrote rather pessimistically to Anderson on November 6, 1875: "It is a little early yet to decide upon the prospects of sale of your books. We are selling *very* few books of any kind now,—and yours are about as 'few' as the rest. We have sold from July 31–to date of your books

| | |
|---|---|
| Maalsag | 8 copies |
| Am not Disc | 3 copies |
| Julegave | 5 copies |
| Norse Mythology | 8 copies |

We have about 18 copies of your Mythology on hand. I do not think we shall sell more than that number during this winter."

All books, however, were not equally poor properties and Lawson could give quite other figures for O. M. Peterson's *Fuldstændig norsk-amerikansk brev- og formularbog* (Complete Norwegian-American Letter and Form Book), a practical guide to writing letters and contracts, published in April, 1875. "We have sold since that date 184 copies, and we shall probably sell 100 more this winter, notwithstanding that there are half a doz others selling it. I state these facts thinking they may interest you," Lawson concluded.

However unsuccessful the first attempts to publish Norwegian-American fiction and belles lettres seem to have been from a purely business point of view, *Skandinaven* and other publishers clearly felt that it was part of their cultural responsibility to include some such titles on their lists. From 1876 original fiction, poetry, and drama were regular features of Norwegian-American publishing for half a century. Moreover, the establishment of publishers among the immigrants, from the first modest newspapers like *Nordlyset, Democraten,* and *Emigranten,* to the large professional businesses like *Skandinaven* and Christian Rasmussen's enterprise, was not only a precondition for a Norwegian-American literature but actually the main encouragement for the early would-be writers to realize their ambitions. The availability of outlets for poems, essays, and stories, as well as for books, was the impetus needed for the earliest literary efforts. Writing for Christian Rasmussen, the aging Knud Langeland looked back on the history in which he had played such a central role and commented on the changes that had taken place during the 1870s and early 1880s "in what we may call Scandinavian-American literature. Before this time the original works of Scandinavian writers in America could be counted on the fingers of one hand, and the books that were commonly read by our compatriots were either homilies or books like *The Adventures of Gjest Baardsen.* Because of the work of several publishers we now have a public that is able to appreciate the importance of good books and there is good reason to believe that this improved taste may gradually lead to the creation of an independent literary culture in our mother tonque here in our new homeland."[29]

Although the Norwegian-American commercial publishers were not quite as idealistic as Knud Langeland here makes them appear and *Skandinaven* thrived on the publication of numerous editions of *Gjest Baardsen* and similar popular fare, the Chicago publisher did perform as midwife at the birth of a Norwegian-American literature. After the first novels in 1876 and 1877, however, smaller firms and private publishing became increasingly important. By the second decade of this century the Minneapolis-based church publisher, Augsburg Publishing House, the publisher of Simon Johnson, Dorothea Dahl, Waldemar Ager, Julius Baumann, Ole Edvart Rølvaag, and others, had become a far more important institution for the well-being of a Norwegian-American literature than *Skandinaven*.

## Notes

[1]Knud Langeland, *Nordmændene i Amerika* (Chicago, 1888), 111.

[2]Useful accounts of the founding and later history of *Skandinaven* are Johs. B. Wist, "Den norsk-amerikanske presse. II. Pressen efter borgerkrigen," in Wist, ed., *Norsk-amerikanernes festskrift 1914* (Decorah, Iowa, 1914), 45–56, and Jean Skogerboe Hansen, "*Skandinaven* and the John Anderson Publishing Company," in *Norwegian-American Studies*, 28 (Northfield, Minnesota, 1979), 35–68. Further information may be found in Jean S. Hansen, "History of the John Anderson Publishing Company of Chicago, Illinois" (M.A. thesis, University of Chicago, 1972), a copy of which is deposited in the archives of the Norwegian-American Historical Association.

[3]Census figures for 1860 suggest that Solberg's population estimates are grossly overstated.

[4]Suckow had been employed as a secretary by Ole Bull in connection with the ill-fated Oleana project in Pennsylvania. Johan Holfeldt, the first secretary-treasurer of the Press Association, had also been an agent for Ole Bull, while the father of Carl Solberg, editor of *Emigranten* from 1857, had been director of the colony. So in this indirect manner as well, Ole Bull had an influence on the growth of a Norwegian-American culture.

[5]This advertisement appears in most issues of *Emigranten* from December 22, 1854, into 1857. The information on businesses in this paragraph and the following one is from advertisements in this newspaper.

[6]One day in October, 1866, Rasmus B. Anderson had been to Ole Monsen's bookstore in Madison and observed that an order was being filled for his friend P. P. Iverslie. He must have written of the coincidence, for Iverslie replied, in English, "It was singular that you should happen to call at Ole Monsen's just when he had the package ready for me. I had sent for two books, one of which is the life of Tordenskjold." P. P. Iverslie to R. B. Anderson, October 26, 1886, in R. B. Anderson Papers, Wisconsin Historical Society, Madison. Other references to letters to Anderson are to this collection.

[7]One example of this advertisement is November 21, 1864.

[8]Examples may be found in *Emigranten* for July 30 and September 17, 1866. Ole Monsen's advertisement on the latter date presents roughly the same variety. The advertisements for both booksellers are frequently repeated with minor variations. When Gulliksen had started advertising in 1860 his list was almost exclusively made up of religious books. See *Emigranten*, January 23, 1860.

[9]The firm Ole Trøan & Bro. had advertised a forthcoming edition of

*Gjest Baardsens levnedsløb* in *Fædrelandet*, October 25, 1866. The more enterprising Monsen had his edition off the press a month later. For Monsen's output see *Emigranten*, January 1, November 15, 1866, and January 21, 1867. John Anderson (*Skandinaven*) brought out many editions of *Gjest Baardsen*, one as late as 1921, and also published *Genoveva af Brabant* in 1891. Ole A. Buslett's *Sagastolen* (1908) is one example of a novel that mentions *Gjest Baardsen*.

[10]*Fædrelandet*, February 1, April 5, August 2, and October 25, 1866; *Skandinaven*, June 1, 1866. Ole Trøan was a printer employed by *Skandinaven*. A few years later Trøan was involved in a confidence fraud and is not heard from again after the scandal that followed. See *Skandinaven*, February 16 and March 16, 1870.

[11]Lloyd Hustvedt, *Rasmus Bjørn Anderson: Pioneer Scholar* (Northfield, Minnesota, 1966), interprets Anderson's life and contributions.

[12]Johnson lived in Madison; questions that otherwise would have been dealt with in conversation were therefore the occasion of letters, most of these from Victor F. Lawson, who succeeded his father as partner in the firm. Lawson preferred English and used this language in his correspondence with Johnson. All letters to Johnson are in the John A. Johnson Papers, NAHA.

[13]M. Falk Gjertsen and J. B. Frich, eds. *Referat af forhandlingerne i en fri-konferents paa Rock Prairie, Wis., mellem nordmænd, der bekjende sig til den evang. lutherske kirke, fra 13de til 22de november 1872* (Chicago, 1873).

[14]Information on these and other businesses has been culled from the advertising pages and the book notices in contemporary Norwegian-Amerian newspapers. Wist's pioneering press history has also been useful.

[15]*Skandinaven*, August 5, 1868.

[16]See advertisement in *Skandinaven*, August 26, 1868.

[17]Wist, "Pressen efter borgerkrigen," 87.

[18]These particular advertisements may be found in *Fædrelandet og Emigranten* (La Crosse) for the dates mentioned, but they were also printed in both *Skandinaven* and *Budstikken* (Minneapolis).

Reading societies and libraries may not always have been as well served as the competitors boasted. On August 9, 1874, a farmer wrote to R. B. Anderson about the library they had established in their settlement and asked advice on books to order in addition to those they had bought, first for $130 from a firm in Bergen, Norway, and then for $20 from Relling in Chicago. Anderson sent advice on how best to spend the $30 they now had, but to little purpose. On December 20 the farmer wrote back thanking him for the advice but explaining that the Chicago bookseller had not had the books they demanded and had sent them some others instead.

[19]Johnson Papers.

[20]The 1870 census puts the total Norwegian-born population at 114,246. Ten years later it was 181,729. *Historical Statistics of the United States: Colonial Times to 1970* (Washington, 1975), 1:117.

[21]Wist, "Pressen efter borgerkrigen," 84–86.

[22] Alfred Søderstrøm, *Minneapolis minnen. Kulturhistoriskt axplockning från qvarnstaden vid Mississippi* (Minneapolis, 1899), 430–432; Wist, "Pressen efter borgerkrigen," 175–177.

[23] To some extent this protection of the American publishing business in general was counteracted by a kind of book dumping that probably had some effect on Norwegian-American book production: the tendency to import remaindered Norwegian books for which there was no longer a market in Norway. In a letter to Rasmus B. Anderson, David Schøyen wrote that the publishers of *Skandinaven* had decided to give their subscribers a choice of several books available in their bookstore "and that it moreover is cheaper to buy remaindered unsellable books in Norway than to produce original books here in America." He added that they had "done a good business" with his American history (September 17, 1877). In the 1870s the Norwegian publisher and bookseller Fredrik Beyer in Bergen raised new capital for his business by travelling in the Midwest and selling his considerable stock of religious books and textbooks that no one would buy in Norway. See Finn Glambeck & Leif Christensen, *Tankens verktøy. F. Beyer 200 år 6. juni 1971* (Bergen, 1971), 92.

[24] The title page has 1874 for year of publication but the printing took much longer than expected. A notice in *Skandinaven*, February 16, 1875, announces that *Den norske maalsag* will be published around March 1. Lawson explained the delay in a letter to the author dated May 4: "The composition cost us more than we had expected—that story was tough on the 'intelligent compositor.' The spelling of almost every word had to be observed. The reason the title page bears the date 1874 is because it was printed when the first form was printed—last fall—when we confidently expected to have the book ready before newyear." Anderson Papers. In 1874 there had been a long debate on the *landsmaal* in the columns of *Skandinaven*.

[25] In an essay in *Budstikken* for June 29, 1875, Erik Leopold Petersen uses the image "European yardstick" ("europæisk alenmaal") in a similar context and he may well be the author of this anonymous review as well.

[26] "There has been a misunderstanding about Askevold's book—we shall make an estimate of its cost at once." Lawson to Anderson, April 27, 1875, Anderson Papers.

[27] Johnson Papers.

[28] "Frithjof," "Til det norsk-amerikanske Publikum," August 31, 1875. One clergyman, who evidently had not subscribed, protested Anderson's views. Signing himself "Bjørn," he published a letter to "Mr. Frithjof" on September 21 questioning the notion that a clergyman had any such responsibility and referring to the poor quality of what had been presented as Norwegian-American literature in the journal *For Hjemmet*: these efforts "have been nothing but deplorable choleric nonsense." The reference is to the second and third Norwegian-American novels in serialized form written by N. S. Hassel.

[29] Knud Langeland, "Lidt skandinavisk-amerikansk Literaturhistorie,"

in *Fortællinger for folket af forskjellige forfattere* (Minneapolis, n.d.) This volume opens with a biographical sketch to commemorate Knud Langeland as the man who "laid the cornerstone for a Scandinavian-American literature." Langeland died in 1886 and the book must have been published after 1887, the year Rasmussen moved his business to Minneapolis. Langeland's short essay seems intended as an introduction to a full account of both the Scandinavian authors that were most popular among the immigrants and those writers who had laid "the first foundation for a Scandinavian-American literature."

# 9

# Who Was Herm. Wang?

*by Ingrid Semmingsen*

In Johannes B. Wist's knowledgeable survey of the Norwegian language press in America after the Civil War one reads as follows: "Older readers of *Verdens Gang* in Kristiania will remember a familiar pseudonym that appeared in the latter part of the 1870s under several well-written satiric articles about such matters as military life on a drill ground or politics and the authorities. At the time, these articles created something of a stir and contributed greatly to the popularity of *Verdens Gang*. Later similar articles appeared in the same journal and from the same pen about the police in Kristiania, articles that were read with interest all over the country. The pseudonym was 'Herm. Wang.' In time it became just as well known in America as it once had been in Norway. The real name that for a long time was hidden behind this *nom de plume* is Ole S. Hervin. He was born in Stange, Hedmark, in 1852, attended the military academy for petty officers, and became a sergeant in 1873. Besides holding a military commission he was also for a time a policeman in the capital. He emigrated to America in 1880, and was here associated with various newspapers, among them *Budstikken, Nordvesten, Skandinaven*, and *Nationaltidende*. The last he edited in 1895–1896. In 1901 he started a small monthly in St. Paul called *Smuler* (Crumbs) in which he gave, in his own characteristic way, his opinions on 'men and forces' among us. *Smuler* appeared regularly until 1912. Since then it has been published occasionally. Hervin has a sharp pen. As a writer he possesses a good deal of originality and a great fund of humor."[1]

It is easy to subscribe to most of what Wist wrote in 1914. In addition it may be possible to put the life and work of Ole S. Hervin into a broader historical perspective in regard both to Norway and to the Norwegian-American milieu.

Ole Simensen Hverven—Americanized into O. S. Hervin—was the son of a cotter. But his father, born in 1825, was the son of a freeholder. The situation is typical of the social development in the eastern lowlands of rural Norway at the time. Ole's father was one of the many victims of the downward social mobility that resulted mainly from the population pressure caused by decreasing infant and child mortality. Ole's mother was the daughter of a cotter. His parents were not married when Ole was born, nor did they marry until two years later, presumably because they could not afford to do so. This is also typical of the social conditions at the time. By 1865 three more children had been added to the family, according to the census of that year.[2]

The farm Hverven (today Verva) was one of the largest in the municipality of Stange. According to the census of 1875 seven cotters' houses belonged to the farm. It also had a blacksmith's shop, and Ole's father was the blacksmith. The combination of blacksmith and cotter was not an unusual one in these districts. The occupation of blacksmith gave considerable esteem to a cotter and usually allowed him more favorable terms than the ordinary cotter's contract. The shop must also have been of great value to the farm and its owner.

Young Ole was a bright boy. When he was confirmed in September, 1867, at the age of fifteen, the pastor gave him very good marks. He ranked second among the confirmands. Out of a total of twenty boys he was one of nine who scored "very good" both in "knowledge" and in "diligence at work and general behavior."[3] Many years later Hervin gave an amusing, ironic, but possibly somewhat romanticized account of how this happened, which also involved an element of social criticism. In this account he praised his teacher in the elementary school as an excellent man who did not pay too much attention to all the baffling questions in the big Pontoppidan catechism, or their complicated answers. But the pastor was different; he wanted all the answers given verbatim. Hervin claimed to have had religious doubts already at that age. He knew, however, that confirmation was socially a "must," an entry to the world of adulthood.

After consulting an older man, whom he later in a poem called "the Anti-Christ of the community," he decided to follow his advice: to dissemble until confirmation was over. In playing the hypocrite, Ole was helped by his ability to read a text upside down. One by one the young girls and boys were called to stand in front of the pastor, who had the catechism lying on the table before him. The pastor praised Ole for having prepared himself well, but in reality he had done very little homework. He just read the text from the book lying in front of him, an ability he had developed at an early age by looking at his father's newspaper. This, incidentally, suggests that the father was an unusual cotter. In the Norway of the 1860s very few cotters had the means and the intellectual keenness to subscribe to a newspaper.

A showdown came, however, on the final examination day at the church. This time the pastor was standing as he directed his questions, and young Ole could see only the back of the book. He floundered, stammered, and stuttered, and was therefore moved one place down in the rankings. In his reminiscences he admitted that the pastor did not seem to bear any grudge against him. On the contrary he gave him a suit of clothes. In the same account Hervin also told of a young girl whom he admired. She had doubts similar to his own, but while he had been of the opinion that he ought to "cry out his protest" at the top of his voice, she felt that he should show patience and respect for other people's beliefs if they were honest and true. She insisted that the main thing was to remain true to oneself, that they were part of a leaven that in time would permeate all of humanity and make freedom, truth, and happiness into more than empty words. They might see the dawn of a better morning, but they would not be able to lift the sun over the ridge of the hill with their own hands.

"Browneyes," as he called this girl in both prose and poetry, died young. In more mature years, he felt no grief at remembering her, for she had been his guardian angel. He saw her as an image of honesty and good will, and he tried, he said, to be an interpreter of her bright, optimistic principle of life.[4]

Three years after his confirmation, at the age of eighteen, Ole was accepted as a student at a military academy for the education of petty officers in Kristiania. It offered a three-year course and it was free. The students got clothes and even an allowance, however small, for their daily expenses. The school provided an opportunity for boys from the countryside with an intellectual bent who did not have the means to continue their education beyond the basic common school. The school in Kristiania was a good one that gave some theoretical education besides the military training. It had a small library of its own, and it offered a course in English as an elective.

According to the military rolls, Ole Hverven became successively a first corporal, an unpaid sergeant, and finally, in July, 1874, a salaried sergeant, commissioned for six years. He took part in various military exercises between 1874 and 1878, either with his batallion or with the entire brigade, or as a sergeant in training young recruits who were called up for their first service. He is described as being five feet, five inches tall, well built, with dark hair and brown eyes (the last characteristic surprised some of his descendants in America who remembered him as having blue eyes). In the census of 1875 his civil profession is given as "dyer."[5]

During this period Ole Simensen Hverven married Nicoline Hansen, who was born in Sande in 1854. As was the case with Ole's parents, the marriage took place only after their first child, Hulda, was born in 1875. They soon married, however, and the census of 1875 states that Ole supported both mother and child, and that they lived together on the outskirts of Kristiania.[6]

His economic situation was not very good in the late 1870s. As a salaried sergeant he obtained a fixed wage amounting to about twenty-five cents per day in American money. In addition he received extra pay for taking part in exercises every summer with his batallion or his regiment. Still it must have been hard to raise a family on the income he was able to bring home. Poverty therefore was probably the reason Nicoline and Ole did not marry until after their first child was born. It also explains why, in order to earn some extra money, he chose to do military service for another man who was conscripted. Until 1879 this could be done in Norway. The well-to-do could be released by paying another man to do their service. Strained economic conditions and a growing family also explain why he worked temporarily in the police force in Kristiania. He may even have started his journalistic career with *Verdens Gang* — at the time one of the most outspoken representatives of the political left in Norway — in order to earn some extra money as a free lancer.

He must also, however, have had a real urge to write, to express himself and to comment on the events of the day, mostly events in the city of Kristiania. He himself definitely belonged to the opposition party — to the critics of the conservative national and municipal authorities. In one of his articles he criticized the lack of staircases from the roof of the recently constructed market hall down to the galleries where the butchers had their stands. Housewives ought not to try to jump down three or four meters. Consequently they had to make a detour and descend to the square below where they had to force their way through a crowd of farmers who were offering their products in the square in order to reach the galleries. It would not have cost much to build such stairs during the construction of the bazaars. To add them afterward would be very expensive. He found that few customers were able to advance to the butchers' counters, and there were long faces among them. One could even hear "American wishes" being expressed. For just as the Americans would like to have wars or bad harvests in Europe in order to take over trade and commerce, these butchers wished for storms and sleet to chase away their competitors in the open air of the square below.[7]

Authorities in Kristiania, he wrote a little later, spent large sums on the erection of a monument in the center of the town, but neglected the upkeep of crowded streets in the outlying neighborhoods where poor people lived. A person who was hoping for an inheritance from a long-lived aunt or uncle could not gain it more quickly than by advising the old kinsman to walk in Helgesen Street on a dark night. If the relative should miraculously get by the hundreds of holes deep as the height of a man, the poisonous gas inhaled in passing the garbage dump would surely contribute to the shortening of life. Yet authorities and conservatives frowned when the people who lived in these parts of the city wanted to make use of their right to vote.[8]

1879 was an election year, and Herm. Wang also commented on the intense political debate of the year, which was especially violent in the capital, and ridiculed conservative press contributions. Very often articles in the newspaper *Aftenposten* were his target, perhaps because *Aftenposten* had numerous subscribers from the middle and lower social strata. Hervin was journalistically very active from the summer of 1879 onward. The heated political atmosphere apparently released his abilities, or perhaps he was stirred by Bjørnstjerne Bjørnson's speeches. He was obviously an ardent admirer of the great poet. In consideration of Hervin's later views it is tempting to assume that Bjørnson's radical political attachment as well as his religious development away from orthodoxy and dogma over to the Darwinian theory of evolution inspired the young petty officer who had known religious doubts at an early age.

Why did he use a pseudonym? The explanation is simple. His critical articles with their satire directed against national and municipal authorities would have made his position in the military ranks impossible, with consequences that would have been fatal to his economic situation. He did not even spare his military superiors, the officers of higher rank. In an article titled "Plain Words" he criticized a lieutenant colonel who had given vent to his displeasure with the petty officers by saying that he would dismiss all of them if he had the opportunity. Herm. Wang commented: "Whether this remark will serve to strengthen discipline or not, the colonel himself knows best. But so much is certain: If the petty officers are such miserable individuals that the outburst is justified, the colonel who himself has appointed them has not shown good judgment in choosing among the numerous applicants for vacant positions. Or else the service under him is a veritable school of moral deteriorioation. At the time—it is now some time ago—when he treated his subordinates considerately, he never had reason for dissatisfaction." Fortunately, Herm. Wang continued, "there existed only one colonel in the Norwegian army who would not find it beneath his dignity to tell his subordinates that he wanted to make conditions 'hot as Hell' for them."[9]

In the fall of 1879 Ole Simensen Hverven made a dramatic decision. He sent in an application to be relieved of his military obligations as a commissioned petty officer in order to emigrate to America. According to a newspaper note, he had written in his application to the authorities that he wanted to emigrate because he was a freethinker and a republican—like Bjørnson at the time.[10] At a formal meeting of the Norwegian cabinet on the 12th of December the permission was granted. In the tortuous language of the time he was told that he was relieved "with the condition that he is bound by his military obligations until his departure and that the permission to leave the country must be used before the end of March next year."[11]

Ole went to America alone the first time, but he was back in Norway by the end of 1880 as a representative of the Cunard Line. He put notices in the newspapers offering his services to prospective emigrants and as a consequence was accused in an anonymous letter to the newspaper of recruiting emigrants. His wife Nicoline, with their three children, left Norway in February, 1881, on a prepaid ticket to Chicago. Hervin may have accompanied them or he may have gone back to America somewhat later as guide to a group of emigrants traveling with Cunard. The family soon moved to St. Paul, the city that became their permanent residence. Two brothers and a sister joined them there during the following years.[12]

By July, 1880, O. S. Hervin was already active in the Norwegian-American milieu. He took part then in a mass meeting of Norwegians in Minneapolis that passed a resolution to pledge support to the Norwegian political leader Johan Sverdrup and the liberal opposition in the so-called "veto fight" then under way, which was testing the limits of the royal veto. The resolution was sent to Sverdrup and to *Dagbladet* and *Verdens Gang*. Hervin then made a motion that it also be sent to the peasant leader Søren Jaabæk and one other representative in the Storting because they both had publicly declared that they were republicans, that is, opponents of monarchy.[13]

Hervin continued his journalistic activity without interruption, partly by sending articles back to *Verdens Gang* in Norway and partly by working for *Skandinaven* in Chicago. He did not take part in a big excursion organized in the summer of 1880 by the Northern Pacific Railroad for Scandinavian "editors, consuls, and journalists of all levels." He did go with the Chicago & Northwestern Railroad through northwestern Minnesota, visiting Norwegian settlements and land offices which cooperated with the Cunard Line. In an article sent back to *Verdens Gang* he played on social dissatisfaction in Norway. No hats in the hands out here in the free West, no question about what newspaper you read when you are trying to get work, no contempt for the common man, no oppressor and no slave. As a postscript he added that if anybody wanted further information, his address was in care of the agent of the Cunard Line in Chicago. In an article to *Skandinaven* he told about one S. D. Peterson, who provided most of southwestern Minnesota with agricultural machinery, and who besides, as an agent for Cunard and other lines, sold a good many tickets every year to compatriots who wanted relatives and friends to emigrate. In every article he praised the fertility of the land, but admitted that the winters might be hard.[14]

Being in principle an adherent of the republican form of government, he obviously felt drawn to the Republican party in America. Late in 1880 he wrote to his Norwegian journal that he rejoiced in Garfield's victory in the presidential elections. "It would have been a great loss to the cause of freedom if the Democrats with their 'States rights' views had succeeded in dividing this great union into small, insignificant states. A strong republic here means progress for republican thought all over the world."[15] Despite these sympathies, the liberal Democrat Luth. Jæger made Hervin editor of his newspaper *Budstikken* in Minneapolis, in the late summer of 1881, while he himself left on a trip to Norway. This was surely a token of confidence in the young man so recently arrived from the old country.[16]

It would be tedious to follow in detail O. S. Hervin's journalistic career during the 1880s and 1890s. It is doubtful that at any time he made enough money from journalism alone to support his fast-growing family. Together, he and his wife reared nine children, while a tenth died young. He kept his ties with the Cunard Line through its representative in the Twin Cities, A. E. Johnson Co., on Washington Avenue South, a strongly Scandinavian district. According to family tradition he made several trips to the Scandinavian countries and guided groups of emigrants to land for settlement in the Middle West, presumably land owned by the Johnson company. Sometimes he wrote in *Smuler* about his travels for the company and about the people he met in the various places he visited. He wrote with a humorous but mostly friendly irony, as when he mentioned prohibitionists who did not always refuse a glass of beer. But his economy was always strained and his appointment to a position at the Sons of Norway headquarters may have given him and his family a degree of economic security they had never experienced before.[17]

The first issue of *Smuler*, in the spring of 1901, opened

with an article carrying the title "No Apology." Here Hervin recorded that he had started to write "smuler" more or less regularly for *Skandinaven* about twelve years earlier, and that he had received many letters from readers, most of them very positive. There was, however, one letter that made him wonder. The letter writer said that *Smuler* was the driest, simplest, and emptiest twaddle he had ever read. He continued: "I know what I am talking about. When the newspaper arrives, the first thing I read is *Smuler*." The effect of the letter and subsequent reflection was that Hervin decided to publish his commentaries as a separate periodical. He went straight to the printing office and ordered the vignette that was to become his trademark—the head of a buck with big curved horns. At the time he did not pursue the idea further because of other work and then because of bad times.

Now he evidently thought that it was time to put the old plan into effect and he sent out a circular inviting subscriptions. Many of those solicited reacted by giving him advice about how to edit the periodical. "I suppose that most of the scribbling idiots among my countrymen have shared with me the affluence of their wisdom. . . . Some of the ideas received in this way will be salted, hung up to dry, cured, and then brought to the market as my own."

He then said that *Smuler* would have no definite program. "Let this be said to console those who have expressed fear that I shall be too radical to get entry into the houses of respectable citizens or too conservative to be able to see anything of value outside one single political party. I shall be radical enough to agree with the Synod pastor in many matters when I believe that he is right and I shall be that much of a conservative that once in a while I shall maintain that Lazarus [the poor man] does not have a monopoly on being right. I shall take things as they come and speak freely to the right and to the left. Politics I shall handle with great care. I am forced to this, if for no other reason, because of the fact that I am myself a Republican and my fellow staff member, Jeremias Pedersen, is a Populist. We cannot start by disturbing the peace in our own kitchen. Otherwise we won't have time to disturb other people's."[18]

This was the kind of humor of which he was to show many examples in the issues of *Smuler* that appeared during the following years.

In another article in that first issue he took up a matter that in different forms was to attract his attention for many years, namely the unfriendly relation between the church and the lodges. He found no rational cause for the antagonism, since the latter dealt with matters of this world, mainly through insurance of various kinds, whereas the task of the church was to convert sinners and save souls for a coming life. "The struggle is as a rule more bitter on both sides in a war that has begun without any reason worth mentioning, and that continues with just as good reason."

To illustrate with a touch of comedy that he was an expert in the field, he made up a nonsense list of all the associations, lodges, and other institutions he belonged to: "I shall begin by confessing that I am a Freemason, an Odd Fellow, a Druid . . . and a member of the Independent Scandinavian Workers' Association (I.S.W.A.) and that in addition I have been a member of some other secret organizations." As a "traveling agent" he was, although under another name, a member of a Lutheran congregation. "In a similar way I am also Methodist, Unitarian, Freethinker, Catholic, Adventist, Theosophist, Spiritualist, and a few other things in addition. I once thought of becoming a Jew, but there were some ceremonies of admission that I did not care for, and furthermore I am too fond of fried pork and blood sausages and pickled pig's feet."[19]

In a more serious vein he criticized the church for being too rigid in not permitting lodge members or Freemasons to be godfathers. On the other hand he asked the members of lodges to reflect on the fact that in America the various churches were voluntary associations. They had the same right to deal with their own affairs as the lodges. He found that in this respect the church was in general more liberal than the lodges. "The church opens its broad portals liberally and hospitably to wretched individuals, to the publican and the sinner, to the lame, blind, and crippled—people for whom the narrow and secret doors of the lodges are closed. The church welcomes the Negro, the Indian, and the Chinese, whereas an Odd Fellows association debates with statesmanlike solemnity the question of admitting a person with one-sixteenth Negro blood in his veins—when he is honest enough to tell them about it." The Freemasons are just the same.

He pointed out that lodge members should be aware of the difference between the State Church of Norway that every one automatically grew into and the separation of Church and State in America that changed the churches into private institutions.

Today it is not easy to grasp the antagonism that existed between the lodges of the Sons of Norway and the Norwegian churches in America around the turn of the century. The pastors evidently felt that the lodges of the Sons of Norway invaded the territory of the church with their use of rituals and ceremonies. Some of the pastors also disliked the practice of insurance against the various misfortunes of life. They believed that human beings should trust in God and accept what His will decided for them. The Sons of Norway people were not irreligious, but many of them were reformists. They wanted to improve *this* world through various popular movements.[20] Therefore when someone had written that it brings joy to the Lord to take a pious soul up to Heaven—in this case a married man—Hervin, the lodge member, asked: What about the widow who was left with five children? Should she be happy about it? And he wondered: When would the theologians stop representing the Lord as a butcher, a hangman who is gratified when his children suffer and die? To Hervin death was a calamity and he favored insurance to reduce some of its most disastrous consequences, whereas many of the church people at the time felt that insurance was a challenge to the almighty God.[21]

When he wrote in a more serious vein, he showed himself to be a convinced Darwinian evolutionist. Evolution to him was synonymous to progress, although he recognized that the road was uneven and sometimes rough. Again he aimed at the pastors. They were not called to quarrel about interpretations of dogma. "To guide and to protect us, that is what you are called to do." The upward path of progress is steep and rough, sometimes darkish too. "We are in need of enlightenment. Here you could help and give compensation for the 'board' we pay you. Until the sun of real freedom rises and chases away the darkness of old prejudices, most of us must toil and struggle by ourselves in the twilight."[22]

Almost every issue of *Smuler* had an attack, sometimes several, on the church and the pastors—their dogmatism, their differing interpretations of the Bible—attacks that were not always of the most refined sort. Derision, ridicule, and irony were his weapons. He seems to have had little sympathy for the low-church, evangelistic faction among the Norwegian churches in America. In his introductory article he had presented himself as a secret member of the Synod under a false name, and some years later he admitted that the Synod was the church toward which he felt most drawn.[23]

However, when he started his monthly this attraction was totally overshadowed by his antipathy toward one of the most prominent members of the Synod, Professor Rasmus B. Anderson, who had recently returned to the church and become the editor of the newspaper *Amerika* in Madison, Wisconsin. When Anderson began his long campaign against modern Norwegian literature, denouncing it as depraved and blasphemous, Hervin rose up in righteous anger and as early as 1899 in *Nordvesten* made a frontal attack on the famous RBA. It was not to be the last, as the great Anderson not only carried on his war for many years against authors like Alexander Kielland and Arne Garborg, but even included Henrik Ibsen and his old friend Bjørnstjerne Bjørnson in his list of "immoral" Norwegian writers.

Hervin's indignation at the attack on what to him were the most valuable expressions of Norwegian culture may have been an important factor in his decision to start his own periodical. At any rate, from the founding of the monthly

*Smuler* in 1901 Anderson was the chief target of Hervin's ridicule and sarcasm. He used various techniques. For example, he never used the title "Professor" R. B. Anderson but named him "Pastor Anderson" or "Pastor Kvelve" (the name of the ancestral farm in Norway), or even "Bishop Kvelve," the "bishop in Madison" — or simply Rasmus. He also created a new name for Anderson's views as they appeared in *Amerika*. They were "kvelverier" — "Kvelveries," that is, absurdities, in Hervin's opinion.

It is safe to say that Anderson went overboard in his criticism of Norwegian literature, and few were able to follow him to the end. Hervin may not have been the most important among Anderson's adversaries, but he was one who counted, and Anderson did not spare him. Hervin got his share of insults from Anderson's rich fund of abusive language; for example, "Bishop Kvelve" called Hervin "herr vin" ("Mr. Wine") — a reminder that the St. Paul editor had little sympathy with the prohibition movement.[24]

When the Synod pastor H. G. Stub made a speech in St. Paul on Bjørnson's seventy-fifth birthday, in December, 1907, Hervin wondered why this event had not aroused a new howl from the zealous "Pastor Kvelve" just to keep the comedy going. The greatest honor Bjørnson received on his birthday, Hervin wrote, was that he did not get a greeting from the reigning Swedish Bernadotte or from "Pastor Kvelve."[25]

Hervin continued his fight against RBA and the "kvelveries" throughout the existence of *Smuler*. He ridiculed Anderson's condemnation of Bjørnson's novel *Mary* (1906). He did so by publishing a rather lugubrious story of minimal literary value about Oline Rotterud (rotte = rat) and her male acquaintances. He also took part in an angry debate about Anderson's advertising principles and his practice of these principles — "cleansing" the texts of the advertisements without removing them from the newspaper. Hervin changed the name of the most debated one — the patent medicine Kuriko — to Fjuskiko (Cheatiko). Analyses had proved that Kuriko contained fourteen percent alcohol along with some laxatives. In 1908 he wrote a satiric tale about Kuriko: On Saturday evening an old woman takes a spoonful of this wonderful fluid that "rejuvenates the old and gives strength to the young." It will have a beneficial effect before breakfast the next morning. Then she gets a dose of the "pure doctrine" at 10 o'clock on Sunday morning, with perhaps one more in the evening, and hopes it will last through the coming week until the rush for the dollar gets the upper hand once more and the process begins all over again. The church's teaching is a kind of patent medicine. Like Kuriko it contains "spirits" — Kuriko fourteen percent wine spirits, the pure doctrine ninety-seven percent "pope spirits."

Yet he became somewhat milder over the years. In 1910 he admitted that Kvelve himself was a pleasant and lovable person. But he still maintained his aversion to the "kvelveries," because to him they represented the principle of hypocrisy.[26]

Another of Hervin's targets was the prohibitionists, especially the best writer among them, Waldemar Ager — "Brother" Ager. Time and again Hervin praised Ager as the editor of *Reform*, but felt that he saw only one issue. He quoted a statement by Ager: "If you put a silver dollar close up to your eyes, the entire world with all its misery is hidden from you." According to Ager the metaphor explained the continued success of the saloon traffic. "Yes," answered Hervin, "but then it also explains the existence of prohibitionism. Without the saloon, no *Reform* next week, and that would indeed be a pity. Consequently something good derives even from the saloon." He continued in the same vein: "Personally I dislike both the saloons and the prohibitionists. I acknowledge, however, that the Creator, who has let the one grow out of the other, has a better understanding of what serves mankind. I wish there were no saloons, but I am willing to wait for the fulfillment of that wish as long as Ager publishes *Reform*."

At this point he became almost philosophical. He believed, he wrote, in a supreme power — one might call it God, fate, or evolution. Evolution was *his* creed. In the evolutionary process, everything would contribute its share to the progress and happiness of mankind. He wrote: "A pile of manure stinks in the beginning. But sunshine and air transform the manure, and soon we see the grass grow and sniff the fragrance of flowers as they cheerfully sway in the wind."[27]

At another time he seemed to doubt his optimistic picture of the role of the saloon. What would the prohibitionists do, he asked, if and when they attained their goal? He felt sure that a fight against tobacco would come next. What else could all the speakers and agitators do? Then in due course a campaign against cards and kisses would begin, soon followed by speeches against all other things that mankind so far has used to make existence tolerable. "Then when all of us have become compulsory Sunday angels, we will easily be able to afford a rope to hang ourselves. Life won't be worth a shilling anyhow." The quotation is a good example of his bittersweet humor and irony. Another example: *Minneapolis Tidende* had expressed concern about divorced couples who despite their divorce continued to live together and had suggested two possibilities: They could be charged with illegal cohabitation, or they might be persuaded to remarry. Why not just leave them alone, Hervin asked.[28]

He was a skeptical person not only with regard to religion but also in more practical matters among his countrymen in America. For instance he predicted no bright future for Det norske Selskab (The Norwegian Society). He had his doubts from the very beginning. In 1901, when plans were discussed, he told his readers that it would be impossible to find "a common hat" that would suit all Norwegian heads. He admitted that they had their Norwegianness in common. "In all my ungodliness I am at least as Norwegian as any Synod pastor. We can meet on level ground to talk about high mountains, blue lakes, *rakefisk*, and cloudberries without stepping on each other's religious corns. If we are careful, we may even remain friends as long as we stay inside the four walls of the society. But, when the meeting is over, we will go back to our various businesses, each to his own *stabbur* [storehouse], and we shall have the same yawning abyss be tween us, over which no bridge can be built." He foresaw future conflicts in the composition of the board of the society. Should a Mason be president and a man from the Church vice-president? Was it possible to imagine a saloonkeeper and a temperance man together on the committee for organizing a banquet? Could the *målmann* (supporter of "New Norwegian") Dr. Leland write a program together with Editor Lange from Bergen? "Is it possible that a sulphurous pastor could read a non-sectarian Lord's Prayer" together with Herm. Wang who could be "a Mason, a journalist, an Odd Fellow . . ." and he goes on to repeat the comic list from the first issue of *Smuler*. "Oh no, we shall keep our Norwegianness, but in small groups, each in our own duck pond . . . Well, I do not say that a Norwegian Society is impossible, only that we, the eventual members, are impossible."[29]

One might think that Hervin's skepticism at this early stage was due to his suspicion that the archenemy Rasmus B. Anderson would be one of the leading figures in the coming society. But even when Anderson refused to join, Hervin remained dubious. "Even if the changeling grows a bit, he still resembles his illegitimate father, Rasmus Kvelve. The child smells Kvelve although the bishop has rejected him."[30]

He was negative also in response to the first issue of *Symra*, the periodical that Johannes B. Wist edited from 1906, with one surprising exception. He was enthusiastic about Pastor U. V. Koren's account of his experiences as a pioneer pastor. That account reminded Hervin "of the most beautiful chapters in the Acts of the Apostles." "There is elevation and inspiration in this contribution."[31] He had a strong dislike of *nynorsk*, the "New Norwegian" that was based on rural dialects in Norway and that some authors tried to introduce among Norwegians in America. He declared himself satisfied as long as he had the language of Holberg and Ibsen. He pretended that he did not understand the Telemark dialect of Torkel Oftelie in *Telesoga*, and he was delighted when he found an attack on New Norwegian neatly formulated by Knut Hamsun. Why shouldn't we write the old Dano-Norwegian as we have always done, he concluded. But fighting and quarreling—that seemed to him to be the national heritage.[32]

Posing as the defender of a pure Norwegian language he sometimes made fun of authors or journalists who wittingly or unwittingly used American loanwords in Norwegianized forms, with a different meaning in the two languages: for example, "Han reiste prisen," that is, he raised the price, whereas "reise" in Norwegian means "travel, go away." In this as in many other small matters he liked to tease and have fun, to play with words and expressions. He quoted a short notice from a newspaper about an old woman who had died "without doctor's help," and commented: "When I think of it, both people and livestock used to die that way in the old days, before doctors and vets were invented. So it is possible. It can be done." When Hervin read about thirty cases of smallpox in Utah of which one died, he reasoned: when the "case" died, the patient ought to be alive.[33]

Hervin rarely, if ever, commented on the discussions in the *Kvartalskrift* (Quarterly) of the Norske Selskab about the importance of maintaining Norwegian ways and Norwegian language in America. Being a part of the largest wave of Norwegian emigration in the heyday of Norwegian nationalism, he seems to have taken it for granted that a certain degree of Norwegian culture would be preserved. Probably he was one of those who thought bilingualism possible and valuable. He was interested in the various differences and even antagonisms inside the Norwegian-American community with regard to culture, religion, and politics, and he wanted to bring these differences up into the light, lay them bare, not cover them up. Although he did not say so explicitly, he seems to have seen himself both as a carrier of what he deemed valuable in Norwegian culture and a bridge builder into the broader American community. His defense of the purity of the written Norwegian language did not prevent him from letting the pseudonymous "Lars Lægmand" blame the pastors for slinging "the European slime" over everything American and hindering Norwegians from becoming acquainted with American conditions. He argued that Anglo-

American literature was the greatest in the world, not only in quantity but also in quality. It had Shakespeare, Bacon, Darwin, Spencer, Emerson, Poe, and a multitude of others. Worst of all, the pastors kept the children from learning English properly.[34]

Once in a while Hervin commented on European and especially Scandinavian affairs. He was skeptical, but perhaps less anti-British than many Americans during the Boer War. At least, as he told his readers, he had little respect for the "political heroes" in and out of Congress who wanted to help the Boers, but showed no sympathy for Finland, a country that, tied hand and foot, was being devoured inch by inch by the Russian spider — exactly the same animal that was behind the so-called fight for freedom of the Boers. His perspective is of some interest even now. To him the main question was whether the Muscovites or the Anglo-Saxons should govern the world. "The Russians devour Finland, Manchuria, and Poland and gag their victims so that their cries cannot be heard. England fights the Boers in full electric light. The whole world can debate every movement. That is the difference." Moreover, he thought that England was fighting to make the Boers peaceful citizens with the obligation to respect the rights of others, while Russia wanted to make the Finns into slaves. The Boer War had started because the Boers did not give full freedom to all citizens. His final statement brought the issue back to America: "We had exactly the same kind of war in this country when the slaveholding Southern states wanted to disrupt the Union."

To Hervin Russia was the Big Bad Wolf in Europe, and he criticized England and Sweden for not seeing this. The Swedes armed instead to fight against Norway.[35]

He remained a Norwegian nationalist. In 1894 he wrote a poem in homage to the pure Norwegian flag (without the union mark in the upper corner), and he defended the Norwegian-born consul for Norway and Sweden in New York who had "forgotten" to show up at a dinner in honor of a visiting Swedish bishop — a dinner where the consul was supposed to propose the toast to King Oscar.[36]

The dissolution of the union between Sweden and Norway in 1905 delighted him. "One of the brightest chapters is just now being added to our saga of freedom," he exclaimed in his June, 1905, issue. In prose and poem he commented on the various events of the year. The old republican even applauded the Norwegian adoption of monarchy and the election of a new king — for practical reasons. He consoled himself with the thought that the Norwegian ship of state would plow republican waters even if it was adorned with a gilded figurehead. He added that the best excuse for electing a new king when they had got rid of the old one was that their neighbors in Sweden and Denmark had kings. Norwegian Americans should not blame the people at home when they found that they had to make a deal. But there was no reason to be jubilant about it, either. One had to accept the situation with calm resignation.[37] However, when the king of Norway, as a friendly gesture, honored some prominent Norwegian-American men with the royal order of St. Olav, he again let satire have a free run. Why not establish a popular industry among Norwegians in America by cutting wooden St. Olav crosses, he suggested. Why not make different models for the various professions?[38]

What were Hervin's views regarding American politics? In Norway he had been deeply moved by liberal, democratic, and even republican ideas. Coming to America in 1880, he would naturally applaud the election of Garfield. Like many Norwegians he continued to support the Republican party. Although he made his application for American citizenship as early as 1880, he did not become an American citizen until 1897.[39] He was never touched by populism, and he disliked William Jennings Bryan. Among Republican voters he may be characterized as an urban liberal or progressive. He was obviously an admirer of Theodore Roosevelt, although he seems to have had his doubts about imperialism. Yes, the Constitution follows the flag, he wrote ironically, but it does not always catch up. The flag goes first, and then the Constitution must try to crawl after it to the place where the flag, so to speak, has struck roots in new ground. During the coal strike of 1902 and the ensuing shortage of coal he considered himself one of the common soldiers in the battle against the coal trust. He used no coal during that winter; instead he burnt birch wood and exchange newspapers and by so doing kept his house warm. Even in this connection he could not resist a dig at Rasmus B. Anderson: "Incidentally, I have noticed that *Amerika* burns with a blue flame." On other occasions he praised the president for having supported the Mormon senator from Utah, Reed Smoot, who was of Norwegian-Swedish descent, when the latter had to fight for his place in the Senate, and for having himself sat down beside a Negro at a banquet.[40] While he evidently remained an admirer of Roosevelt, he expressed his admiration in a humorous vein. In 1910, when Teddy was hunting lions in Africa, Hervin wrote: "A big lion with teeth torn to pieces has been observed in Africa. It tried to bite Roosevelt. It did not know him."[41]

In the later years of *Smuler's* existence Hervin was to a large extent engaged in a debate on socialism, with Emil Mengshoel, editor of *Gaa Paa*, the socialist journal published in Minneapolis, as his chief antagonist. Mengshoel and his wife Helle were real Socialists, even Marxists. Mengshoel, whose social background in Norway was not unlike Hervin's, but who was more than ten years younger, had first been exposed to socialistic impulses when he attended the military school in Kristiania; Helle had pleaded the case of women workers during a strike in the capital in 1889.[42] Laurits Stavnheim — otherwise a good friend and a lodge brother — was another defender of socialism. Hervin agreed that the Socialists ably elucidated the evils of society as it existed, but he objected to the rigidity of their thought. He felt that they were unable to explain in detail how their system would work, and he feared that it would bring loss of freedom — a value that was of supreme importance to him.

Hervin now and then reprinted attacks on himself from other newspapers, sometimes proving himself very generous in this respect. In 1906 he printed *in extenso* an article by Christian Bødtker, the editor of *Revyen*, Chicago, under the

heading "A Gentleman Socialist."[43] Hervin characterized
Bødtker as a man who wanted to discuss matters in an honest
and decent way, and who did not resemble other socialists
except in his tendency to be boringly long-winded. In his
own reflections on the article, Hervin first said that it had
been a pleasure to print it in full because it was fair and well
written. Furthermore, he disagreed only slightly with the
content and felt that "Brother" Bødtker was a socialist of another kind than Mengshoel and Stavnheim. Bødtker seemed
to Hervin to be an evolutionist like himself. Hervin declared
that he would gladly vote for public ownership of railroads
and trusts at the first opportunity, but he did not think that
public ownership was equivalent to socialism. Socialism was
a creed, and the Socialists were a sect in which the leaders,
like the pastors, ordered the people how to vote. In the list
of people able to give orders to voters he now also included
the factory owner and the saloonkeeper. As a path to improvement, Hervin continued to believe in enlightenment
and liberation from authority.

On another occasion he defended women's rights. A Socialist had written that in a socialist society the liberation of
women would follow of itself. Hervin replied: "On the contrary. I maintain that the liberation of women will make socialism superfluous. Our society will be able to improve, to
repair itself, as soon as women are really put on an even foot-
ing with men. Men do not have the moral right to introduce
socialism or any other form of government before women
are regarded as equals and take part in the decision."

He may even be regarded as an early ecologist. Mankind
should remember that ants and butterflies were also part of
God's creation. He voiced his displeasure with gold digging
because it destroyed nature to get possession of a metal that
in itself had no value. His granddaughter recalled that Hervin
"would never have a Christmas tree in the house, because he
didn't believe in cutting down the trees." Ecologist or conser-
vationist, in this respect too he was in agreement with Theodore Roosevelt.[44]

It should perhaps be added that although the tone was

sharp between Hervin and Mengshoel, the distance between them was not great. They were both self-taught intellectual left-wingers. They both wanted to discuss and even provoke. But there was a difference. Mengshoel had a vision of a Utopia, a conviction, and even, as Hervin maintained, a creed. Hervin wanted different points of view to be clarified through discussion and debate. He was of a much more skeptical nature than Mengshoel. He could write that nobody rejoiced in the Socialist victory in Milwaukee in 1910 more than he did, but his main reason for feeling good was that the Democrats were beaten in the election.[45]

Individual freedom and personal responsibility were values that Hervin emphasized both in his campaign against the prohibitionists and in his debates with Mengshoel.

Who were the subscribers to *Smuler* and how many were there? It seems reasonable to assume that most of them lived in the Twin Cities or elsewhere in the Middle West. He sent his journal to a great many newspapers and periodicals and evidently received exchange copies containing articles that gave him material for reflection and eventual satirical or approving comment. Occasional copies, now kept in the University Library in Oslo, identify some of the readers. Professor Laur. Larsen at Luther College and some of his colleagues were subscribers, and one copy carries the name of Bishop Wexelsen of Oslo. The complete and elegantly bound four-volume copy of *Smuler* in the library of NAHA at St. Olaf College was donated by the widow of the poet Julius Baumann.

It is impossible to form any idea of circulation figures. In 1903, Hervin noted with pleasure that the one dollar subscription money was flowing in, with the consequence that the *Smulemand* could now afford to buy a new overcoat to replace his seven-year-old one.[46] In later years complaints and pleas for subscription money appeared with increasing frequency, and in 1912 he finally gave up. After that date only a few issues came out at irregular intervals.

Johannes B. Wist wrote about *Smuler* that it was primarily the editor's own "crumbs" that gave "color and character" to the periodical, although there were other contributors. Many odd pseudonyms appear, like "Jens Jernspett" (iron rod), "Lars Lægmand" (layman), "Jakob Jonsok" (Midsummer Night) and "Reverend Per Pram" from the Norwegian settlement "Sutterud" down in Arkansas and his antagonist the teacher "Ræverud". There was also "Julius Apostata," the defender of both Voltaire and Darwin in lengthy debates with "Peter Olsen," who interpreted the Bible. The signature "MOT" and perhaps Julius Apostata are identifiable as the physician and poet Knut Martin Olsen Teigen, who lived in the Twin Cities in the first decade of the century and whose poem *Amnor* got enthusiastic praise from Hervin.[47]

The editor of *Smuler* had a genuine journalistic talent. He wrote a clear and fluent nineteenth-century Dano-Norwegian. Although he can not be called a great poet, he shows an unusual sense of rhythm and rhyme in the poems he printed in *Smuler* and afterward published under the title *Ved Hovedkirken* (At the Main Church). His taste for literature made him include people like the lyric poet Julius Baumann and the novelist Simon Johnson among his favorites. He was well-read and knowledgeable in many fields. He was reflective and independent. He told himself he did not have to write according to a certain formula like so many other journalists. In his sense of humor he had few equals among Norwegian-American writers of the time. He was not a champion of "Norsedom" in the debate about the maintenance of Norwegian culture in America, though he consistently defended what he perceived as the Norwegian heritage in literature, religion, and politics, and tried to make his views known among his countrymen, mostly through humor and satire. At the same time, he was open-minded in relation to the larger American community. In many ways he may be seen as an assimilationist.

Within the Norwegian-American community he was very much a dissident. He found *Decorah-Posten* toothless, *Skandinaven* much too conservative, and Rasmus B. Anderson's *Amerika* stupid and reactionary. His best friends among journalistic colleagues were people like K. M. O. Teigen, Anton B. Lange, active in *Scandia* in Duluth and later Chicago, Christian Brandt, who worked for many different newspapers, and Christian Bødtker from *Revyen* in Chicago. Men with whom he disagreed, but whom he respected and liked to debate with included Waldemar Ager, Laurits Stavnheim, Emil Mengshoel, and possibly H. A. Foss of *Normanden*.

O. S. Hervin is representative in many ways. For one thing he is a spokesman for eastern Norway in his lack of enthusiasm for causes like temperance and language reform. Further he is representative of socially mobile Norwegian groups, groups that were fired by social dissatisfaction and ambition. He was one of those who sought the remedy in education, a country boy with an intellectual bent. Such people were a minority within their group, but they did exert considerable influence in Norway, and in America as well, as teachers, journalists, publishers, and literary personages. Few of them, at least the literary ones, climbed very high on the social ladder. O. S. Hervin certainly did not. In the sociologist's categorization he would be a white-collar worker, but only from the lower middle class. His granddaughter described their house as "two-story but rather small and poor. Dad told me that grandfather would not take any advertising for his *Smuler*, being proud and idealistic, and even with the other things he did, the family was always poor. Dad said he had to go to work when he was twelve years old in order to get shoes. He was the seventh of ten children, and there was never enough money to go around."

The best known of these people lived in small towns — like Rølvaag, Wist, and Ager. But they were also found in the cities. In addition to those already mentioned they included men like Luth. Jaeger and Nicolay Grevstad. Many lawyers and medical doctors belonged to the same group. Together they formed a liberal and intellectual enclave to which historians have paid little attention. It may be worth noticing, however, as part of a more urbanized culture in Norwegian and Scandinavian America, with traditions back to 1848 — to the labor leader Marcus Thrane and the Chicago liberal

Gerhard S. C. H. Paoli—and with a heritage down to our own times. If so, it would involve a study not only of the press but also of the various professions, the medical, the legal, and the scholarly. While it is true that the majority of Americans of Norwegian descent have been conservative in many respects, it is also true that in every period there has existed a liberal strand. This part of the picture has been neglected and the neglect has had harmful consequences for the contact with corresponding groups in the mother country. This trend could perhaps be reversed by the rediscovery of a tradition that is more than a century old.

## Notes

[1]Johannes B. Wist, "Pressen efter Borgerkrigen," in *Norsk-amerikanernes festskrift 1914* (Decorah, Iowa, 1914), 100. Wist may have exaggerated the effect of these articles. An unsigned article about life on a drill ground appeared in *Verdens Gang* for July 14, 1875. The article, obviously written by a petty officer, shows sympathy for the common soldiers, most of them country boys. It is less aggressive than later articles signed Herm. Wang, but it may have been written by him. It has not been possible to find the pseudonym Herm. Wang before 1879. His journalistic activity in Norway seems to have been limited to 1879–1881.

[2]Census of 1865, Municipality of Stange, farm number 31, Hverven, in the National Archives, Oslo. The medieval form of the name of the farm is Hervin.

[3]The parish record from Ottestad Church in Stange states that Ole Simensen was confirmed September 22, 1867. All such records are in the National Archives, Oslo.

[4]"Et Konfirmationsminde," in *Smuler*, 22 (February, 1903), 4–10. A versified account of the event is found on the pages just preceding. "Browneyes" is also treated in a poem titled "Verduvia," in *Smuler*, 31 (November, 1903), 1. Hervin's poems have been collected under the title *Ved Hovedkirken* (At the Main Church).

[5]The military rolls of Kristiania Batallion, 1874–1879, in the National Archives, Oslo. Ole Simensen Hverven has the number 163.

[6]This information is from the 1875 census for Kristiania, in the National Archives, Oslo. A computerized edition of this census is available at the Institute of History, University of Oslo.

[7]*Verdens Gang*, July 17, 1879. The articles from the pen of Herm. Wang are listed in J. B. Halvorsen, *Norsk forfatter-lexicon*. The list is relatively complete for the articles in *Verdens Gang* in 1879–1881, but less complete for articles in Norwegian-American newspapers. For a more complete list of

the latter see the catalogue of Norwegian-American authors prepared in manuscript by Thor M. Andersen in the Oslo University Library's Norwegian-American Collection.

[8]*Verdens Gang*, July 31, 1879.

[9]*Verdens Gang*, September 16, 1879.

[10]*Bergens Aftenblad*, April 7, 1881, and Halvorsen, *Norsk forfatter-lexicon*. O. S. Hverven's application to the Army Department could not be found in the National Archives. The Protocol of the Norwegian Cabinet gives no indication of motives. The fact that Herm. Wang is mentioned in Halvorsen suggests that he was a person of some notoriety at the time.

[11]Protocol of the Norwegian Cabinet in Kristiania, December 12, 1879, in the National Archives, Oslo.

[12]Emigration protocols in the State Archives, Oslo.

[13]*Verdens Gang*, August 10, 1880.

[14]*Verdens Gang*, August 26, 1880, and *Skandinaven*, August 31, 1880.

[15]*Verdens Gang*, December 2, 1880.

[16]Wist, "Pressen efter Borgerkrigen," 66.

[17]Obituaries from various newspapers and periodicals in the Norwegian-American Historical Association archives, Northfield, Minnesota. Karen Hervin, Portland, Oregon, a great-granddaughter of O. S. Hervin, is the source of the family tradition.

[18]*Smuler*, 1 (1901), 1–4.

[19]*Smuler*, 1 (1901), 12–16.

[20]Odd S. Lovoll, *The Promise of America* (Minneapolis, 1984), 187–189.

[21]*Smuler*, 3 (July, 1901), 10–13, and 7 (November, 1901), 24–25.

[22]Lars Lægmand, "Sermoner til vor Geistlighed. Den tiende Preika," in *Smuler*, 23 (March, 1903), 11–29.

[23]*Smuler*, 1 (1901), 1.

[24]*Nordvesten*, June 6, 1899. R. B. Anderson's fight against modern Norwegian literature is superbly treated by Lloyd Hustvedt, *Rasmus Bjørn Anderson: Pioneer Scholar* (Northfield, Minnesota, 1966), 249–283. There was a bit of competition between Hervin and A. B. Lange of *Scandia*, Chicago, about who had been the first to take up the fight against RBA. See *Smuler*, 31 (November, 1903), 29.

[25]*Smuler*, 21 (January, 1903), 21, 29. See also 19 (November, 1902), 27.

[26]About *Mary*, see *Smuler*, 68 (December, 1906), 4–5. RBA had called it "unchaste from cover to cover." The story of Oline Rotterud is in *Smuler* in 1906. On Anderson's fight for the removal of advertisements for patent medicines see Hustvedt, *Rasmus Bjørn Anderson*, 274–283, and *Smuler*, 83 (March, 1908), 15–19. On hypocrisy, see 82 (February, 1908), 30–31, and 102 (July, 1910), 4.

[27]*Smuler*, 31 (November, 1903), 16–18.

[28]*Smuler*, 83 (March, 1908), 25.

[29]*Smuler*, 7 (November, 1901), 5–8.

[30]*Smuler*, 28 (August, 1903), 22. Hervin was replying to Laurits Stavn-

heim, who had written that RBA had strengthened the Norwegian Society by withdrawing from it.

[31]*Smuler*, 58 (January, 1906), 18.

[32]On Ibsen and Holberg, *Smuler*, 78 (October, 1907), 1; on *Telesoga*, 100 (April, 1910), 14; on Hamsun, 104 (September, 1910), 3; on the national heritage, 27 (July, 1903), 8.

[33]*Smuler*, 21 (January, 1903), 31.

[34]*Smuler*, 23 (March, 1903), 16–17.

[35]*Smuler*, 12 (April, 1902), 21, and 28 (August, 1903), 21.

[36]On Consul Ravn in New York, see *Smuler*, 7 (November, 1902), 11–14. The poem "17de Maj Flaget" was reprinted in *Bergens Tidende*, 169 (1894), from *Norden* (Chicago), May 12, 1894. It was also included in Ludvig Lima, *Norsk-amerikanske digte* (Minneapolis, 1903), 149–151.

[37]*Smuler*, 50 (June, 1905), 19–22, 27–28, and 58 (January, 1906), 7.

[38]*Smuler*, 82 (February, 1908), 21–29.

[39]Information from Karen Hervin.

[40]On imperialism, see *Smuler*, 3 (July, 1901), 29; on banquet with Negro, 8 (December, 1901), 28–29; on lack of coal, 22 (February, 1903); on support of Senator Smoot, 78 (November, 1907), 29.

[41]*Smuler*, 100 (April, 1910), 20.

[42]Records are in the Archives of the Norwegian Labor Movement, Oslo.

[43]*Smuler*, 57 (January, 1906), 18–25. Notes and articles on socialism appear in almost every issue of *Smuler*, together with a lengthy discussion between a rationalist and a Bible-reading fundamentalist. On socialism see for instance 78 (October, 1907), 7–9, and 82 (February, 1908), 16–17.

[44]On women's rights, see *Smuler*, 60 (April, 1906), 9; on ecology, 52 (August, 1905), 8; on gold digging, 66 (October, 1906), 2; on Christmas tree, letter from granddaughter of O. S. Hervin to her niece, Karen Hervin.

[45]*Smuler*, 102 (July, 1910), 5.

[46]*Smuler*, 21 (January, 1903), 30. In "Salt for the Buck," in 101 (April, 1910), 26, he complained about his bad mood around Christmas time because he had had no money for a "Christmas dram." When Stavnheim's *Vor Tid* had to close in 1910, Hervin got the subscription list. Apparently it was of little help.

[47]Professor Orm Øverland, University of Bergen, suggested that MOT, who began his contributions in the autumn of 1903, was the pseudonym of Knut Martin Olsen Teigen. In fact Hervin says so himself in *Smuler*, 54 (October, 1905), 31. Hervin here praises MOT for his contribution to *Smuler* with aphorisms called "Hickory-Nödder" (Hickory-Nuts). He also hopes for new contributions from Teigen in the future. Professor Øverland also came forward with the idea about "Julius Apostata." Hervin himself probably wrote the letters from the "Sutterud settlement down in Arkansas"; he may also be the author of the poems in the later years of *Smuler* signed "Busterud'n." Hervin said in *Smuler*, 11 (March, 1902), 2, that up to that time he had written all of the "smuler" himself. From then

on he was willing to receive contributions provided they were written "paa smulevis," in the spirit of *Smuler*. Wist, in "Pressen efter Borgerkrigen," 86–88, also mentions that other "more or less sharp pens" contributed to the periodical, but maintains that Hervin gave it its distinctive character. Hervin praised *Amnor* in a poem in *Smuler*, 7 (November, 1901), 1–2, and again in a poem for Teigen's *Vesterlandske digte*, 53 (September, 1905), 1–4. The next issue, 55 (November, 1905), 9–12, carried a review by Julius Baumann.

# 10

## "The Best Place on Earth for Women": The American Experience of Aasta Hansteen

### by Janet E. Rasmussen

The enduring popular image of Aasta Hansteen has been of an impassioned, eccentric, umbrella-wielding reformer. Gunnar Heiberg's play *Tante Ulrikke* (1884) captured this side of her. Ibsen's dynamic heroine Lona Hessel, who insists upon unveiling social hypocrisy in *Pillars of Society* (1877), is also frequently said to have been modeled on Aasta Hansteen. The daughter of Christopher Hansteen, a distinguished early professor at the University of Oslo, Aasta Hansteen (1824–1908) was well known in the intellectual and upper-class circles in Norway's captial, for her unconventional behavior set her apart from her contemporaries. Aasta Hansteen had the distinction of being Christiania's first female portrait painter, the first Norwegian woman to deliver public lectures, the first woman to publish in the *nynorsk* language, and, along with Camilla Collett, a pioneer in the Norwegian women's movement. Hers was a rich and fascinating life, but one which until recently has remained largely unexplored.[1]

Aasta Hansteen lived in the United States for nine years, between 1880 and 1889. She spent six and a half years in the Boston area and two and a half years in the Midwest, primarily Chicago. Thus her American experience was an urban one. The reasons she chose Boston as her initial residence are obscure; one can only speculate that the rich cultural environment and the established women's movement made it an attractive destination. She could count on a small annual income from Norway, which she supplemented by painting portraits on commission; her life-style was of necessity extremely modest. This was, nevertheless, an important and eventful time for her. A study of her experiences in, and responses to, the American scene opens up new perspectives on Aasta Hansteen as a person, artist, and reformer. In addition, it enriches our understanding of the two environments in which she lived.

As she later expressed it, Aasta Hansteen decided to emigrate because the ground was burning beneath her feet. Hostility, it seemed, surrounded her in Norway. Hansteen's defiance of convention and vocal opposition to traditional theological views about women generated a steady barrage of criticism and scorn. With good reason she felt isolated, unappreciated, and misunderstood. Her decision was also prompted by the knowledge that in the New World the struggle for women's rights was well under way. She eagerly anticipated the opportunity to observe the inspiring suffrage leaders about whom she had read. Thus a combination of "push" and "pull" factors motivated Aasta Hansteen to go abroad at the age of fifty-five. Together with her foster daughter Theodora Nielsen, she sailed from Christiania on April 9, 1880.[2] In the euphoria of departure she wrote in her pocket calendar, "My misery is over." In her first published communication from the United States, she confirmed her happy decision: "Since I left Christiania, my principal emotion has been an indescribable feeling of liberation."[3]

On Wednesday, May 5, Aasta Hansteen arrived in Boston. She at once began to seek out progressive individuals and organizations. May was an excellent month for her orientation to begin, for it was the time when many groups, including the suffrage associations, held their "anniversary meetings." There was thus opportunity to sample America's flourishing club and organizational life before the summer hiatus. As the weeks passed, Aasta Hansteen met or observed such leading reformers as Lucy Stone, Julia Ward Howe, Mary Safford, Mary Livermore, and Wendell Phillips. Her sole paid occupation during the first months consisted of writing five reports for the Christiania newspaper *Verdens Gang*, an assignment apparently agreed upon before she left Norway. These articles made it clear that she was keeping up with the Boston press, in particular *The Woman's Journal* (referred to as "Kvindernes Ugeblad"), and that she was very favorably impressed by the liberal Boston intellectuals with whom she came in contact.

October brought a flurry of activity surrounding the visit of Bjørnstjerne Bjørnson. It also marked Aasta Hansteen's transition from newcomer to working artist. Her initial project was a portrait of Alice Blackwell, daughter of the editors of *The Woman's Journal*, Lucy Stone and Henry Blackwell, who was then twenty-three years old and a student at Boston University. On October 28 she noted that Alice Blackwell had been received, presumably for a sitting, and that she had earned her first dollar. Soon she was engaged in other projects as well; the most exciting of these was a portrait of Bjørnson, to be underwritten by local Scandinavians. Hansteen expected this portrait to open doors for her throughout the Scandinavian community. The festivities for Bjørnson, especially a grand reception in Paine Memorial Hall on October 7 with a thousand persons in attendance, made a considerable impression. There were other stirring occasions at which Aasta Hansteen was present, including a rally hosted by the Scandinavian Republican Club. Her health and spirits appear to have been good; Bjørnson characterized her as "optimistic and well."[4] On one occasion he visited her to sit for his portrait, having sent a postcard in advance asking to be directed to her "jomfru-bur" (maiden bower). Aasta Hansteen's calendar indicates that Bjørnson visited on December 3 and that they enjoyed a meal of oyster sandwiches and beer.

In January, 1881, Aasta Hansteen called upon Boston's foremost art dealers, Williams & Everett, and offered them a small Rhine landscape. They purchased it for $20. In late

February she engaged an atelier in The Studiobuilding, where she worked and displayed her paintings from March to June. The Studiobuilding, 112 Tremont Street, was a well-known center for Boston's professional artists. Aasta Hansteen rented studio 36; this location put her in touch with colleagues like Mrs. Jessie Noa, who worked in studio 33. Jessie Noa's reputation was a fine one. At the time of her death *The Boston Evening Transcript* characterized her as the "eminent Boston pastel portrait artist."[5] So the announcement concerning Aasta Hansteen which Jessie Noa sent to *The Woman's Journal* may be regarded as a solid endorsement. Here "Madame Hansteen" was presented as "an artist of high reputation in Christiania" and the public was invited to inspect her work at the Studiobuilding. Mrs. Noa singled out for special mention the painting "Moses Praying for Victory" and concluded by noting: "her fine drawing would make her an excellent teacher; we therefore hope she will meet with encouragement."[6] Mrs. Noa's announcement appeared in *The Woman's Journal* in early May, but there is no indication of an influx of visitors or orders as a result. Still, the spring of 1881 offered the most promise for Aasta Hansteen's connections with, and involvement in, the Boston art world. Had she given the Studiobuilding and her new contacts more time, a steady business might have evolved. But her financial situation was too precarious; she was forced to pawn several items and her relationship with the landlords at 28 East Brookline Street deteriorated. America was proving a demanding environment for an aging artist whose command of English was very limited.

On June 2, 1881, Aasta Hansteen reached the decision to travel to the Midwest on a lecture tour. The handsome sum of money Bjørnson had earned during his recently concluded lecture tour no doubt made the thought of her own tour among the Scandinavians highly tantalizing.[7] Aasta Hansteen raised the necessary travel funds by borrowing $80 against some of her paintings and obtaining a personal loan of $20 from the local consul. Her initial destination was Chicago but she clearly planned to travel on from there to a number of other Scandinavian settlements. A letter to *The Woman's Journal* told of her intention to stay on in Chicago until late August, "because it is very pleasant here among so many of my compatriots, and the season is not favorable for lecturing," and suggested that later correspondence would cover her experiences in places like Madison, La Crosse, and Minneapolis. This same letter contained a description of her Chicago lecture, held on July 10, 1881, in Aurora Turner Hall: "The audience was not large—about two hundred persons—but it was quite sympathetic with the subject and with my points of view, and I had much applause. The Scandinavian newspapers, Norwegian, Swedish, and Danish, were very favorable to me before and after the lecture."[8] Indeed she had prepared the way for her lecture tour by sending announcements to three Midwestern newspapers—*Budstikken* and *Folkebladet* in Minneapolis, and *Norden* in Chicago. The Chicago lecture proved to be a positive emotional experience; at the same time it must have disappointed her from a financial point of view. The crowd apparently generated an income of only $17.

While waiting to continue her lecture tour, Aasta Hansteen spent the summer getting acquainted with the Chicago Scandinavians and painting their portraits. At the end of July she received four commissions and during the hot and humid days of August she worked long, steady hours in an effort to keep up with the mounting bills. She had arrived in Chicago on June 26 and spent several weeks with a Vingaard family before moving to 151 Morgan Street, where she was charged about $4.50 a week for board. September found her adopting new strategies for obtaining portrait orders. The lecture plans had been laid aside; Aasta Hansteen was absorbed with her new friends and with prospects for foster daughter Theodora to develop her musical talent. Except for a brief trip to Minneapolis in 1882, Chicago remained her home for the next two years.

Having completed the first round of paintings and anxious for more work, Aasta Hansteen arranged to exhibit the

Bjørnson portrait which she had brought along from Boston. In late September it was placed on display at Melanders' (presumably L. M. Melander & Bros., photographers). The death of President Garfield on September 19 prompted her to begin his portrait and by mid-October it, too, could be viewed at Melanders'. A second Garfield portrait was then completed and exhibited at A. Reed & Sons, piano dealers, on State Street. In November socialist reformer and editor Marcus Thrane sat for his portrait. Throughout the winter and into the spring of 1882 individual Scandinavian immigrants appear to have accounted for most of her portrait painting.

At the same time her work received exposure in Chicago's bustling art colony through the elegant but short-lived gallery known as The Cosmos. The Cosmos was the brainchild of Marie Brown, a New York native who according to *The Chicago Tribune* "has made a name for herself in Eastern literary and art circles by her masterly translations of Swedish literature and her interesting and successful lectures on Scandinavian art." Brown was a true Scandinavian enthusiast, as her later writings on Leif Ericson testify, and she welcomed Aasta Hansteen as an exhibitor. The Cosmos occupied space in Haverly's Theatre Building and was officially opened on November 23–24, 1881. It boasted expensive furnishings and a Scandinavian Room, and individual paintings were displayed with great care. Aasta Hansteen attended the gallery opening and in December exhibited four paintings there. *The Chicago Tribune* referred to three of these — portraits of President Garfield and Bjørnstjerne Bjørnson and a "Norwegian Peasant Girl."[9] By January, 1882, The Cosmos was encumbered with heavy debts. A move and an attempt to sell $100 shares in the enterprise could not save the venture; by June it had folded and Marie Brown had left for Sweden. Among the Hansteen papers in the Norwegian National Archives is a small red notebook originally used to record the names and addresses of Cosmos subscribers.

As had been the case in Boston, Aasta Hansteen found herself despairing over the tiny trickle of income she received from her work. But Chicago offered her the advantage of a substantial support network. Her move to 242 North Clark Street on the near north side in late September, 1881, put her in close proximity to two other Scandinavian artists — William Torgerson, a Swede who specialized in marine paintings, and John Olson Hammerstad, a Norwegian landscape painter, both of whom were located at 3 North Clark Street. She may or may not have known Torgerson well; Hammerstad later proved to be an important inspiration. This was not a fashionable studio area — Torgerson was encouraged by *The Chicago Tribune*'s art critic to leave it: "he should come over and establish himself in the region of studios and take the place among artists which of right belongs to him" (December 11, 1881). But North Clark Street was an ethnic neighborhood where Aasta Hansteen felt comfortably at home and where she could afford to live. She began to take her dinners at a restaurant operated by Mrs. Thora Hansteen on Milwaukee Avenue, the thriving commercial center of the early Scandinavian community. Mrs. Hansteen was presumably Thora Lange Hansteen (1845–1930). What the family connection was, if any, is unknown.

One of Aasta Hansteen's most important contacts in Chicago proved to be Dr. Gerhard Christian Paoli (1815–1898). G. S. C. H. Paoli attained a high status within his profession, serving twice as president of the Chicago Medical Society. He also acquired a reputation as a champion of social and political reform. He took a strong interest in opening the medical field to women and taught for many years at Women's Medical College of Chicago. In local Scandinavian circles he was known in particular for his leadership, along with Marcus Thrane, of the Freethinkers' Society. Dr. Paoli introduced Aasta Hansteen when she delivered her speech at Aurora Turner Hall and later invited her to parties and meetings in his home on Webster Avenue. On November 4, 1881, Paoli married Sarah Corning Magnusson; it was the second marriage for both. Among their friends the Paolis counted Ole Bull and Jenny Lind, figures whom Aasta Hansteen greatly admired. Their political and philosophical stance coincided with hers and they enjoyed the same generational outlook. Aasta Hansteen not only found considerable comfort in their acquaintance but enjoyed their practical assistance as well.

During the summer of 1882, after a slow period when she turned to the retouching of photographs for extra income, Aasta Hansteen demonstrated a burst of artistic energy. In rapid order she produced four thematic paintings, sharing the conception and development of each with her Norwegian colleague J. O. Hammerstad. This "Kunstneralliance" (artistic alliance), as she called it, obviously provided important inspiration and encouragement. The paintings bear intriguing titles, in particular the composition called first "Noble Deeds of American Women" and later "Europe Pays Homage to American Women." These paintings all sold within a few months, thanks to the good offices of Dr. Paoli, but the professional relationship with Hammerstad was short-lived. On August 28 Aasta Hansteen recorded his comment to her: "He felt that I was a better writer than painter." The diary makes no further mention of him. Taking into account the various portraits and crayon drawings which she completed, the four thematic paintings, and the other professional activities noted in late 1881 and during 1882, this must be regarded as Aasta Hansteen's most productive artistic period while in America. Unfortunately the paintings themselves have not yet been located.

Little is known about Aasta Hansteen's activities in Chicago during 1883, but it seems that while in the Midwest her attention rested primarily on supplementing her annual income by selling paintings or exchanging them for room, board, and other services. She wrote one article which appeared in *Den nye Tid*, sent two letters to *The Woman's Journal*, and was the subject of an article by Jakob Bonggren in *Svenska Amerikanaren*. Her social contacts were based squarely in progressive Scandinavian circles as represented by the Scandinavian Freethinkers' Society and members of the radical press. She oriented herself in the larger progressive movement to a certain extent, though one looks in vain for references to suffrage meetings. The unpublished poem "Til-bageblik" (Retrospective View) which she composed on July 30, 1883, on the steps of the Methodist Episcopal Church, La Salle Street, illustrates the sincere optimism that she maintained in Chicago despite difficult financial straits. One stanza reads, freely translated:

> "The Atlantic's strong breeze, the prairie's
> sharp storms lie between us and narrow-mindedness.
> Our courage stirs in spite of all that
> we have suffered, in spite of want and the
> daily, frightening struggle for
> bread. For here life's seeds and opportunities
> swirl about us, in
> the refreshing wind."[10]

Aasta Hansteen's diary breaks off in October, 1882; thus the last year of her stay in Chicago remains very thinly documented. In November, 1883, she returned to Boston. *The Woman's Journal* noted this fact with a brief statement in its "Concerning Women" column on December 1.

While living in Chicago she briefly revived the plan for a lecture tour to other Midwestern cities. *Budstikken* passed along word on March 14, 1882, that Aasta Hansteen could soon be expected in Minneapolis and other nearby communities. Two weeks later the same newspaper announced that the Minneapolis appearance had been set for Sunday, April 2, in Nordens Hall: "She will treat the woman question as it has developed among us Norwegians. Since Miss Hansteen is one of the women who first functioned as a spokesman for this cause in our homeland, we expect to receive from her a presentation that is as interesting as it is substantial."[11] She left Chicago on March 31, traveling on a free pass supplied by the emigration department of the railroad. Upon her arrival in Minneapolis on Saturday evening, April 1, she drove immediately to the residence of Mrs. Oline Muus, where she received a friendly welcome.[12] The following day she delivered a speech at Nordens Hall for an audience of some 100 persons. The subject was woman's social position and the lecture followed the main lines of the one given in Chicago the year before; however, certain unexplained practical difficulties appear to have marred this Minneapolis appearance. According to the diary, Aasta Hansteen delivered her speech without benefit of manuscript, silk dress, or admission tickets.

In order to boost the income from the trip, Mrs. Muus helped arrange a benefit concert for the following Monday, April 10, in Harrison Hall. The program consisted of six musical numbers which framed a speech by Aasta Hansteen entitled "Tidsbetragtninger og Strøtanker" (Contemporary Meditations and Aphorisms). The musical numbers were performed by local talent—"kvartetten 'Freja,' frøken Wetterhal, herr Selmer Johnson, frøknerne Kjelstrup"—and tickets cost 25 cents. Since Aasta Hansteen listed ticket sale income at $45, paid attendance at this evening of entertainment was presumably 180. Her financial situation was so difficult that she apparently abandoned all plans to travel to other cities and instead returned directly to Chicago on Wednesday, April 12. The Minneapolis trip was no triumph. *Budstikken*'s report on her first speech expressed disappointment at its "somewhat fragmented form" and the financial return was not what Aasta Hansteen had hoped.[13] But neither was the venture a disaster. It provided her an opportunity to meet Mrs. Muus, on whose behalf she had written strong appeals, and to see another segment of the Norwegian-American community.

After her return to Boston Aasta Hansteen shared lodgings with the Clarke family, an arrangement which lasted throughout her remaining five years in America. It has not been possible to trace this family through city directories or other sources; the name may have been spelled either Clark or Clarke. One is led to believe that they had no connection with Scandinavia; when disagreements erupted, Aasta Hansteen labeled them "uforskammet [insolent] Yankees." The first year their address was 11 Tremont Street, a residence she described as cold, leaky, and unhealthy.[14] Then in April, 1885, the Clarkes and she moved to the country. Here Aasta

Hansteen felt her optimism and strength return. She recalled this summer in Clarendon Hills in a letter to her American friend Mrs. Lyon Livingston Machynleth: "What lovely surroundings, beautiful landscape! Oh, to see the trees of peach, cherry, and apple in bloom, it is beneficial for the human soul!"[15] They spent four months in this pleasant rural area some seven miles from the city center. Aasta Hansteen interpreted this summer as a turning point. In early 1885 she had been on the verge of returning to Norway. She had informed her family to expect her and had even bought a steamship ticket. To sister Nanna she wrote that joy at having escaped Norway sustained her during the first years in America, but as time went by circumstances grew more and more confining. Now, however, her financial situation improved and she settled into a new way of life in America.

Because she was no longer responsible for Theodora's support, Hansteen could now adapt her expenditures to fit within the limits of her $200 annual income. This meant a number of restrictions upon household services, but at the same time it brought a new measure of freedom—there was no longer pressure to generate extra income through the sale of paintings. Instead she adopted a frugal and largely self-sufficient life-style. She learned to cook, wash clothes, and make her own dresses. These practical skills were not easy to acquire at the age of sixty, but she wrote proudly of her accomplishments to her sister Nanna. One letter offered an extensive list of the various dishes which she had learned to prepare, including fish soup, oyster stew, roast beef, and oatmeal porridge. The notation of "pengeknibe" (short of funds), frequent in the early years in America, virtually disappears from the later diaries.

There was a dramatic shift in her creative pursuits at this same time. She let the paintbrush and charcoal rest and turned with enthusiasm to research and writing projects. Her new financial independence was the key to this redirection of energies. As she wrote to her friend Agnes Mathilde Wergeland, "In this way I am independent and can manage my own time, can study the sciences, and write books."[16] In composing an essay entitled "Sejr" (Victory) on June 8, 1885, she pledged herself to the pen; as she wrote in her calendar two years later: "Anniversary 'Sejr!' Two years ago I took up my pen again, nevermore to let it rest." Through the summer and fall of 1885 she produced a series of Norwegian-language manuscripts which may be found among her papers at the National Archives in Oslo. The titles are revealing of her philosophical and political interests: "Evolutions-filosofi" (The Philosophy of Evolution), "Det franske Folk" (The French People), "Verdenshistoriske Vendepunkter" (Turning Points in World History), and "Dyreriget og Menneskeheden" (The Animal Realm and Humankind). She continued writing over the next four years, in part reworking some of the same materials. In addition, she focused on English translations of her own works and those of her literary hero, Henrik Wergeland.

With the exception of a few articles in specialized publications like *The Woman's Journal*, Aasta Hansteen's attempts to enter the American publishing scene did not succeed. Her limited command of the English language remained a major stumbling block. When she sent the text of *Church of Christ in the Nineteenth Century* to editor B. F. Underwood of *The Open Court*, he returned it stating that it was not in acceptable form. It might be published if "some practiced writer put it in good English, at the same time condensing it."[17] Such setbacks did not dampen her productivity. In the summer of 1887 she began submitting material to *Nylænde* (New Ground), in Christiania. In November she mailed the first of three articles to *Framåt* (Forward) in Gothenburg and the first of two articles to *Kvinden og Samfundet* (Woman and Society) in Copenhagen. These three journals were all geared to supporters of the women's movement.

Her dream of seeing a major article appear in English remained unfulfilled, however. Efforts in this direction had begun in the late 1870s when she commissioned a translation of her 1878 treatise *Kvinden skabt i Guds billede*. Repeated submissions of this manuscript also failed to net a positive result, but a breakthrough finally occurred in 1888. After Aasta

Hansteen revised and edited sections of the English text, three installments appeared as *Woman Created in the Image of God* in the spiritualist periodical *The World's Advance Thought* (Portland, Oregon) during 1888–1889. She was naturally delighted by this turn of events, as she was by the appearance in *The Woman's Journal* for April, 1888, of her descriptions of Norway's feminist pioneers. While her ambition to become an "American" writer was never realized, Aasta Hansteen did have the satisfaction of returning home to Norway with some American publications. She continued to seek visibility in America throughout the rest of her life. There were further successful submissions to *The World's Advance Thought* and further unsuccessful negotiations concerning the publication of *Woman Created in the Image of God* as a monograph.

By the summer of 1888 Aasta Hansteen could look back on three years of steady involvement with writing projects. She had seen articles published on both sides of the Atlantic and was following with intense interest the blossoming of the Scandinavian women's movement. Prompted in part by her Norwegian friends in Boston, she began to think seriously of returning home. A new wave of depression and loneliness had engulfed her and this time Norway seemed to present a positive alternative. In August, 1888, she was inspired with the idea of undertaking a lecture tour of the Scandinavian countries, and in late February, 1889, she sent a notice to *Dagbladet* and *Verdens Gang* in Christiania formally announcing her intention to return and deliver a series of speeches. In early May, 1889, exactly nine years after her arrival in Boston, she left the Clarke household to begin the trip back across the ocean. The leave-taking sparked a renewed feeling of emancipation and optimism. Aasta Hansteen had pictured her emigration as a matter of self-preservation. The return to Norway was a matter of following her heart.

Aasta Hansteen experienced two sides of "Norwegian America" during her nine-year stay in the New World. On the one hand, she ran up against the hierarchy and ideology of the Norwegian Lutheran Church as transplanted to America. On the other hand, she encountered the fellowship of the Scandinavian Freethinkers and the patriotism of liberal nationalists. Her personal orientation naturally led her to lash out at the first group and embrace the second.

Part of her journalistic mission while abroad was to describe the backward state of affairs among conservative Norwegian Americans. Her favorite example here was a case involving Pastor Bernt Julius Muus, whose wife Oline had challenged his authority to dispose of her inheritance. For this display of insubordination, she had been publicly censured by her husband and the Norwegian Synod. Aasta Hansteen was outraged by this action and described for *The Woman's Journal* the situation among "these antiquated people, who, like a phenomenon from the dark middle ages, are living in the last decades of the nineteenth century in the prosperous and thriving states of Wisconsin and Minnesota, in the middle of America."[18] She concluded a second article by quoting an unnamed acquaintance, "If these are Christians I will try the heathen for a while."[19]

It pained Aasta Hansteen to present her countrymen in this unflattering light: "I do not feel proud, in telling you about this Norwegian church party, and I wish you not to think all the Norwegians are in that way — without brains and without hearts."[20] Fortunately, Aasta Hansteen had ample opportunity to associate with Norwegian Americans who shared her reformist views. In Chicago she was a participant in the activities of the Scandinavian Freethinkers' Society. The Society met twice monthly. According to the 1882 city directory its president was Marcus Thrane and its vice-president Dr. Gerhard Paoli, both of whom Aasta Hansteen counted as personal acquaintances. At one of the society's meetings Dr. Paoli spoke about the Italian patriot Giuseppe Garibaldi. The group was also known to celebrate the birthday of the radical political theorist Thomas Paine. The newspaper *Den nye Tid* (The New Era) held an autumn fair which Aasta Hansteen attended in both 1881 and 1882. She described one feature of the fair as "three blood-red Socialist banners above the door."

In Boston Aasta Hansteen was drawn into the social activities of the Norwegian Society of Boston. This group had originally been formed in 1853 but had languished for some years before it was revitalized in 1872. During the 1880s the organization was quite active; major efforts were directed to the visit of Bjørnstjerne Bjørnson and to the completion and dedication of the Leif Ericson statue. The meeting place of the society was the Boston Turnverein Clubhouse, or Turner Hall, located at 29 Middlesex Street. Aasta Hansteen participated in several of the society's programs. She spoke at "Promulgationsfesten" on June 9, 1884, at the "sexa" following the unveiling of the Leif Ericson statue on October 29, 1887, and at the thirty-fifth anniversary celebration on September 19, 1888.[21] On this last occasion she presented a portrait of Bjørnson to the society. In her presentation speech she expressed certainty that the portrait would inspire the Norwegian Society to endorse full national independence for Norway. Her comments emphasized further the liberal, patriotic character of the organization: "The Society has become a place for the liberal Norwegians in Boston to gather. We hope that it increasingly will serve as the headquarters for those who believe in progress and patriotism."[22]

The high point of national sentiment which Aasta Hansteen experienced abroad may well have been the festivities surrounding the long-awaited dedication in 1887 of the Leif Ericson statue. The Boston newspapers described a day full of impressive activity, involving prominent figures from civic and political life.[23] In the evening two sexas were held at which leaders of the Scandinavian community spoke. The Norwegians gathered at Turner Hall. Aasta Hansteen later used an amended version of the speech she gave there as the introduction to *Kvinden i det nye Norge* (Woman in the New Norway, 1893). In her address she talked of a "new Norway" which promised to rival Norway's golden age, if only it would grant appropriate social recognition to women. Aasta Hansteen's intense patriotism found an outlet in these organized celebrations; but as the years in America passed, such socializing also awakened a feeling of homesickness. In October, 1888, she spent an evening at a social in the Norwegian Lutheran Church in Boston. The rather lengthy summary of the evening in her pocket diary noted the familiar songs and typical games in which she had joined. The very authenticity of this Norwegian gathering underlined her sense of alienation from American society and triggered her longing to return to the country and the people that she loved.

When Aasta Hansteen left Christiania in the spring of 1880, the shock waves from Ibsen's *A Doll's House* were still being felt. Norway boasted no feminist organization and no feminist journal. Role models and moral support had to be sought abroad. Because of this, the American women's movement exerted a powerful influence upon Aasta Hansteen and her generation. For these Norwegian activists the American movement served two related functions. First, it represented a source of inspiration and energy; and second, it offered a revealing contrast to Norwegian conditions. Aasta Hansteen's writings from, and about, America point up the symbolic importance of American feminism. This is true in particular because Hansteen indulged a tendency to idolize American leaders and to prophesy the dawning of a new age whose sun was rising "in the West." Woven into this general rhetoric are specific concerns that spring from the American context but that reflect the author's own ideological bias. Aasta Hansteen believed strongly in the spiritual power of women, in the appropriateness of public female leadership, and in the need to cement the bonds of sisterhood.

By 1871 Aasta Hansteen was acquainted, at least superficially, with American women's struggle for independence. In a newspaper article she pointed to America as the home of women's liberation but noted that only vague and incomplete reports had thus far reached Norway.[24] Soon afterward she learned about Elizabeth Cady Stanton and Susan B. Anthony, two of America's leading feminists. Her introduction to these women came through the Swedish *Tidskrift för Hemmet* (Home Journal) and its editor, Sophie Leijonhufvud, as well as through *L'Espérance*, a journal published in Geneva by

L'Association Universelle des Femmes. Elizabeth Cady Stanton and Susan B. Anthony symbolized for Aasta Hansteen the best of the new movement; by 1873, when hard at work on *Kvinden skabt i Guds billede*, she wrote to the two suffrage leaders seeking advice about publication possibilities in the United States. Her inquiries, written in French, went unanswered, and so it was not until May of 1881 that Aasta Hansteen came into contact with her admired models. The occasion was a New England suffrage meeting held in Boston and Hansteen was apparently not disappointed. In her diary she wrote, "Now I have seen them!"

An intriguing diary entry from October 2, 1879, suggests that the actual decision to emigrate was connected with another well-known American woman. "Victoria C. Woodhull. Resolved to emigrate to America" the entry reads. Victoria Woodhull's fame rested both on her involvement with spiritualism and on her candidacy for the presidency of the United States, the first woman to run for the office. It is unclear how Aasta Hansteen came to know of her endeavors, but the impression she made must have been considerable. On November 15, 1879, Hansteen sent a dispatch to Woodhull and in preparation for emigration she included Woodhull's name in a list of New York addresses.[25]

Once settled in Boston Aasta Hansteen met women like Julia Ward Howe, Lucy Stone, and Mary Livermore and was introduced to the organized life of the women's movement. To judge from her diaries, Aasta Hansteen found women's congresses and suffrage meetings to be wonderfully inspiring occasions. A favorite response was "herligt" (glorious). In fact the second newspaper report she sent back to Norway consisted of a detailed description of the New England Woman's Club. What impressed her in particular was the manner in which American women presented themselves from the podium. She was struck by their eloquence, bearing, and intelligence. In a speech given to the Norwegian Suffrage Club in 1898, Aasta Hansteen expressed her admiration in this way: "The greatest result of the women's movement, the effect which also is felt in Europe, concerns this flock of impressive

pioneers who have shown the world true womanhood, genuine femininity — so different from the pitiful model which
for such a long time was forced upon us as the correct female
posture." Earlier in the speech she singled out American
women as "the most advanced and the most superior in ability and character of any women in this century."[26]

Since Aasta Hansteen had been ridiculed for holding
public lectures in Norway, it proved exhilarating for her to
encounter accomplished female orators and moderators. In an
unpublished manuscript she remarked: "I sought out a great
country, better suited for a woman who wished to engage in
thought and to speak those thoughts." Hansteen herself
found few opportunities in the United States to do public
speaking, however. Her limited knowledge of English handicapped her, especially in the beginning. She delivered her
welcoming remarks to the New England Woman's Club in
French and her few formal lectures were directed specifically
to Scandinavian-American audiences. Yet, as her written descriptions show, she was an appreciative and sensitive observer of public discourse. She was attracted in particular to
the strong personalities who led the women's movement and
her perception of American feminism was based in large measure upon them.

Another significant discovery for Aasta Hansteen was
the fellowship she encountered in America. One of the first
feminists she met received her with the gracious words: "We
belong to a sisterhood." The fact that she no longer felt alone
is articulated in the verse composed during this period. There
is among her private papers a small, unpublished collection of
America poems. The poems are sentimental and rather sim-
plistic, but they provide a useful index to her moods. In
"Arbeidsglæde" (Joy of Work, 1886) she celebrates her movement from isolated individual to member of a community.
The text, freely translated, runs in part:

"In Norway I was deserted,
shrouded in loneliness,
all the others were 'we'
but not me.

Here in freedom's land,
here I am blessed,
here I too am 'we.' "

Hansteen also commented on what she perceived as an absence of ridicule and malice among American women.

Certain key images recur in the prose and poetry. These
focus on sun, light, and warmth. In America Aasta Hansteen
encountered the sunflower in use as a feminist symbol. The
plant was interpreted as a visual sign of woman's claim to
light and air and Hansteen took upon herself the task of introducing this symbol into Scandinavia. Her first article on
the subject appeared in the Swedish journal *Framåt* in 1888;
an expanded version was printed in Norway in 1894.[27] The
campaign achieved definite success in Norway, where the
sunflower was adopted as the official symbol of the Norwegian Feminist Society and its journal. Aasta Hansteen's
seventieth birthday was celebrated by her friends as a special
sunflower festival. The sunflower image points up the optimistic spirit which Aasta Hansteen brought back from
America. A short poem composed in 1867 during a time of
great personal anguish described a feeling of being engulfed
by flames. In 1896 Aasta Hansteen added this short verse:

"But now the flames have turned to
sunbeams
and sunflowers."[28]

Traces of Aasta Hansteen's contact with American feminism are scattered throughout her writings. They reveal that
she especially valued the religious strain which often infused
the American movement. She took particular note of *The
Woman's Bible*, a project begun by Elizabeth Cady Stanton,
and the prominence of women preachers in the New World.
Her avid interest in spiritualism was no doubt piqued by the
extent to which women were given leading roles in spiritualist congregations. She understood as well that the American
legal and social structure provided women with enviable
protection and opportunities. In 1875 she had compared
Norway's marriage laws with the American and concluded

that the latter provided women with "the greatest justice as well as protection."[29] During her stay in America she felt compelled to remark on the social conventions which permitted women to voice their opinions, earn their own keep, and walk the streets without harassment.

Norway had been comparatively slow to provide publication outlets for women. Hansteen understood the necessity for periodicals dealing with women's issues and her American stay offered the opportunity to study a leading publication at close hand. During the summer of 1880 she paid her first visits to the Boston office of *The Woman's Journal*. Through that office she also received from time to time copies of Scandinavian publications such as the Danish *Kvinden og Samfundet* (Woman and Society). Of major importance to Aasta Hansteen's perception of the changing political climate in her homeland was the appearance in 1887 of a Norwegian periodical for women. *Nylænde* (New Ground), edited by Gina Krog, reached Aasta Hansteen in Boston on Midsummer Day, 1887. She welcomed this channel of communication and immediately began to make use of it. Gina Krog later indicated that it was *Nylænde* that had called Aasta Hansteen home from her exile abroad—"and she came home to us and grew near and dear to us."[30]

The warm and genuine enthusiasm which Aasta Hansteen displayed for the American women's movement and her clear endorsement of its models were integral elements of her American experience and a necessary prerequisite for her characterization of America as "det første sted paa jorden for kvinder" (the best place on earth for women).[31] But it should be stressed that she remained on the periphery of the organizations themselves. Shortly after her arrival in Boston, she reported that she had become a member of the New England Woman's Club; however, the club membership records do not include her name and her pocket calendars suggest no involvement with their activities in subsequent years. It was typical of Aasta Hansteen that she took no role in the day-to-day work of such organizations. Her basic stance was rather that of observer and commentator.

The American influences which left a deep mark on Aasta Hansteen overlapped and to a certain extent blended together. Feminism, spiritualism, and free religion were movements that shared advocates and rhetoric, and Aasta Hansteen drew freely from all of them. The radical circles made no distinction between reform in the spiritual and social spheres; they represented a confluence of efforts to define and implement a new moral order. Hansteen's overriding concerns were undoubtedly female autonomy and female spirituality. Issues like *The Woman's Bible* and the sunflower badge were therefore natural ones for her to promote. But one might argue that it was precisely the multi-faceted milieu of American progressive thought that in particular appealed to this visionary and wide-ranging reformer.

Her decision to return to Norway was influenced by the desire to function in a more visible, public capacity, unhampered by the language barrier. Aasta Hansteen was clearly encouraged by changes on the Norwegian scene which made such action possible. The intervening nine years had brought increased tolerance for Norwegian women who appeared and wrote publicly. In a letter written from Boston on December 26, 1887, to her sister Nanna, Aasta Hansteen expressed happy astonishment that such was the case: "It is wonderful that women now can use their talents and energies." By 1889 the Norwegian feminist movement had taken firm root, and Aasta Hansteen could be welcomed home as one of its pioneers.

## Notes

[1]For a comprehensive look at Aasta Hansteen's career and a detailed review of her years in America, the reader is referred to *Furier er også Kvinner, Aasta Hansteen 1824–1908* by Bente Nilsen Lein, Nina Karin Monsen, Janet E. Rasmussen, Anne Wichstrøm, and Elisabeth Aasen (Oslo, 1984). The author gratefully acknowledges the courtesy and generosity of the Hansteen family in making available much pertinent material, including Aasta Hansteen's notebooks and calendars from the period. Sincere appreciation is also extended to the Norwegian Foreign Ministry and to the Norwegian Research Council for their support of this project. Eva Lund

Haugen provided key assistance with local source materials in the Boston area and Rolf Erickson with Chicago sources. All translations from the Norwegian are the author's.

[2]Not much is known about Theodora Mathilde Nielsen. To judge from a photograph taken in 1880, she was then perhaps eighteen years old. Theodora took voice lessons in Chicago and received further training at a conservatory in Boston. She lived with Aasta until 1884, and later resided with various families. By 1907, she apparently was living in Colorado with Aasta's friend Mrs. L. L. Machynleth. The relationship between Aasta and Theodora was sometimes stormy; Aasta apparently wanted more undivided attention than Theodora was prepared to give her.

[3]Aasta Hansteen, "Över Atlanterhavet," in *Verdens Gang*, June 15, 1880.

[4]Eva Lund Haugen and Einar Haugen, eds. and trans., *Land of the Free: Bjørnstjerne Bjørnson's America Letters, 1880–1881* (Northfield, Minnesota, 1978), 83.

[5]*The Boston Evening Transcript*, April 17, 1907.

[6]"A Norwegian Artist," in *The Woman's Journal*, May 7, 1881, 149; the painting singled out for mention by Mrs. Noa was completed in Paris in the mid-1850s and bore the title "Moses, som beder om sejren, understøttet af Aron og Hur." It is now part of the collection at the Norwegian-American Museum in Decorah, Iowa.

[7]Haugen and Haugen, *Land of the Free*, 170.

[8]See *The Woman's Journal*, July 30, 1881.

[9]The "Art in Chicago" Sunday column of *The Chicago Tribune* carried information about The Cosmos and Marie Brown on October 23, October 30, November 27, December 11, and December 18, 1881, and January 1 and June 18, 1882. According to Aasta Hansteen's diary, the fourth painting exhibited at The Cosmos was a portrait of her father. Marie Brown's later writings included "The Norse Discovery," in *The Index*, August 5, 1886, and *The Icelandic Discoverers of America* (London, 1887).

[10]The stanza in the original Norwegian reads as follows:

"Nu er
Atlanterhavets friske bris, —
præriens hvasse storme, mellem os
og sneverheden. Dette hæver modet,
trods alt hvad vi har lidt, trods nød
og daglig, ængstlig kamp for brødet.
Thi her jo livets frø og muligheder
rundt om os flyve, med den friske vind."

[11]*Budstikken*, March 28, 1882.

[12]As discussed below, Mrs. Muus was at this time the center of a substantial controversy in Norwegian-American circles. Aasta Hansteen had defended her in two articles in *Budstikken*, August 3 and October 6, 1880.

[13]*Budstikken*, April 11, 1882. Carl G. O. Hansen gives a brief descrip-

tion of Aasta Hansteen's appearance in Minneapolis in his book *My Minneapolis* (Minneapolis, 1956), 111–112.

[14]Letter to Nanna Hansteen, November 5, 1886, in possession of the Hansteen family. This address was probably in the area of the city known as Roxbury.

[15]Letter to Mrs. Machynleth, March 14, 1900, in manuscript collection, University Library, Oslo. Aasta referred to the summer residence as being in Clarendon Hills; the mailing address was Dale Street, Roslindale.

[16]Maren Michelet, *Glimt fra Agnes Mathilde Wergelands liv* (Minneapolis, 1916), 140.

[17]Letter from B. F. Underwood, dated May 30, 1887, in Hansteen papers, National Archives, Oslo. *The Open Court* began publication in Chicago in 1887 as a successor to *The Index*, a well-known weekly published in Boston by the Free Religious Association; Underwood had previously served on *The Index* editorial staff. Hansteen's monograph *Kristi kirke i det 19de aarhundrede* was published in Christiania in 1897.

[18]*The Woman's Journal*, July 30, 1881.

[19]*The Woman's Journal*, May 20, 1882.

[20]*The Woman's Journal*, July 30, 1881.

[21]"Sexa" was a colloquial term for a supper held about 6 p.m., usually as part of a festive occasion. "Promulgationsfesten" celebrated the vote of the Storting on June 9, 1880, which was understood to be a declaration ("promulgation") of the Storting's right to interpret the Norwegian constitution and to ignore a royal veto in constitutional matters.

[22]The manuscript of Aasta Hansteen's speech was made available by the Hansteen family; a draft is in the Hansteen papers.

[23]The plan to erect a statue of Leif Ericson originated with Ole Bull and was carried on after his death by Sara Thorp Bull and a number of Bull's admirers.

[24]*Dagbladet*, January 9, 1872.

[25]Victoria Woodhull also aroused the interest of Norwegian author Kristofer Janson (1841–1917). He discusses her in *Amerikanske forholde* (Copenhagen, 1881). By 1880 Woodhull was living in England, so there was in all likelihood no contact between her and Hansteen.

[26]Aasta Hansteen, "Tale ved festen i K.S.F.K. den 17de februar 1898," in *Nylænde*, April 1, 1898, 98–102.

[27]"Brev fra America: Solblomsten," in *Framåt*, February, 1888; and "Solblomsten," in *Nylænde*, January 1, 1894.

[28]Included in a letter to Randi Blehr, February 12, 1896; printed in "To dikt av Aasta Hansteen. Meddelt av lektor Sigurd Blehr," in *Norges Kvinder*, September 24, 1929.

[29]*Stud. med. Anton Gjerdings forhold til Baronesse Jaquette Liljenkrantz*, Part 4 (Copenhagen, 1876), 4.

[30]*Nylænde*, January 15, 1912.

[31]Letter to Agnes Mathilde Wergeland, dated Boston, New Year's Day, 1886. Printed in Michelet, *Glimt fra Agnes Mathilde Wergelands liv*.

# 11

## "Dear Sara Alelia": An Episode in Rølvaag's Life

*by Einar Haugen*

Ole Edvart Rølvaag, author and professor, is characterized in the "official" biography by his colleagues Theodore Jorgenson and Nora O. Solum as "an inveterate letter writer."[1] They quote extensively from his letters in an effort to give an intimate, personal picture of the man and his work, but the possibilities the letters provide are far from exhausted. While doing research on Rølvaag in the archives he founded at St. Olaf College, it became apparent that an edition of his letters is long overdue. Rølvaag's letters cast light not only on his own life and writings, but also on a large segment of the Norwegian America of his day. It is no coincidence that his first published novel, *Amerika-breve*, in 1912, was written in epistolary form.[2]

Among the letters in Rølvaag's hand collected in the archives there was one that especially called attention to itself by being marked "restricted." It was accompanied by a covering letter from Bishop Eivind Berggrav of Oslo to President Clemens Granskou of St. Olaf College. The "restricted" letter, written in 1927, was brought to this country in 1956. Berggrav asked that the letter be restricted for at least ten years, a period that is now long past.

The letter was mysterious in more than one way. Although unmistakably written in Rølvaag's flowing, hand-

269

some script, it was not signed "O. E. Rølvaag" or "Ole," as
were most of his letters. It was signed "Norenius" and addressed to a person whom he called "Sara Alelia," suggesting
a desire for anonymity. The bishop explained that the letter
was written to a close friend of his family. She was a woman
who in a moment of desperation had halfheartedly attempted
suicide by walking out on the thin ice of a nearby body of
water. He added that she was a "widow, highly gifted, but
also very self-centered and ambitious for recognition, frustrated."[3] But he did not reveal her name.

No one at the Norwegian-American Historical Association was aware of her real name or the reason for Rølvaag's
curious pseudonym; and they had no knowledge of other
such letters. The contents of the letter, to be examined later,
were deeply moving, expressing Rølvaag's concern about the
recipient's well-being. He urged upon her his philosophy of
active concern for one's fellow beings as the best guarantee
of happiness. Neither the letter nor the peculiar disguise is
mentioned in any biography or study of Rølvaag's life. Even
the members of his own family could not solve the riddle.

In preparation for a book on Rølvaag, I was able to pursue my researches in Norway.[4] Even the experience of a visit
to his birthplace on the island of Dønna in northern Norway
did not solve the riddle of Norenius. But the answer came
during study in the archives of the University of Oslo Library, which provided a truly serendipitous solution. Librarian Øivind Anker, among other things well known for his
work on Bjørnson, was able to inform me that in that very
year (1980) a collection of letters from Rølvaag had been
turned over to the library. Anker had personally received the
letters from the recipient's daughter, a well-known Norwegian art weaver, Else Halling. A number of these were addressed to "Sara Alelia" and signed "Norenius."

Anker was able to identify "Sara Alelia" as Marie Halling
Swensen (1877–1964), usually known as Mimmi Swensen.
She had been married to the Reverend Johannes Swensen
(1862–1920).[5] She came of a family distinguished for their
work in education and the church. Her father, Honoratus

Halling (1819–1886), was a minister, known for his efforts on behalf of the laboring classes and for his authorship of numerous works of a religious nature, including at least one novel. He was also the founder and first editor of a still existing religious journal, *For Fattig og Rig* (For Poor and Rich).[6] His son, Marie's brother Sigurd, was an educator who founded a private school in Oslo known as "Hallings skole," where even King Olav studied in his youth.

It is therefore not surprising that Mimmi Swensen had literary ambitions of her own. But these were hardly encouraged by the men around her. Her position as a pastor's wife in the small town of Holmestrand on the Oslo fjord south of the capital may also have been inhibiting. She appears to have published only one book, a collection of rather sentimental short stories for and about children, entitled *Bedstevenner* (Best Friends), in 1913. But she found opportunities for self-expression through her family friendship with Eivind Berggrav, who asked her to review books for his journal *For Kirke og Kultur* (For Church and Culture) while he was still the head of a school in Holmestrand. She also gave public readings of literary works and lectured on literary personalities. She had three children, two of whom grew to adulthood and are still, as far as I know, alive. One of them, Else, is the aforementioned weaver, now residing in Oslo.[7] It was therefore a simple matter to get in touch with her and learn more about her mother. Miss Halling not only granted permission to make use of the letters she had turned over to the University Library, but also provided additional information, including pictures and clippings of her mother's writings from various periodicals.

It appeared that at the time of her marriage in 1896 Mimmi was only nineteen, while her clergyman husband was thirty-six. Some hints in the correspondence suggest that this May-and-September marriage was not entirely harmonious. Since the daughter Else was unmarried, the responsibility of taking care of her mother in later years fell upon her. It seems that the mother was often unhappy and was not above taking

The Reverend Johannes Swensen, Marie (Mimmi) Halling Swensen, their daughter Else, born in 1899, and their son Erik, born in 1902.

*Courtesy of the University of Oslo Library*

it out on her daughter. It is clear from Mimmi Swensen's enthusiastic reception of Rølvaag's first novel published in Norway that she was deeply fascinated by his portrait of Beret, the heroine of *I de dage* — (1924) and *Riket grundlægges* (1925), which together became *Giants in the Earth* (1927). "In Beret's thoughts," she wrote, "lies the significance of all yearning for emigration, then and now."[8] In an interview on her eighty-fifth birthday she referred with animation to her earlier correspondence with Rølvaag.

Knowing her name made it possible to go back to the NAHA archives and locate some of her letters to Rølvaag. Only nine have been found, beginning with a card dated November 8, 1924, which accompanied her review of *I de dage* — . She wrote on the card that this "is among the most beautiful books ever written. . . . There are descriptions and lines so fine that reading them has been to me like a devotional meeting." And she adds, with a sigh, "I envy you."[9] Most of these letters are from 1926; the last is dated January 1, 1927. But it is clear from his replies that she had written many more, the last on July 9, 1931, to which he replied on August 9, 1931, just three months before his death on November 5. The Oslo collection contains thirty-six letters from Rølvaag and one fragment (to which may be added the Northfield letter) dated from June 18, 1926, to the one in August, 1931. Even this collection is not complete, as appears from the fact that she has numbered his earliest surviving letter "9" and the third one "18." From her letters one can see how she followed his literary output, writing reviews of *Peder Seier* in 1928 and of *Den signede dag* in 1931, and giving a public lecture on his life and work in 1926. According to accounts in local newspapers, the auditorium was packed and her lecture was received with "vigorous applause."[10]

But what about Sara Alelia? The solution appears in his letter of September 13, 1926. Up to that time their salutations have been fairly formal. But once Mimmi Swensen had made the contact in 1924, she not only wrote long letters, but also showered him with clippings, books, and even gifts. Appropriately enough, one of these was a letter opener, which he received together with a book entitled *Prestedatteren* (The Minister's Daughter), a Norwegian translation (1922) from the Swedish of Hildur Dixelius (1879–1969). The title of the original, published in Stockholm in 1920, was *Prästdotteren*; the story was continued in *Prästdotterens son* (1921) and *Sonsonen* (1922).[11] It was not surprising that Mimmi would be fascinated by the title and subject matter of this novel since she, like Dixelius, was a minister's daughter. The book had sufficient quality to win translation not only into Norwegian but also into English, in 1926, as *The Minister's Daughter*. It won the approval, interestingly enough, of two American woman novelists. Zona Gale called it a book "which no lover of the unique art of Sweden should miss," and Ruth Suckow characterized it as "an austerely imagined, finely proportioned book."[12] Rølvaag found it interesting, even though he held that "artistically there are many and considerable defects." Still he thought it "a great work of art . . . the book fascinates quite strangely from the first sentence. Only a great poet could write such a book."[13]

At all events, the names we have been seeking come from this novel. Sara Alelia is a young woman married to a pastor several years her senior. In her loneliness she lets herself be seduced by a passing Don Juan, who abandons her when she is about to bear his child. The first volume of the trilogy ends with her retirement to a remote farm in northern Sweden to bring up the child on her own. Mimmi's accompanying letter, which is not preserved, must have expressed her identification with the young woman, for Rølvaag replied: "Well, well, if you are Sara Alelia, then I am Norenius." This prominent character in the novel is neither her husband nor her seducer, but a gruff and eccentric local curate to whom Sara turns for comfort, alternately teasing him and treating him as a father figure. Rølvaag comments: "I have all of his defects and even a few more. But Sara is outstanding in her goodness, just like my friend in Hillestad [that is, Mimmi]." He addressed her as "Sara Alelia" for the first time in a letter of November 8, 1926, and began signing himself "Norenius" on December 18. In the novel Norenius is blunt and outspoken, and Rølvaag plays a similar role by scolding her for what he calls her "whimpering." He reminds her of her talents, her children, and her potentialities for benefiting humanity. He warns her that if she doesn't change her ways, he would be tempted to give her a good spanking. He even addresses her at times affectionately as "little Sara Alelia."

During the remaining years of his life she served as his contact with current literary trends in Norway, while he was concerned with filling her in on his earlier books, so far unknown outside Norwegian-American circles. He was happy to hear of her lecture about his work and wanted her to know as much as possible about it. In keeping her informed he often commented interestingly on his books. For example, he surprisingly wrote of his bitterly satirical *To tullinger* (1920, translated as *Pure Gold*, 1930) that "artistically it is my best work," although he fears that she will "throw up over it." "I regretted the praise it got," he continued, perhaps feeling it has been over-praised, and so "I sat down and wrote without a thought of such things as intrigue and structure — just wrote from a full heart, and that became *Længselens baat*" (1921, translated as *Boat of Longing*).

She was indeed pleased with *Boat of Longing*, particularly the lyricism of the Norwegian sections, the tale of Nils Vaag's youthful years in Nordland. But, in close agreement with most critics of the book, she was less enthusiastic about the two central sections, the story of his life in Minneapolis and in the North Woods. Rølvaag advised her to reread the section on the old woodsman (the "Stril") whom Nils met up north. "I maintain that this is one of the best things I have done; at least I am not aware that the homelessness and rootlessness of the emigrant has been more strongly asserted than in him; nor the joyless heart that often becomes the special feature of the emigrant."

Returning to his general philosophy of literary realism, he expressed his conviction that "the art of the future will aim at the character portrayal of people. It is easy to make plots, but extremely difficult to create human beings. And life is so delightfully interesting that there is not a single person who would not be suitable as the protagonist in the most exciting novel if only the artist with the glint of genius in his eye was there to catch him." He wrote that he had tried to do this, but without success, in his youthful book, *Paa glemte veie* (On Forgotten Paths), published in 1914. He did not share the extreme pietism of his heroine Mabel, "but the air was so stifling around me that I had to try to portray a human being who really attempted to walk the path of the cross."[14]

He was still hoping to get his first book, *Amerika-breve*, republished in Norway and even enlisted her in his campaign.[15] He had not yet found his translator, Lincoln Colcord, and he complained about the problems of getting his novel out in English: "It is not easy to make Per and even less Beret speak English naturally." To speak candidly, he wrote, "all translation is sinful—a sin against the characters, who are too tender and delicate to rise up and protest."[16]

He commented somewhat resignedly on his fellow author Waldemar Ager's novel *Gamlelandets sønner*, which he had persuaded his Norwegian publisher to print in 1926.[17] The Norwegian reviews were apparently not enthusiastic, and he confessed to his own disappointment that "I almost cried when I read the novel." "Brilliant as journalism, but there is nothing in it. He fails to catch hold; the material eludes his grasp, as do the characters. I put the book down and said, 'Now Ager won't get any farther—poor man.' " He granted Ager an alibi in his lack of time to work on the book and in his family situation. In the same letter he returned to *To tullinger* with its picture of miserliness: "The book was more of a sensation here than any other published among us Norwegians in America. People wrote about it and ministers preached about it from their pulpits. But it also won me many enemies: I was accused of slandering the Norwegian Americans. Ah, it was lively in those days."[18]

In the meantime his American translator, Lincoln Colcord, had entered his life, and Rølvaag made his first contact with the larger world of American publishing.[19] In May, 1927, he could send Mimmi an early copy of *Giants in the Earth*. Now he could predict: "It is possible that this book about Per Hansa and Beret will make my name known from one end of America to the other."[20]

In March, 1928, his new-won fame got him an invitation to attend the Ibsen centennial in Oslo, making it possible for him to meet Mrs. Swensen for the first and only time. They had been anticipating such a possibility for some two years. In 1926 he had written: "After the first feeling of strangeness is overcome, I think time will fly as we talk for hours about all possible topics—both permitted and forbidden. We would both be the richer for it!—But we must not dream of it. . . . Let us think of it as something beautiful that could happen to us."[21] Busy days at the centennial limited them to one meeting. Afterward he wrote: "Dear, dear Sara, don't be grieved that things are like this for me! It was by accepting all this hullabaloo that I could get to Norway and spend those hours with you: let us be grateful for that!"[22] From that time on, he addressed her with the informal pronoun "du" instead of the formal "De."

By August, 1928, he could report on the completion of *Peder Seier* (translated as *Peder Victorious*): "There are many mad whims in it, but I am myself well satisfied." He knew he had written the truth, "life as I think I have seen and experienced it."[23] But, like Ibsen, "I feel a strange emptiness in my body after saying goodbye to these dear folk. . . . We have shared good and bad together, have even—all of us— been to Hillestad and visited Mrs. Mimmi Swensen!. . . . I think this is the most original book I have written. . . . There may be more of myself in it than in any of my others—unless that might be *Længselens baat*." He wonders: "Will you find genuine, unfalsified people in it?" Her review was reassuring: "Rølvaag's book is realistic and alive." She admired his descriptive ability, his faith in life and in human goodness; she commended his "yearning for harmony . . . as the great goal among races and peoples."[24]

In March, 1931, he informed her that *Den signede dag* was completed: "It is a bit wordy; this was unavoidable in a portrayal of a society—not just the little Norwegian one, but the American as well, and here even the Irish! You can't conceive how much Irish and Catholic lore I've had to dig my way through before I could draw those figures!"[25] Once more she commended the realistic portrait of the fusion of peoples in the American Midwest. "With the poet's gift he has lent beauty to everyday life, from the time they pioneered down to Beret's deathbed—the most moving episode he has given us in this book. If the picture of a life is to be truthful, everything must be included, and Rølvaag does that, rendering the inner life and the yearning behind the struggles of the pioneers."[26]

If most reviewers saw a marked diminution of power in Rølvaag's last books, the account of his own failing health in these letters goes far to explain it. There may have been other reasons too, such as his deeper empathy with the first than the second immigrant generation. But the letters also reveal the problems of a bilingual author. He found it a burden to write first in Norwegian and then have to prepare an English version as well. It took as much time to rewrite *To tullinger* into *Pure Gold* as to write another book.[27]

His proposed solution, to Mimmi's dismay, was to begin writing in English. He actually did start an autobiography in English, which remained a fragment.[28] Already in 1929 he wrote: "This last year my ties with Norway have loosened. . . . One can't live abroad a whole lifetime without putting down roots."[29] In reply to her protests: "This does not mean that the window of memory grows dim; only that one finds less time to look through the pane. But nights are long and sleepless hours are many. . . . I feel the mighty magnetism of this great country."[30]

It was inevitable that to this daughter of the church he would entrust his thoughts on religion. He dismissed the value of prayer: "Neither physical nor spiritual laws can be temporarily suspended and then temporarily put back to work."[31] He was less interested in what people believed than in what they did: "The greatest thing in all religion is goodness. . . . not doing evil to men. . . . But people knew *that* long before Christianity was founded."[32]

"Sara Alelia" survived her "Norenius" by thirty-four

years, dying in 1965 at the age of eighty-eight. In an interview on her eighty-fifth birthday she dwelt on her correspondence with Rølvaag and their meeting.[33] The interviewer noted that she was remembered locally for her readings and lectures: "Lively, vital, and thoroughly familiar with her material, she stood on the rostrum, delighted to read and speak to a grateful audience." She was known for her radical views and the courage of her convictions. We do not have her last letter to Rølvaag (July 9, 1931), but his reply began, "Dear lonely soul," and went on to say that it was one of the most beautiful letters she had written to him.

But the most beautiful letter he wrote to her and one that must have meant a great deal to her was precisely the one that Bishop Berggrav sent back to Rølvaag's college. This specimen of Rølvaag's epistolary art concludes the account of their correspondence.[34]

"March 8, 1927

"Dear Sara Alelia!

"Uff, how sad your last letter was. Now I'm going to tell Sara Alelia a great secret, and this secret is the quintessence of all religion: We were not born into life in order to *get*, to demand. We were given life so that we might *give*. And then give a little *more*. And then again a little more. That is the purpose of it all. That is the answer to every riddle.

"Sara Alelia is unhappy because she is not getting what her heart yearns for. But Sara Alelia should not yearn to *get* things. If she only could—and she perfectly well can!—turn her yearning right around, then she would find satisfaction immediately and her sore heart would be brimming over with a marvelously rich joy. Sara Alelia is like the deer that runs to the water to drink. When he gets there, he lifts his head and drinks dry air; he fails to observe the water, and his thirst is unbearable. Sara Alelia is like a singer who has been granted the most melodious gift of song. Instead of going out among people and singing so they weep from joy, she goes into a narrow black stone chamber where she sits growling, and then she scolds the Lord for not caring about her.

"Sara Alelia is like the brook that got the idea that to reach the sea it had to run *uphill*. And so it really started to run backward. It ran and it ran, struggled and labored on its way to the sea until the cheerful melody of the brook fell silent, the brook stopped its course entirely, and its water — the clear, melodic water — turned slimy and ugly and unfit for people.

"Sara Alelia is like the rose that became aware of its own fragrance and conceived the idea: I must save this fragrance until I have a great deal of it — only then can I charm the children of men. And so the rose hid its fragrance and died of it. But lo — it did not know this itself. Sara Alelia is like the wave that wanted to hear its own song and so it stopped to listen. — After that it never ran again.

"And I could compare Sara Alelia with the star that put out its light to save it, or with the grain of wheat that wouldn't grow so it could save its strength, or with the heart that did not dare to let in the sunlight.

"But what is the use of such parables? None whatever. For Sara Alelia insists that to be happy she must *get*. She must get love and sympathy and happiness. How strange it is that Sara can't hear at all! For out of all that exists there rings the commandment of the Lord to her: You shall get, Sara! You shall get to *give*! Don't you hear at all? You shall get to give. And the Almighty himself has no greater gift to grant than the ability to give, that is God-given. But Sara will not use it except to a few whom she likes very well. 'But lo, if you are good to those who are good to you, what gain have you from that?' She knows this is true, and yet she won't believe it — that's how wicked the good-hearted Sara Alelia can be!

"Now Norenius has preached for Sara Alelia, and he hasn't the strength for any more. For Norenius is poorly and has no strength either for preaching or anything else. But he felt it was exceedingly *bad* of Sara to blame the Lord because the water was not deep enough where she walked through the ice. What if it had been deep enough, would little Sara

then have been any happier? Here, too, Sara's chief fault shows up: when she can't get, she wants to put an end to her getting!
A sermon by Norenius"

## Notes

[1]Theodore Jorgenson and Nora O. Solum, *Ole Edvart Rölvaag: A Biography* (New York, 1939), 221.

[2]O. E. Rølvaag, *Amerika-breve* (Minneapolis, 1912); trans. by Ella Valborg Tweet and Solveig Zempel as *The Third Life of Per Smevik* (Minneapolis, 1971).

[3]Eivind Berggrav to Clemens Granskou, February 20, 1956, in Norwegian-American Historical Association, Northfield, Minnesota.

[4]Einar Haugen, *Ole Edvart Rölvaag* (Boston, 1983).

[5]*Studenterne fra 1880* (Kristiania, 1905), 292–293.

[6]See J. B. Halvorsen, *Norsk Forfatterleksikon 1814–1880*, 2 (Kristiania, 1888), 481–483.

[7]On Miss Halling see Elle Melle, " 'Mosrosen' fra Skotselv som ble Norges store billed-veverske," in *Drammens Tidende*, February 17, 1976; also her own article, "Gamle tepper—ny inspirasjon," in Oslo Kunstindustri-museum *Årbok*, 1972–1975 (Oslo [1975]), 111–118; for her biography, see *Norsk Kunstnerlexikon* 2 (Oslo, 1983), 30–31. She adopted her mother's maiden name for professional reasons.

[8]Review of *I de dage*—, unidentified clipping from Oslo University Library, 1924.

[9]Marie Halling Swensen to O. E. Rølvaag, November 8, 1924, in Norwegian-American Historical Association.

[10]Review of *Peder Seier* in *Jarlsberg*, October 20, 1928; of *Den signede dag*, in same newspaper, undated (1931). For lecture, March 19, 1926, see *Jarlsberg* (*Holmestrandsposten*), April 2, 1926, also unidentified clipping of May 5: "Fru Swensens foredrag."

[11]Information from Örjan Lindberger, Swedish scholar.

[12]*Book Review Digest* (New York, 1927), 211.

[13]Rølvaag to Swensen, September 13, 1926, in Oslo University Library.

[14]Rølvaag to Swensen, September 13, 1926.

[15]Rølvaag to Swensen, October 26, 1926.

[16]Rølvaag to Swensen, November 8, 1926.

[17]Waldemar Ager, *Sons of the Old Country*, trans. by Trygve M. Ager, with an introduction by Odd S. Lovoll (Lincoln, Nebraska, 1984).

[18]Rølvaag to Swensen, December 18, 1926.

[19]Haugen, *Rölvaag*, 93–94; Jorgenson and Solum, *Ole Edvart Rölvaag*, 365–376.

[20]Rølvaag to Swensen, May 14, 1927.

[21]Rølvaag to Swensen, October 26, 1926.

[22]Rølvaag to Swensen, [March 13, 1928].

[23]Rølvaag to Swensen, August 2, 1928.

[24]Swensen, review of *Peder Seier*.

[25]Rølvaag to Swensen, March 13, 1931.

[26]Swensen, review of *Den signede dag*.

[27]Rølvaag to Swensen, August 19 [1929].

[28]"Romance of a Life," manuscript in Norwegian-American Historical Association [1931].

[29]Rølvaag to Swensen, August 19 [1929].

[30]Rølvaag to Swensen, October 20, 1929.

[31]Rølvaag to Swensen, May 25, 1929.

[32]Rølvaag to Swensen, April 25, 1930.

[33]Interview by O. O. B-n, "En midtsommeraften hos fru Mimmi Swensen," in *Holmestrands Blad*, July 3, 1962.

[34]Rølvaag to Swensen, March 8, 1927, in Norwegian-American Historical Association.

# 12

## Norwegian-American Artists' Exhibitions Described in Checklists and Catalogs

*by Rolf H. Erickson*

The catalogs and checklists of the exhibitions at which Norwegian-American artists showed their work are a valuable source of information about the artists, their work, and the times in which they exhibited. There are problems, however. The catalogs and checklists vary greatly in the information they provide. Evaluation of the artists' work is at best seldom more than implied. In addition, the collection of catalogs which has survived is probably incomplete. The catalogs were often discarded after the exhibitions closed; the artists themselves were casual about retaining copies with their own papers. Even so, the catalogs yield information about the artists, their work, and the periods during which they were active.

Artists have always been drawn to the cities. The art exhibition has generally been an urban phenomenon in American life. This is confirmed in the experience of the Norwegian-American artists. The first colony of artists in Norwegian America was formed at the turn of the century in Chicago, then the largest urban settlement of Norwegians in the United States.[1] Later, smaller colonies of artists formed in other urban settings, Minneapolis, Brooklyn, and Seattle. In

283

all I have identified 451 Norwegian artists in the United States.[2]

To date no one has attempted to explain why there were so many artists among urban Norwegian Americans. One explanation may be that they came from a society in Norway which respected the artist/craftsman. It may also be that the talented immigrant who found himself in an urban setting realized that the making of "art" was one of the few means available to him for expressing his creative impulses. A newcomer to the city would not have found an appreciative audience for hand-carved furniture or handmade textiles. Mass-produced goods were on hand and they were cheap. However, drawings, paintings, and sculpture were valued as symbols of sophistication and luxury by urban dwellers.

Art exhibitions can be grouped into a number of categories: juried and non-juried, judged and unjudged, and exhibitions where works are or are not for sale. Organizers of exhibitions have always put together shows using a variety of criteria. A show, for example, can be a juried, commercial show with no judging or awarding of prizes or a show can merely be a collection of works assembled to honor one or more artists without any value being placed on the works or any attempt to market them. Except for the retrospective shows, however, the purpose of most exhibitions was to sell the artists' work.

Exhibition catalogs featuring Norwegian-American artists arrange themselves into three groups: the catalogs of the Chicago colony, exhibitions held in New York City, and exhibitions held elsewhere in the country. The catalogs differ in quality from mimeographed checklists to finely printed pamphlets sporting artistically designed covers and full-color photographs. None, interestingly enough, were published in Norwegian, perhaps indicating a desire of the exhibitors to seek as wide an audience as possible.

The first known catalog was that published by Young's Galleries in Chicago, a commercial firm, for a one-man show of Lars Haukaness' work in 1913, and the first exhibition catalog presenting the work of several artists appeared in 1920 when the Chicago Norske Klub held its first show. The work of the many artists who were active earlier is not documented with any publications. The Lars Haukaness catalog was a handsome one containing, as it did, a thoughtful biography of the artist and ten illustrations. When the exhibition moved to Minneapolis the same catalog was used, and a simple checklist appeared in the local newspapers.[3]

The Chicago Norske Klub produced catalogs for all its exhibitions, 1920 through 1927, 1929, 1930, 1943, 1947, and 1963. The first ten exhibits were juried, commercial shows at which prizes were also awarded. The jurors were selected from outside the Norwegian-American Chicago colony — usually staff members from the Art Institute of Chicago. The jurors lent prestige and credibility to the events. These jurors were charged not only with ruling on what works would be exhibited but also with awarding the prizes, except for the Popularity Prize given on the basis of ballots cast by those attending the exhibition. As these annual exhibitions grew more successful, the artists faced stiffer competition to enter, and the jurors, not surprisingly, faced criticism about their decisions.[4]

It is worth noting that the 1920 catalog contains a list of Chicago Norske Klub members. The 1921 catalog contains biographies of artists Olaf H. Aalbu, Dorothy Visju Anderson, Alexander Baker, Emilie P. Beutlich, Emil Biørn, Olaf Brauner, Oscar B. Erickson, Herbjørn Gausta, Olav Iversen, Sigurd Knudson, Oscar Lumby, Magnus Norstad, Carl Olderen, Leonard A. Simonsen, Sigurd Skou,[5] Elling Tronnes, Enoch Vognhild, Arild Webord, and John S. Wittrup.[6] Lists of prize winners can be found in the catalogs of 1924 through 1927 but those from 1929 and 1930 list the prize winners of only the previous three years. The catalog of 1924 is the first to carry the message that "Under the rules of these exhibitions a prize cannot be given to the same artist two years in succession. This rule, however, does not apply to the prize awarded by popular vote."

First Annual

Norwegian - American

Art Exhibit

by

Chicago Norwegian Club

2346-2350 North Kedzie Boulevard

from

Saturday, December Eleventh

to

Sunday, December Nineteenth

Nineteen Hundred Twenty

The design of this cover resembles the work of Einar Magnus Kling, who served on the exhibition's committee on arrangements. Kling was born in Bergen in 1868, came to New York in 1888, and moved to Chicago in 1892. In Chicago he and his brother Daniel operated an interior decorating business at 1018 North Kedzie Avenue. All photographs are by Howard M. Leeple.

That the exhibitions grew in popularity may be deduced from the statement in the 1923 catalog, which is the first to contain a program assigning organizations specific viewing times; by 1925 the program was quite elaborate:

# PROGRAM

### Friday Evening, 8 P.M.

November Fourteenth

>Official Reception. For Club members and invited guests only.
>Address. Musical program. Refreshments.

### Saturday Afternoon, 5 P.M.

November Fifteenth

>Art Exhibit opens to the Public.

### Tuesday Evening, 9 P.M.

November Eighteenth

>Awarding of Prizes by Jury.

### Thursday Afternoon, 2 P.M.

November Twentieth

>Illinois Seventh Congressional Districts Federation of Women's Clubs.

### Sunday Evening, 9 P.M.

>Awarding of Popularity Prize.
>11 p.m. Closing of the Exhibit.

### Exhibition is Open Daily

>From seven to eleven p.m.; Saturdays from five to twelve p.m. and Sundays from one to twelve p.m.

The exhibitors of 1929 were given a second opportunity to exhibit their work with an invitation to take part in "An Exhibition of Works by Scandinavian-American Artists Given Under the Auspices of the American-Scandinavian Foundation at the Illinois Women's Athletic Club," December 1–10. This was also a juried show and prizes were awarded.

When local Norwegian-American artists learned that the Chicago Norske Klub would not stage the usual annual exhibition in the fall of 1931, several local artists came together to form the Norse Art League.[7] Their goal was to stage two juried exhibitions a year. The first was held March 1–15 and the second December 5–20. Juries from outside the Norwegian colony judged the pieces before the openings so that the catalogs could contain the names of the winners. Members of the Norse Art League were naturally disappointed when sales were poor. The Great Depression was in full force and few of the exhibitions' viewers had the means to purchase art. The Norse Art League simply ceased to exist. Its members scattered; some, such as Lars Fletre and Magnus Gjertsen, returned to Norway. A few, such as Bernhard Berntsen and Michael Hoiland, sought employment in New York. Elmar Berge went to Minneapolis, while August Werner settled in Seattle.[8] It may well have been the arrival of artists from Chicago in New York which gave the Society of Scandinavian American Artists new energy. In January, 1939, the Norwegians in New York formed their own organization, the Norwegian Art and Craft Club.

In 1942 the Norwegian Women's Club of Chicago presented the work of two of its members, Margit Osri and Emilie Beutlich, March 8–18, at the Norwegian Federation Club House, 2512 North Kimball Avenue. A simple checklist was printed. The following year the Chicago colony was saddened by the death of Karl Ouren, long regarded as Chicago's best Norwegian artist. The Chicago Norske Klub held a memorial art exhibit November 25–28 in the club rooms. The checklist contains a photograph of the artist's "Self Portrait" and a biography. Works were for sale. The

AT

## Chicago Norske Klub

2350 North Kedzie Boulevard

FRIDAY, NOVEMBER 14th TO
SUNDAY, NOVEMBER 23rd, 1930

The cover design has been attributed to Emil Biørn, who was born
in Oslo in 1864 and died in Chicago in 1934.

idea of an annual juried show, with prizes awarded, was revived by the Chicago Norske Klub on November 20–23, 1947. Obviously the show was not very successful, since there was not another exhibition until 1963. The 1963 exhibition proved to be the Chicago artists' last hurrah. It was an open, non-juried show containing pieces for sale and not for sale. There was no judging. The Norwegian-American exhibitors were outnumbered by other artists three to one. Prices of the pieces are listed in the catalog for the first time.

One last accomplishment of the Chicago Norske Klub proved to be the building of a club art collection with purchases from the exhibitions. A description of that collection, *The Chicago Norske Klub Collection*, contains a brief history of the Chicago art colony and biographies of Sigvald Asbjørnsen, Christian Ucherman Bagge, Emil Biørn, Ben Blessum, Olaf Brauner, Thoralf Gjesdal, Lars Haukaness, Jonas Lie, Marie Løkke, Karl Ouren, Bernt Rinnan, Halvard Storm, Sigurd Skou, and Even Ulving.[9]

Brooklyn's Norwegian artists first came together as members of the Society of Scandinavian American Artists. The first exhibition of the Society was held at the Brooklyn Museum, January 30 through March 1, 1926, with seventy artists participating. The majority appear to be Swedes (no ethnic origin is noted) but exhibitors Olaf Brauner, Mons Breidvik, Olav Iversen, August Klagstad, Christian Midjø, Sigvard Mohn, Magnus Norstad, Brynjulf Strandenaes, John S. Wittrup, and Trygve Hammer are known to be Norwegian Americans. Two years later, in 1929, the same organization again had the cooperation of the Brooklyn Museum. Sixty-five artists participated, but Olaf Brauner, Mons Breidvik, Trygve Hammer, and Paul Lauritz were the only Norwegian exhibitors. Another exhibition was held by the Society of Scandinavian American Artists at the Brooklyn Museum, April 11–May 15, 1932. Among the eighty-six exhibitors at this exhibition were Norwegians Thorbjorn Bassoe, Bernhard Berntsen, Mons Breidvik, Johan Bull, Gunvor Bull-Teilman, Olga Carstensen, Einar Hansen, Sigvart M.

The Chicago Norske Klub's exhibition in 1929. The white sculpture at the far right—a young woman with a baby at her breast—may be Genevieve Alexandersen's "Motherhood," while the bust in the corner is likely Oskar J. W. Hansen's "Bust of Elijah P. Lovejoy (From the Editorial Hall of Fame)." The three small figures on the left side of the table resemble the work of Lars Fletre and could be "A Vagabond" (the man with a pack on his back), "Male Figure: Study," and "Norwegian Peasant Woman." The large figure to the right of the table is most likely Hansen's "Bronze Figure." The large painting hanging near the ceiling is Lars Haukaness' "From Granvin, Hardanger, Norway." It is still at Norway Center. The large painting on the back wall is Karl Ouren's "Fishers Coming in to Svolvær Harbor." The painting on the far right is Emil Biørn's "The Wake," also part of the Norway Center collection.

Mohn, Karl Ouren, L. Haug Wiig, Maia Wiig-Hansen, Paul Fjelde, Lars Fletre, Trygve Hammer, and Oskar J. W. Hansen. The Society's last exhibition was held at the Squibb Building on Manhattan's Fifth Avenue, September 21–October 11, 1939, with fifty artists participating.

As mentioned earlier, interest in the Society of Scandinavian American Artists appears to have waned; artists in

Brooklyn's Norwegian settlement came together in 1939 to organize themselves as the Norwegian Art and Craft Club. Non-Norwegian members were accepted from the start, however. The club offered classes, arranged meetings at which models were present, and staged exhibitions of members' work. Social activities, dinners, dances, and parties, were a large part of the club's program. Although the Norwegian Art and Craft Club was very active, catalogs were not published for all of the club's exhibitions. Few of the exhibitions were juried shows, and seldom were prizes awarded. The earliest catalog is for an exhibition which opened May 2, 1942, at the Staten Island Museum of Arts and Sciences, followed by an undated catalog for an exhibition which may have been held in 1945, since the catalog refers to "when the club started about six years ago"; it was held at the Norwegian Seamen's Home, 62 Hanson Place, Brooklyn.

There were three exhibitions in 1946, a "Spring Exhibition" held at the Norwegian Seamen's Home, the "8th Annual Fall Exhibition" held November 17–December 1 at the Norwegian Seamen's Home, and the third held December 2–15 at the Brooklyn Public Library. In 1947 two exhibitions were held: March 7–31 at the Brooklyn Public Library and September 14–28 at the Riverside Museum. The latter show was juried. Prices of the works shown are listed. Later that year the Brooklyn Public Library at Grand Army Plaza published a checklist for an exhibition of the work of Norwegian Art and Craft Club member William Torjesen titled *Torjesen Paintings/Brooklyn Scenes/Exhibition/October 27 thru November 17/1947*. A biographical sketch of the artist, who was born in Kristiansand in 1895,[10] and an illustration of one of his paintings are included. In 1949 the club produced a catalog for a "Second New York Exhibition/ April 12th–24th, 1948/ and Memorial Exhibition of Sculpture by Trygve Hammer" held at the Argent Galleries, 42 West 57th Street, New York. It contains a biography of Hammer (1878–1947), who attended school in Oslo and came to the United States in 1903. Prices of Hammer's sculptures available for sale are listed.

This unique and splendidly romantic vision of a Viking appears to be signed "K.O.," which could perhaps be Karl Ouren.

Another Norwegian Art and Craft Club member, Thorn Norheim, director and owner of the Norheim Art Studio, 6007 Eighth Avenue, Brooklyn, and teacher of art, produced the *Art Journal* in conjunction with his "Fourth Annual Student Exhibit" held in May of 1949. It was a juried show and awards were given. The *Art Journal* included endorsements by Norheim's friends and students, and an essay by the well-known American artist, Rockwell Kent, who had been Norheim's teacher. In addition there was a brief history of the Norwegian Art and Craft Club, "And After Darkness Came Light," by August Satre, biographies of eight Norwegian NACC members, Katherine Bie, Olav Flatabo, Olav Nilsen, Thorn Norheim, Captain Peder G. Pedersen, Erling Tjonn, William Torjesen, and Bernhard O. Wahl, as well as biographies of two Swedish members, William Björk and Arvid Skoggard.

On October 9–23, 1949, the Norwegian Art and Craft Club held its "Tenth Annual Fall Exhibition," a juried show, at the Riverside Museum on Riverside Drive at 103rd Street. The last exhibition of the Norwegian Art and Craft Club appears to have been one held November 29–December 17, 1955. The undated checklist contains a statement that "the Norwegian Art and Craft Club was founded 16 years ago by the present President, Mr. Karl Larsen." The exhibition was held at the Brooklyn Public Library's South Branch, 4th Avenue and 51st Street.

In 1979 or 1980 a catalog titled merely "Nygaard" was published for an exhibition of the sculptures of Dr. Kaare Nygaard at Caravan House Gallery, 132 East 65th Street, New York. The catalog is undated and the gallery has not kept records. It may well be that the absence of a date on the catalog was intentional, for the Caravan House Gallery had several one-man shows of Nygaard's work.[11] Dr. Kaare Nygaard, a surgeon, was born in Lillehammer, Norway, in 1903, came to the United States in 1930, and lives in Scarsdale, New York.[12] A second catalog of Nygaard's work was published to coincide with the presentation of one of his pieces in Dallas, Texas, on November 9, 1984.

Minneapolis was the scene of the largest exhibition ever held of the work of Norwegian-American artists. It was arranged for the Norse-American Centennial and opened at the Minnesota State Fair Grounds on June 6, 1925, for four days. It was assembled under the direction of Herbjorg Reque and a committee of twenty drawn from Chicago, New York, St. Paul, and Minneapolis. There were 227 pieces shown, including 22 watercolors, 74 oil paintings, and 19 pieces of sculpture. Luther College lent 37 oils by Herbjørn Gausta; photographs of mural paintings by Thomas Bull and Trygve Hammer were displayed. In addition the committee borrowed 131 paintings to provide a broader display of Norwegian-American art. Four prizes were awarded in the category of oil painting, three for watercolor, and one for sculpture. The jury, selected from outside the Norwegian community, made their decisions before the exhibition opened so that prize winners could be listed in the catalog. All of the work in the Competitive Exhibition was for sale as well as a few items in the Loan Exhibition.

Elsewhere in the country there have been publications documenting the work of Norwegian-American artists. In 1979 the University of Wisconsin-La Crosse Foundation published *A Catalog of the Oyen Collection from the University of Wisconsin, La Crosse/ Including a History of the Oyen Interior Design Firm/ Buildings Decorated by the Oyen Firm/ Employees of the Oyen Firm*. The catalog is well illustrated and provides splendid documentation of the little-known activities of a Norwegian immigrant, Odin J. Oyen, and his interior-decorating firm.

Professor Reidar Dittmann of St. Olaf College, Northfield, Minnesota, put together in 1980 the exhibition, "Scandinavian Paintings in Northfield," which contained the works of some Norwegian immigrant artists, Emil Biørn, Herbjørn Gausta, Lars Haukaness, Karl Ouren, and Svend Svendsen. Brief biographies of the artists are included in the catalog.

In 1982 Mary Towley Swanson, Professor of Art History at Augsburg College and St. Thomas College, was cur-

This exhibition arranged by Mary Towley Swanson and held at the University Gallery, University of Minnesota, October 1–November 7, 1982, was a major exhibition of Scandinavian-American artists. The painting on the cover is "Arctic Scene" by Karl Ouren, who was born in Halden in 1882 and died in Chicago in 1943.

ator of "The Divided Heart: Scandinavian Immigrant Artists 1850–1950," at the University of Minnesota. The catalog is well illustrated and contains the biographies of seven Danes, four Finns, fourteen Swedes, and nineteen Norwegians. The Norwegians are Christian Abrahamsen, Sigvald Asbjørnsen, Ben Blessum, Jacob H. G. Fjelde, Herbjørn Gausta, Trygve Hammer, John Olson Hammerstad, Lars Haukaness, Michael Hoiland, Paul Lauritz, Jonas Lie, Marie Løkke, Peter Lund, Karl Ouren, Herman Schultz, Gulbrand Sether, Sigurd Skou, Svend Svendsen, and Arild Weborg.

Cornell University in Ithaca, New York, was the scene of a retrospective of the work of Olaf Brauner, an immigrant from Oslo who became a professor of art and founder of the Art Department at Cornell University. The catalog, *The Art of Olaf M. Brauner, 1869–1947/ 9 June to 17 July 1983*, contains a complete, well-documented biography of the artist as well as twenty-seven illustrations of Brauner's paintings, five of which are in full color.

Marion J. Nelson, Director of Vesterheim, the Norwegian-American Museum, Decorah, Iowa, has published two exhibition catalogs. *Berntsen and Hoiland; a Retrospective* was published to document an exhibition of the works of Bernhard Berntsen and Michael Hoiland held from July 27, 1983, to May 18, 1984, in Decorah, Iowa, and contains biographical material on the two artists as well as thirty-one illustrations. *Arild Weborg, 1900–1963: the Artist and the Age* contains biographical data and thirty-eight illustrations of Weborg's work. The Weborg retrospective was held in Decorah July 28, 1984, to May 18, 1985.

In 1985 the Life of Maryland Gallery of the Baltimore Life Insurance Company produced a full-color catalog for "The Egeli Family Exhibition: the fine art of eleven family artists." It contains fourteen illustrations and a genealogical sketch, in addition to a biography of the patriarch Biorn Egeli, who came to the United States from Horton, Norway.

In many instances these catalogs and checklists have proved to be the only sources of information about individ-

# THE EGELI FAMILY EXHIBITION
*The fine art of eleven family artists*

SEPTEMBER 3–NOVEMBER 1, 1985
THE LIFE OF MARYLAND GALLERY

The cover painting is Bjorn Peter Egeli's "Self-Portrait." Egeli was born in Horton, Norway, in 1900, came to the United States in his early twenties and died in Valley Lee, Maryland, in 1984. He painted over 600 portraits and his famous subjects bear such names as Eisenhower, Nixon, MacArthur, Auchincloss, Guggenheim, and Du Pont.

ual artists. A profile of an artist begins to emerge from a listing of all the paintings exhibited. In addition, a listing also may be the only record of the paintings themselves. The catalogs, many in fragile condition and very rare, are themselves objects worthy of preservation as remnants of our artistic culture. Copies of the catalogs are available to researchers at the archives of the Norwegian-American Historical Association, Northfield, Minnesota, and at Vesterheim, the Norwegian-American Museum, Decorah, Iowa.

## List of Catalogs and Checklists

### Chicago

Young, J. W. *Exhibition of the Works of Lars Haukaness, from Tuesday, April twenty-second to Saturday, May third, inclusive, nineteen hundred and thirteen, in Young's Art Galleries, third floor Kimball Hall, Jackson Boulevard and Wabash Avenue, Chicago* (Chicago, 1913), 12p.

Chicago Norwegian Club. *First Annual Norwegian-American Art Exhibit by Chicago Norwegian Club/ 2346–2350 North Kedzie Boulevard/ from Saturday, December Eleventh to Sunday, December Nineteenth Nineteen Hundred Twenty* (Chicago, 1920), 12p.

Chicago Norwegian Club. *Second Annual Norwegian-American Art Exhibit/ Chicago Norwegian Club/ 2346–50 North Kedzie Boulevard/ from Thursday, December 1st to Friday, December 9th, 1921* (Chicago, 1921), 12p.

Chicago Norwegian Club. *Third Annual Norwegian-American Art Exhibit/ Chicago Norwegian Club/ 2346–50 North Kedzie Boulevard/ from Friday, November 17th, to Wednesday, November 22nd, 1922* (Chicago, 1922), 12p.

Chicago Norwegian Club. *Fourth Annual Norwegian-American Art Exhibit/ Chicago Norwegian Club/ 2346–50 North Kedzie Boulevard/ from Tuesday, November 13th, to Thursday, November 22nd, 1923* (Chicago, 1923), 10p.

Chicago Norwegian Club. *Fifth Annual Norwegian-American Art Exhibit/ Chicago Norwegian Club/ 2346–50 North Kedzie Boulevard/ from Friday, November 14th to Sunday, November 23rd, 1924* (Chicago, 1924), 20p.

Chicago Norwegian Club. *Sixth Annual Norwegian-American Art Exhibit/ Chicago Norwegian Club/ 2346–50 North Kedzie Boulevard/*

*from Friday, November 13th to Sunday, November 22nd, 1925* (Chicago, 1925), 20p.

Chicago Norske Club. *Seventh Annual Norwegian-American Art Exhibit at Chicago Norske Club/ 2346–50 North Kedzie Boulevard/ Friday, November 12th to Sunday, November 21st, 1926* (Chicago, 1926), 20p.

Chicago Norske Klub. *Eighth Annual Norwegian-American Art Exhibit at Chicago Norske Klub/ 2346–50 North Kedzie Boulevard/ Friday, November 11th to Sunday, November 20th, 1927* (Chicago, 1927), 24p.

Chicago Norske Klub. *Ninth Annual Norwegian-American Art Exhibit at Chicago Norske Klub/ 2350 North Kedzie Boulevard/ Friday, November 15th to Sunday, November 24th, 1929* (Chicago, 1929), 24p.

*An Exhibition of Works by Scandinavian-American Artists Given Under the Auspices of the American-Scandinavian Foundation at the Illinois Women's Athletic Club/ 111 Pearson Street/ Price, 25 Cents/ December 1st to December 10th, 1929* (Chicago, 1929), 16p.

Chicago Norske Klub. *Tenth Annual Norwegian-American Art Exhibit at Chicago Norske Klub/ 2350 North Kedzie Boulevard/ Friday, November 14th to Sunday, November 23rd, 1930* (Chicago, 1930), 20p.

Norse Art League. *Norse Art League First Semi-Annual Art Exhibit/ Open from 5 P.M. to 12 P.M. Daily March 1 to 15, 1931/ Den Norske Kafe Banquet Hall/ 2741–45 W. North Avenue* (Chicago, 1931), 6p.

Norse Art League. *Norse Art League's Exhibit/ Second Semi-Annual/ December Fifth to Twentieth Nineteen Thirty One/ Den Norske Kafe/ 2741–45 West North Avenue, Chicago, Illinois* (Chicago, 1931), 1 leaf folded.

Norwegian Women's Club. *Norwegian Women's Club 7th District Art Exhibit Presenting Work of Margit Osri/ Emilie Beutlich/ 1942/ March 8th to March 18th Inclusive/ Norwegian Federation Club House/ 2512 N. Kimball Avenue–Chicago* (Chicago, 1942), 1 leaf.

Chicago Norske Klub. *Karl Ouren Memorial Art Exhibit Sponsored by Chicago Norske Klub/ 2350 North Kedzie Boulevard Chicago, Ill. From Thursday, November 25th thru Sunday, November 28th, 1943/ Exhibition Open Daily from Seven to Eleven P.M. and on Sunday from Four to Eleven P.M.* (Chicago, 1943), 1 leaf folded.

Chicago Norske Klub. *Norwegian-American Art Exhibit/ Chicago Norske Klub/ 2350 North Kedzie Boulevard from Thursday, November 20th to Sunday, November 23rd, 1947* (Chicago, 1947), 1 leaf folded.

Chicago Norske Klub. *Art Exhibit November 20 through December 1, 1963/ Chicago Norske Klub/ 2350 North Kedzie Boulevard/ Chicago, Illinois* (Chicago, 1963), 1 leaf folded.

## New York City

Society of Scandinavian American Artists. *Exhibition Scandinavian-American Artists/ Jan. 30th–March 1st 1926/ Brooklyn Museum* (Brooklyn, 1926), 19p.

Society of Scandinavian American Artists. *Scandinavian-American Artists/ Brooklyn Museum/ April 9–May 7 1928* (Brooklyn, 1928), 17p.

Society of Scandinavian American Artists. *Scandinavian-American Artists/ Brooklyn Museum/ April 11–May 15 1932* (Brooklyn, 1932), 43p.

Society of Scandinavian American Artists (?). *Scandinavian-American Artists Catalogue 1936/ Art Galleries in the Squibb Building/ September 21–October 11/ Seven Forty Five–Fifth Avenue, New York* (New York, 1936), 1 leaf folded.

The Norwegian Art and Craft Club. *The Norwegian Art and Craft Club/ 4806–4th Avenue, Brooklyn, N.Y./ Exhibition at the Staten Island Museum of Arts and Sciences/ Stuyvesant Place and Wall Street/ St. George, Staten Island/ Opening Saturday, May 2nd, 1942/ Reception 7–10/ Program by: Betty-Ann Goodwin/ DeWitt Durgin Lash/ Erling Lee/ Exhibition Continued Throughout May, 1942/ Open Daily from 10–5 — 7–10 p.m. Sundays from 2–5 p.m.* (Brooklyn, 1942), 12p.

Norwegian Art and Craft Club. *Norwegian Art and Craft Club's Exhibition at the Norwegian Seamen's Home/ 62 Hanson Place, Brooklyn, N.Y.* (Brooklyn, 1945?), 1 leaf folded.

Norwegian Art and Craft Club. *Norwegian Art & Craft Club/ Spring Exhibition 1946/ Norwegian Seamen's House; 62 Hanson Place, Brooklyn, N.Y.* (Brooklyn, 1946), 1 leaf folded.

Norwegian Art and Craft Club. *Norwegian Arts and Crafts Exhibition/ December 2nd to 15th 1946/ Brooklyn Public Library/ Grand Army Plaza/ Brooklyn 17, N.Y.* (Brooklyn, 1946), 2 leaves folded and stapled back to back.

Norwegian Art and Craft Club. *8th Annual Fall Exhibition by Norwegian Art & Craft Club/ at Norwegian Seamen's House; 62 Hanson Place, Brooklyn, N.Y./ Exhibition Remains Open From November 17 thru December 17, 1946* (Brooklyn, 1946), 1 leaf folded.

Norwegian Art and Craft Club. *Paintings by American Scandinavians/ Norwegian Art & Craft Club Exhibition/ Brooklyn Public Library/ Grand Army Plaza/ March 7th thru March 31st, 1947* (Brooklyn, 1947), 1 leaf folded.

Norwegian Art and Craft Club. *The Riverside Museum/ 310 Riverside Drive, N.Y.C./ Exhibition Norwegian Art & Craft Club/ Sept. 14 thru Sept. 28, 1947* (Brooklyn, 1947), 1 leaf folded.

Brooklyn Public Library(?). *Torjesen Paintings/ Brooklyn Scenes/ Exhibition/ October 27 thru November 17, 1947/ Brooklyn Public Library/ Grand Army Plaza* (Brooklyn, 1947). 1 leaf folded.

Norwegian Art and Craft Club. *Norwegian Art & Craft Club/ Second New York Exhibition April 12th–24th, 1948 and Memorial Exhibition of Sculpture by Trygve Hammer (Sponsored by the Club)/ Argent Galleries/ 42 West 57th St., New York 19, N.Y.* (Brooklyn, 1948), 1 leaf folded.

Norheim, Thorn. *Art Journal/ Norheim Art Studio/ 6007 Eighth Avenue/ Brooklyn 20, New York 1949* (Brooklyn, 1949), 58p.

Norwegian Art and Craft Club. *Norwegian Art & Craft Club Tenth Annual Fall Exhibition October 9th–23rd, 1949/ Riverside Museum/ 310 Riverside Drive at 103rd St., N.Y. 25, N.Y./ Open Daily 1–5 Closed Mondays* (Brooklyn, 1949), 1 leaf folded.

Norwegian Art and Craft Club. *Exhibition Norwegian Art and Craft Club at South Branch Brooklyn Public Library/ 4th Avenue & 51st Street/ November 29–December 17* (Brooklyn, 1955?), 1 leaf folded.

Caravan House Gallery. *Nygaard* (New York, 1979?), 20p.

Parke, Stephen P. *Catalog of Sculpture by Nygaard* (White Plains, New York, 1984), 20p.

*Elsewhere*

Fine Arts Committee, Norse-American Centennial. *Norse-American Centennial Art Exhibition/ Minnesota State Fair Grounds/ June 6–7–8–9, 1925* (Minneapolis, 1925), 21p.

Rausch, Joan M. and Dr. Leslie F. Crocker. *A Catalog of the Oyen Collection from the University of Wisconsin, La Crosse/ Including a History of the Oyen Interior Design Firm/ Buildings Decorated by the Oyen Firm/ Employees of the Oyen Firm* (La Crosse, Wisconsin, 1979), 64p.

St. Olaf College, Northfield, Minnesota. *Scandinavian Paintings in Northfield/ Works by Immigrant Artists and Others/ an Exhibition on the*

*Occasion of the "Norway Today" Symposium/ April 9 to 21, 1980/ in Steensland Gallery/ St. Olaf College/ Northfield, Minnesota* (Northfield, 1980), 8p.

University Gallery, University of Minnesota, Minneapolis. *The Divided Heart: Scandinavian Immigrant Artists/ 1850–1950/ October 1–November 7, 1982; University Gallery, University of Minnesota* (Minneapolis, 1982), 40p.

Peters-Campbell, John R. *The Art of Olaf M. Brauner/ 1869–1947/ 9 June to 17 July, 1983/ Exhibition and Catalogue/ Herbert F. Johnson Museum of Art/ Cornell University, Ithaca, New York* (Ithaca, New York, 1983), 36p.

Nelson, Marion J. *Berntsen and Hoiland/ a Retrospective.* Published as *Vesterheim Newsletter,* 19 (Decorah, Iowa, Spring, 1985), 8p.

Nelson, Marion J. *Arild Weborg 1900–1963. The Artist and the Age.* Published as *Vesterheim Newsletter,* 20 (Spring, 1985), 8p.

Life of Maryland Gallery, Baltimore, Maryland. *The Egeli Family Exhibition/ The fine art of eleven family artists/ September 3–November 1, 1985/ the Life of Maryland Gallery* (Baltimore, 1985), 1 leaf folded with insert.

# Notes

[1] The census of 1900 counted 22,011 persons who indicated that Norway was their country of birth, making Chicago by far the most "Norwegian" of the large urban centers of the United States. Other cities which counted large numbers of Norwegian-born citizens were New York (11,387), Minneapolis (11,532), St. Paul, Minnesota (2,900), and Seattle (1,642). *Twelfth Census of the United States, 1900: Population,* 1, 798–802.

[2] The list has been compiled from the catalogs listed here, the archives of the Norwegian-American Historical Association, the reference files of Vesterheim, the Norwegian-American Museum, and volumes one and two of *Norsk Kunstner Leksikon* (Oslo, 1982 and 1983).

[3] An undated and unidentified newspaper clipping from the archives of the Norwegian-American Historical Association gives the dates of the exhibition of Lars Haukaness' work at the Radisson Hotel in Minneapolis as November 18–29, 1913.

[4] Interview with Dr. Oscar John Olsen, Park Ridge, Illinois, March 11, 1980.

[5] The artist also spelled his surname "Schou."

[6] The artist also spelled his surname "Whittrup."

[7] Interview with Reidar Rosenvinge, Chicago, September 20, 1979.

[8] Interview with Josefa Hansen Andersen, Chicago, January 15, 1986.

304    *Rolf H. Erickson*

[9]Rolf H. Erickson, *The Chicago Norske Klub Collection/ A Catalog of the Art at Norway Center/ 2350 North Kedzie* (Chicago, 1982).

[10]*Art Journal* (Brooklyn, 1949), 25.

[11]Erik J. Friis, "Carver of the Invisible, Dr. Kaare Nygaard — Surgeon and Sculptor," in the *Norseman*, 1980, no. 2, 46.

[12]Nathan Cabot Hale, *The Spirit of Man: The Sculpture of Kaare Nygaard* (Oslo, 1982), 45 and 89.

# Some Recent Publications

*compiled by C. A. Clausen*
*with Norwegian listings by Johanna Barstad*

BOOKS AND PAMPHLETS

Andersson-Palmquist, Lena. *Building Traditions Among Swedish Settlers in Rural Minnesota.* Stockholm, 1983. 121 pp.

Angel, Marc. *La America: The Sephardic Experience in the United States.* Philadelphia, 1982. x, 220 pp.
> "The history of the some thirty thousand Levantine Jews who migrated to these shores between 1890 and World War I."

Archdeacon, Thomas J. *Becoming American: An Ethnic History.* New York, 1983. xviii, 297 pp.
> A one-volume survey of the American immigrant experience.

Barthel, Diane L. *Amana: From the Pietist Sect to American Community.* Lincoln, Nebraska, 1984. 210 pp.

Bodnar, John et al. *Lives of their Own: Blacks, Italians, and Poles in Pittsburgh 1900–1980.* Urbana, Illinois, 1982. 286 pp.

Bruflot, Arnfinn. *På andre sida av havet.* Oslo, 1986. 54 pp.
> A poetic description of the United States during the immigration era and today.

Carini, Mario. *Milwaukee's Italians: The Early Years.* Milwaukee, 1984. 12 pp.

Cazden, Robert E. *A Social History of the German Book Trade in America to the Civil War.* Columbia, South Carolina, 1984. 801 pp.

Chan, Anthony B. *Gold Mountain: The Chinese in the New World.* Vancouver, British Columbia, 1983. 224 pp.
> "Chinese immigrants to Canada had a very harsh life. Canada allowed them to come to build railways and to seek gold in the Fraser Valley, British

Columbia. When the railway was built, the country did its best to discourage the Chinese from staying."

Chao, Evelina. *Gates of Grace.* New York, 1985. 372 pp.

"The theme of the New Land is the theme of America. In *Gates of Grace,* Evelina Chao gives us a modern, Eastern variation on that theme, showing a Chinese family working its way slowly and painfully into America in San Francisco, New York, and Washington, D.C., in the 1950s and 1960s."

Christianson, J. R., ed. *Scandinavians in America: Literary Life.* Decorah, Iowa, 1985. 342 pp.

The proceedings of SIMCON II, a conference at Luther College, Decorah, Iowa, which focus on the literary life of Scandinavians in America, mainly in the century 1850–1950.

Cinel, Dino. *From Italy to San Francisco: The Immigrant Experience.* Stanford, 1982. viii, 347 pp.

". . . much more than a history of Italians in a single city. His analysis of immigrant origins will be of great value for all immigration scholars and is a contribution to Italian social history."

Clark, Dennis. *The Irish Relations: Trials of an Immigrant Tradition.* Rutherford, New Jersey, 1982. 225 pp.

Detjen, David W. *The Germans in Missouri, 1900–1918: Prohibition, Neutrality, and Assimilation.* Columbia, Missouri, 1984. 244 pp.

Dittmann, Chrisma S., compiler. *Norwegian-American Imprints in the St. Olaf College Library.* Northfield, Minnesota, 1986. 122 pp.

Eisen, Arnold M. *The Chosen People in America. A Study in Jewish Religious Ideology.* Bloomington, Indiana, 1983. x, 237 pp.

Erickson, John, ed. *Petersen fra Peterson.* Translated by Karl Pedersen. Peterson, Minnesota, 1985. 49 pp.

A collection of letters and other writings pertaining to the founding of Peterson, Minnesota.

Fosdal, Roberta Lien. *Norwegian Roots, American Branches: the Kjetil and Bergit Lien Family History.* Jefferson, Wisconsin, 1984. 253 pp.

Friedman, Murray, ed. *Jewish Life in Philadelphia, 1830–1940.* Philadelphia, 1983. 353 pp.

Friedman, Philip S. "The Danish Community of Chicago." *The Bridge,* 8,1: 5–95 (1985).

This whole issue of *The Bridge* is devoted to Friedman's study of the Danish community in Chicago.

Friis, Erik J., ed. *The Scandinavian-American Bulletin.*

This bulletin is published monthly by the Scandinavian-American Business Association of Greater New York. It carries articles of interest about all the Scandinavian countries. A special feature is "The Scandinavian of the Month," a brief article by the editor honoring a person of Scandinavian blood who has achieved distinction in some particular field.

Georges, R. A. and Stern, S. *American and Canadian Ethnic Folklore: An Annotated Bibliography.* New York, 1982. xix, 484 pp.

Gjerde, Jon. *From Peasants to Farmers: The Migration from Balestrand, Norway, to the Upper Middle West.* New York, 1985. xiv, 319 pp.

Glasrud, Clarence A., ed. *A Heritage Fulfilled: German-Americans.* Moorhead, Minnesota, 1984. 237 pp.

Hale, Frederick. *Swedes in Wisconsin.* Madison, 1983. 32 pp.

Hale, Frederick. *The Swiss in Wisconsin.* Madison, 1984. 40 pp.

Harney, Robert F., ed. *Polyphony: The Bulletin of the Multicultural History Society of Ontario.*

Some issues of this periodical are devoted to a single topic. Recent issues include:

Vol. 3, no. 1 (Winter, 1980–1981): problems of creating trustworthy guidebooks for emigrants.

Vol. 3, no. 2 (Fall, 1981): aspects of Finnish life in Canada.

Vol. 4, no. 1 (Spring–Summer, 1982): the role of the ethnic press in Ontario.

Vol. 5, no. 2 (Fall–Winter, 1983): immigrant or ethnic theater in Canada.

Vol. 6, no. 1 (Spring–Summer, 1984): the more than sixty ethnic presences in Toronto.

Herscher, Uri D., ed. *A Century of Memories, 1882–1982: The East European Experience in America.* New York, 1983. 189 pp.

Hess, Earl J., ed. *A German in the Yankee Fatherland: The Civil War Letters of Henry A. Kircher.* Kent, Ohio, 1983. xi, 169 pp.

Hoerder, Dirk, ed. *Essays on the Scandinavian-North American Press: 1880–1930.* Bremen, 1984. 161 pp.

Hoff, Stein. *Drømmen om Galapagos. En ukjent norsk utvandrerhistorie.* Oslo, 1985. 211 pp.

Norwegian emigration to the Galápagos Islands.

Hoglund, A. William. *Immigrants and their Children in the United States. A Bibliography of Doctoral Dissertations, 1885–1982.* New York, 1986. xxviii, 491 pp.

A listing of 3,543 dissertations on immigrants to the continental United States since 1789 and their children.

Holubetz, Sylvia H., ed. *Farewell to the Homeland: European Immigration to Northeast Wisconsin, 1840 to 1900.* Green Bay, Wisconsin, 1984. 150 pp.

Jones, George F. *The Salzburger Saga: Religious Exiles and Other Germans Along the Savannah.* Athens, Georgia, 1984. 209 pp.

Jones, Peter D'A. and Holli, Melvin G., eds. *Ethnic Chicago.* Grand Rapids, Michigan, 1984. ix, 625 pp. Revision of the 1981 edition.

Klepp, Hans. *Fem år av mitt liv.* Lillehammer, 1983, 178 pp.

About Klepp's stay in the United States, 1929–1933.

Kloss, Heinz, ed. *Deutsch als Muttersprache in den Vereinigten Staaten. Teil II: Regionale und Funktionale Aspekte.* Wiesbaden, 1985. 297 pp.

Kopp, Michael and Ludwig, Stephen. *German-Russian Folk Architec-*

*ture in Southeastern South Dakota.* Vermillion, South Dakota, 1984. 36 pp.

Landelius, Otto Robert. *Swedish Place-Names in North America.* Translated by Karin Franzen, and edited by Raymond Jarvi. Carbondale, Illinois, 1985. xvii, 348 pp.

Lee, Knute. *Survivor.* Detroit, 1984. 223 pp.

The author of this autobiography grew up in Spring Grove, Minnesota, was a navy pilot during World War II, and later taught religion at various Lutheran institutions.

Lovoll, Odd S., ed. *Norwegian-American Studies,* Vol. 30. Northfield, Minnesota, 1985. 340 pp.

Published by the Norwegian-American Historical Association. The contents are listed individually by authors in the following section on articles. "This volume of *Norwegian-American Studies* . . . makes evident the rich opportunity for scholarly research that Norwegian settlement in the Far West provides; six of the nine articles in the collection are devoted to this topic." The volume is dedicated to the memory of Peter A. Munch.

Lovoll, Odd S., ed. *Scandinavians and Other Immigrants in Urban America.* Northfield, Minnesota, 1985. 214 pp.

The proceedings of a research conference at St. Olaf College, October 26–27, 1984.

Lupul, M. R., ed. *A Heritage in Transition: Essays in the History of Ukrainians in Canada.* Toronto, 1982. viii, 344 pp.

Mandel, David. *Settlers of Dane County. The Photographs of Andreas Larsen Dahl.* Introduction by John O. Holzhueter, foreword by George Talbot. Dane county, Wisconsin, 1985. 84 pp.

Andreas Dahl emigrated to America in 1869 and supported himself as an itinerant photographer, especially of Norwegian-American subjects.

Miller, Randall M., ed. *Germans in America: Retrospect and Prospect.* Philadelphia, 1984. 132 pp.

Miyamoto, S. F. *Social Solidarity among the Japanese of Seattle.* Seattle, 1984. xxiv, 74 pp.

Mortensen, Enok. *Den lange plovfure.* Copenhagen, 1984. 232 pp.

"In the postscript to his novel, *The Long Plow-furrow,* Enok Mortensen notes that it is a fictional book portraying the Danish pioneer minister's role and significance in the great immigration of the nineteenth century."

Pedersen, Erik Helmer. *Drømmen om Amerika.* Copenhagen, 1985. 320 pp.

A survey of Danish immigration to and settlement in America. A volume in *Politiken's* series on Danish history.

Petersen, Peter L. *A Place Called Dana.* Blair, Nebraska, 1984. 231 pp.

The Centennial History of Trinity Seminary and Dana College, 1884–1984.

Procko, Bohdan P. *Ukrainian Catholics in America: A History.* Washington, D.C., 1982. xiv, 170 pp.

Puskas, Julianna, *From Hungary to the United States (1880–1914)*. Translated by Maria Bales and Eva Pálmai and edited by F. Mucsi. Budapest, 1982. 225 pp.

". . . the first English-language history of emigration to come out of East Central Europe. . . . a condensed, and translated, version of a much longer book that originally appeared in Hungarian."

Qualey, Carlton C., ed. *The Immigration History Newsletter.*

Published twice a year by the Immigration History Society, it contains articles, bibliography, listing of works in progress, and other material of interest to scholars in the field of ethnic history.

Rippley, La Vern J. *The Immigrant Experience in Wisconsin*. Boston, 1985. 220 pp.

Rochlin, Harriet and Fred. *Pioneer Jews: A New Life in the Far West*. Boston, 1984. 243 pp.

"Whether in the mines, on the farms and ranches, or in trade, commerce, and the professions, Jewish pioneers in the West made good."

Rølvaag, O. E. *When the Wind is in the South and Other Stories*. Translated by Solveig Zempel. Sioux Falls, South Dakota, 1984. 88 pp.

Roos, Rosalie. *Travels in America 1851–1855*. Translated and edited by Carl L. Anderson. Carbondale, Illinois, 1982. xviii, 152 pp.

A Swedish woman's impressions of the Antebellum South.

*Samtiden*. 93: 1–80 (3, 1984).

This issue deals with Norway in America and America in Norway and includes articles on Norwegian-American topics by John R. Jenswold, Helge Dahl, Hans Fredrik Dahl, Nils Johan Ringdal, Terje I. Leiren, Arvid Bryne, Kjetil A. Flatin, Cæcilie Stang, and others.

Sandburg, Carl. *Ever the Winds of Chance*. Urbana, Illinois, 1983. xiii, 172 pp.

". . . a rough draft—written in 1955 but never completed—of an account of Sandburg's third decade, 1898–1908."

*Scandinavian Review*. 73: 1–159 (Winter, 1985).

Seventy-fifth anniversary issue, containing articles on Scandinavian-American history by Dorothy Burton Skårdal, A. William Hoglund, Valdimar Björnson, Odd S. Lovoll, and Ulf Beijbom.

Scarpaci, V. *A Portrait of Italians in America*. New York, 1983. xxxii, 240 pp.

Schultz, Arthur R. *German-American Relations and German Culture in America: A Subject Bibliography 1941–1980*. White Plains, New York, 1985. 2 vols., xxiv, 1279 pp.

Scourby, Alice. *The Greek Americans*. Boston, 1984. 184 pp.

Seller, Maxine Schwartz, ed. *Ethnic Theatre in the United States*. Westport, Connecticut, 1983. viii, 606 pp.

"Twenty individual essays, each treating the theatrical-historical experience of a different ethnic group."

Sherman, William C. *Prairie Mosaic: An Ethnic Atlas of Rural North Dakota.* Fargo, 1983. 152 pp.

"Each of the six regional maps is accompanied by a supporting text detailing the settlement history of all major ethnic concentrations."

Solensten, John. *There Lies a Fair Land.* St. Paul, Minnesota, 1985. 176 pp.

An anthology of Norwegian-American writing, with graphics by Arch Leean.

Sørbøl, Kjell. *Ei Roeslekt i Noreg og Amerika.* Gol, Norway, 1985. 123 pp.

A family history from both sides of the Atlantic.

Standal, Ragnar. *Mot nye heimland. Utvandringa frå Hjørundfjord, Vartdal og Ørsta.* Ørsta, Norway, 1985. 688 pp.

An article based on this study appeared in *Norwegian-American Studies*, 29 (1983), as "Emigration from a Fjord District on Norway's West Coast, 1852-1915."

Steele, M. A. *Knute Rockne: A Bio-Bibliography.* Westport, Connecticut, 1983. xii, 318 pp.

Stegner, Wallace and Etulaine, R. W. *Conversations with Wallace Stegner on Western History and Literature.* Salt Lake City, 1983. 207 pp.

Conversations with the noted Norwegian-American author.

Thomas, R. D. *Hanes Cymry America: A History of the Welsh in America.* Washington, D.C., 1983. xxi, 517 pp.

Translated by Phillips G. Davis from the Welsh original which was published in 1872.

Tjossem, Wilmer L. *Quaker Sloopers: From the Fjords to the Prairies.* Richmond, Indiana, 1984. 80 pp.

Trommler, Frank and McVeigh, Joseph, eds. *America and the Germans: An Assessment of a Three-hundred-year History.* Philadelphia, 1985. 2 vols.

*Utvandrere fra Grong til Amerika.* Grong, Norway, 1985. 24 pp.

Immigrants from Grong in Trøndelag to America.

*Utvandring frå Voss til America. Eit 150-års minne/Emigration from Voss to America: The 150th Anniversary.* Published as *Gamalt frå Voss*, no. 17. Voss, 1985. 246 pp.

Norwegian and English text.

Ward, Robert E. *A Bio-Bibliography of German-American Writers.* White Plains, New York, 1985. 1xx, 377 pp.

Weiss, Bernard J., ed. *American Education and the European Immigrant, 1840-1940.* Urbana, Illinois, 1984. xxviii, 217 pp.

Wendelius, Lars. *Bilden av Amerika i svensk prosafiktion 1890-1914.* Uppsala, 1982. v, 204 pp.

Pictures of America in Swedish prose fiction, 1890-1914.

Wickberg, Edgar, ed. *From China to Canada: A History of the Chinese Communities in Canada.* Toronto, 1982. viii, 369 pp.

Wiff, Patricia. *The Lefse and Lutefisk Belt: A History of the Village and Township of Martel, 1840–1920.* Spring Valley, Wisconsin. iii, 270 pp.

Wright, Rochelle and Robert, eds. *Danish Emigrant Ballads and Songs.* Carbondale, Illinois, 1983. ix, 302 pp.

The volume includes both the Danish originals and English translations.

Wyman, Mark. *Immigrants in the Valley: Irish, Germans, and Americans in the Upper Mississippi Country, 1830–1860.* Chicago, 1984. xiii, 258 pp.

## ARTICLES

Abrams, Elliott. "Unforgettable Scoop Jackson." *Readers Digest,* February, 1985, 81–85.

Senator Henry M. "Scoop" Jackson (1912–1983) of the state of Washington was the son of Norwegian immigrants.

Arestad, Sverre. "Norwegians in the Pacific Coast Fisheries." *Norwegian-American Studies,* 30: 96–129 (1985).

Barton, H. Arnold. "The Life and Times of Swedish-America." *The Swedish-American Historical Quarterly,* 35: 283–296 (July, 1984).

Berggrav, Ragnvald. "Fra snekker-lærling til mangemillionær. Kjell Nordvik oppretter utdannelsesfond gjennom Nordmanns Forbundet." *The Norseman,* 24–25 (4, 1985).

"From apprentice carpenter to multimillionaire: Kjell Nordvik establishes an educational fund through the Norsemen's Federation."

Berlin, Ira and Gutman, H. G. "Natives and Immigrants, Free Men and Slaves: Urban Workmen in the Antebellum American South." *American Historical Review,* 88: 1175–1200 (December, 1983).

Betsinger, Signe Nielsen. "Jens Kjær: From Horsens to Atlantic." *The Bridge,* 6,2: 42–52 (1983).

Jens Kjær (1866–1959) was a Danish-born artist who spent most of his adult life in the little community of Atlantic, Iowa.

Bjork, Kenneth O. "Reindeer, Gold, and Scandal." *Norwegian-American Studies,* 30:130–195 (1985).

The involvement of Scandinavians in the Alaska gold rush and the attempt to introduce reindeer into the territory.

Christianson, J. R., ed. "Clausens on the Move: Chicago, St. Ansgar, Virginia, 1870–1873." *The Bridge,* 6,2: 27–41 (1983).

Letters throwing light on the work of the famous Danish-born pioneer pastor, Claus Laurits Clausen. Translated by Erik Christianson, J. R. Christianson, and Paul Christianson.

Clausen, C. A. "Some Recent Publications." *Norwegian-American Studies*, 30: 293–310 (1985).

A listing of books and articles, published largely during the years 1982–1984, dealing with immigration history.

Dagman, Stieg-Erland. "Gustaf Mellberg—From Swedish Academician to American Farmer." *Swedish-American Genealogist*, 3: 161–169 (December, 1983).

Dørum, Hallvard. "Einar Haugen. Amerikaner, nordmann og oppdaling." *Bøgda vår. Årsskrift for lokalhistorie*, 1985, 4–17.

"The Emigrant Boy Who Became Governor." *The Bridge*, 16,3: 69–74 (1984).

The story of Adolf Olson Eberhardt, immigrant from Sweden, who served as governor of Minnesota, 1909–1915.

Erickson, Rolf H. "David Johnson—Chicago's First Norwegian." *Swedish-American Genealogist*, 4: 69–71 (June, 1984).

Gulliksen, Øyvind T. "Clarence A. Clausen, drangedøl og amerikaner." *Det var ein gong-: minner frå Drangedal*, 93–127 (8, 1985).

An account of a second-generation Norwegian American and his interest in the culture of his forefathers.

Gulliksen, Øyvind T. "John Lie og Amerika." *Telemark Historie*, 103–130 (6, 1985).

An account of John Lie (1846–1916), a Norwegian novelist and poet whose works became very popular among Norwegian-American readers.

Gunderson, Nancy. "Displaying the Colors." *The Sons of Norway Viking*, 81, 6: 288–290 (September, 1984).

Honors paid to the 15th Wisconsin Regiment, "The Norwegian Regiment," which did valorous work during the Civil War.

Gustavson, Erik. "The Emigration from Karlstad to America." *The Bridge*, 16, 3: 75–78, 83–86 (1984).

Hale, Frederick. "The Dano-Norwegian Department of Chicago Theological Seminary." *The Bridge*, 7, 1: 12–29 (1984).

Hambro, Johan. "Fra verdensmann blant pionérene." *Norges Jul*, 1985, 48–50.

An account of the vain attempt of Nils Otto Tank (1800–1864), a prominent Norwegian, to found a "Herrenhut" settlement near Green Bay, Wisconsin.

Hamre, James S. "Three Spokesmen for Norwegian Lutheran Academies: Schools for Church, Heritage, Society." *Norwegian-American Studies*, 30: 221–246 (1985).

The views of Herman Amberg Preus (1825–1894), D. G. Ristad (1863–1938), and Olaf M. Norlie (1876–1962).

Haugen, Einar "Kristine Haugen. Brubygger og kulturpersonlighet." *Bøgda vår. Årsskrift for lokalhistorie*, 1984, 14–17.

An account of the author's mother, a distinguished Norwegian-American cultural leader.

Havik, Sveinung. "Gullgraverekspedisjonen som skulle til 'Californien,' og som stranda i Rio de Janeiro, Brasil." *Levanger historielag. Årsskrift*, 1985, 26–38.

A gold expedition to California that was stranded in Rio de Janeiro.

Hedblom, Folke. "Swedish Personal Names in America." *Swedish-American Genealogist*, 5: 17–35 (March, 1985).

Hegstad, Patsy Adams. "Scandinavian Settlement in Seattle, 'Queen City of the Puget Sound.'" *Norwegian-American Studies*, 30: 55–74 (1985).

Hollwas, John. "John Reagan's *Emigrant's Guide*: A Neglected Literary Achievement." *Illinois Historical Journal*, 77: 269–294 (Winter, 1984).

The *Emigrant's Guide* is a detailed account of immigration to early Illinois.

Hoyle, Karen Nelson. "Danish Immigrant Contributions to Mainstream American Children's Literature, 1867–1983: An Overview." *The Bridge*, 6, 2: 18–26 (1983).

Hustvedt, Lloyd. "O. A. Tveitmoe: Labor Leader." *Norwegian-American Studies*, 30: 3–54 (1985).

The life and activities of a prominent Norwegian-American labor organizer and editor in the San Francisco area in the first quarter of this century.

Jacobson, Charlotte. "From the Archives." *Norwegian-American Studies*, 30: 311–318 (1985).

A listing, with brief analyses, of recent acquisitions by the Archives of the Norwegian-American Historical Association, Northfield, Minnesota.

Johnson, Rolf. "Tragedy at Sea." *Hallingen*, June, 1985, 23–26.

The trials and sorrows of an immigrant family aboard a sailing ship in 1846.

Karevoll, John. "Sverre Falck Nielsen. Mannen som bygger San Diego." *The Norseman*, 22–23 (5, 1984).

The story of a Norwegian American who has designed and built many of the largest and most noted buildings in San Diego.

Kolle, Nils. "Gjensyn med Castle Garden." *The Norseman*, 18–20 (2, 1985).

Return to Castle Garden, the immigrant receiving station in New York until 1892.

Kolltveit, Bård. "Amerikabåtene." *Norsk sjøfartsmuseum. Årsberetning*, 1983, 137–242.

Includes a summary in English: "The 'America Boats': the Passenger Ships of the Norwegian-America Line."

Kvelstad, Ragnvald. "The Pioneers of Dog Fish Bay." *Norwegian-American Studies*, 30: 196–220 (1985).

Norwegian settlers in the Poulsbo, Washington, area.

Larson, Nels T. A. "Life in Saskatchewan, 1918–1925: A Story of a Pioneering Missionary Family," edited by Samuel Chell. *The Swedish-American Historical Quarterly*, 36: 39–55 (January, 1985).

Leiren, Terje I. "Ole and the Reds: The 'Americanism' of Seattle Mayor Ole Hanson." *Norwegian-American Studies*, 30: 75–95 (1985).

An analysis of the ideas of Ole Hanson, son of Norwegian immigrants, who served briefly as mayor of Seattle (1918–1919) and won national recognition because of his fight against supposedly "red" labor unions and his strong advocacy of "Americanism."

Ljungmark, Lars. "Canada: An Alternative for Swedish Emigration to the New World, 1873–1875." *The Swedish-American Historical Quarterly*, 35: 253–266 (July, 1984).

McCree, Barbro Persson. "John P. Sjolander, Cedar Bayou, Texas." *The Swedish-American Historical Quarterly*, 36: 239–250 (October, 1985).

Sjolander (1851–1939) emigrated in 1871 from Hudiksvall, Sweden, to Texas, where he gained fame as a poet, primarily in the English language.

Moynihan, Daniel Patrick. "The Irish Among Us." *Readers Digest*, January, 1985, 61–65.

The first article in a series on "The Peoples of America."

Munson, Reuben M. "Win One for the Gipper." *The Norseman*, 36–37 (6, 1985).

The story of Knute Rockne, All-American from Voss, Norway.

Næss, Hans Eyvind. "Utvandringen fra Rogaland til Amerika. Hvem dro til Amerika fra Rogaland på 1800-tallet?" *Ætt og Heim*, 1984, 97–110.

Immigration from Rogaland in the nineteenth century.

Nelson, Charles H. "John Elof Boodin, Philosopher-Poet." *The Swedish-American Historical Quarterly*, 35: 124–150 (April, 1984).

Nielsen, John Marken. "Our Mission to the Indians." *The Bridge*, 6, 2: 5–17 (1983).

An account of a Danish Immigrant Churches Mission to the Cherokee Indians in 1892.

"Norwegian Texans: The Norwegian Migration to Texas." *The Norseman*, 36–38 (2, 1985).

O'Connor, David E. "The Swedish Element in Connecticut." *The Swedish-American Historical Journal*, 36: 275–299 (October, 1985).

The great wave of Swedish migration to Connecticut occurred during a thirty-year period, between the mid-1880s and the outbreak of World War I in 1914.

Olsson, Nils William. "Emigrant Traffic on the North Sea." *Swedish-American Genealogist*, 4: 158–163 (December, 1984).

Olsson, Nils William. "The Diary of an Early Swede with a Texas Connection." *Swedish-American Genealogist*, 3: 1–18 (March, 1983).

Petersen, Peter L. "A New Church in a New Land: The Founding of Det danske evangeliske lutherske Kirkesamfund i Amerika." *The Bridge*, 7, 2: 5–21 (1984).

Pickle, Linda S. "Stereotypes and Reality: Nineteenth-Century German Women in Missouri." *Missouri Historical Review*, 79: 291–312 (April, 1985).

Rischin, Moses. "Marcus Lee Hansen: America's First Transethnic Historian." *The Bridge*, 7, 2: 22–52 (1984).

Hansen "was the first and only American historian between the two world wars to conceptualize, legitimate, and give stature and universality to the ethnic dimensions of American life, at least in its European aspects."

Rosten, Leo. "The Jews Among Us." *Readers Digest*, March, 1985, 153–160.

The second article in "The Peoples of America" series.

Rowan, Carl T. "The Blacks Among Us." *Readers Digest*, June, 1985, 72–76.

The third article in "The Peoples of America" series.

Salmonsen, Morris. "Lægepraksis i Chicago." *The Bridge*, 7, 2: 53–68 (1983).

Morris (Moritz) Salmonsen was a prominent native of Copenhagen who spent the years 1872–1912 in Chicago. This article about medical practices among the Scandinavians in Chicago is taken from his book, *Brogede minder. Fra fyrreogtyve års ophold i Chicago* (Varied memories from a forty years stay in Chicago), (Copenhagen, 1913).

Sandal, Per. "Emigrasjonshistoria i bygdebøkene." *Heimen*, 22, 4: 213–218 (1985).

A discussion of the treatment of emigration in Norwegian local histories.

Scott, Larry Emil. "The Poetry of Agnes Mathilde Wergeland." *Norwegian-American Studies*, 30: 273–292 (1985).

Scott, Franklin D. "Changing Swedish Attitudes Toward America and Emigrants." *The Swedish-American Historical Quarterly*, 35: 297–308 (July, 1984).

Selkurt, Claire. "The Domestic Architecture and Cabinetry of Luther Valley." *Norwegian-American Studies*, 30: 247–272 (1985).

"The purpose of this article is to recreate aspects . . . of the material culture, the buildings and furniture of Luther Valley [Wisconsin] during the early period of settlement, as well as to show the persistence of certain Norwegian traditions."

Semmingsen, Ingrid. "Kontakten med Amerika." *Nordmanns-Forbundet*, 106–108 (4, 1984).

A sketch of the cultural relations between Norway and Norwegian America. The author suggests that Norway could and should have done more to strengthen these relations.

Setterdahl, Lilly. "Microfilming of Swedish-American Newspapers." *The Swedish-American Historical Quarterly*, 35: 65–76 (January, 1984).

Smedvig, Hjördis. "Utvandrernes Professor." *The Norseman*, 21–22 (3, 1985).

An article about Professor Ingrid Semmingsen of Oslo University, who is her country's leading authority on Norwegian emigration to America. Reprinted from *Stavanger Aftenblad*.

Steen, Roald. "John Hanson i Forest City." *Nordmanns-Forbundet*, 104–105 (4, 1984).

The story of the man who founded the Winnebago industry.

Stegner, Wallace. "The Scandinavians Among Us." *Readers Digest*, October, 1985, 130–134.

The fourth in the series "The Peoples of America."

Trautman, F., trans. and ed. "Johan Georg Kohl: A German Traveler in Minnesota Territory." *Minnesota History*, 49: 127–139 (Winter, 1984).

Vanberg, Bent. "Lawrence Olav Hauge." *The Norseman*, 39 (2, 1985).

Introducing the president of the Norwegian-American Historical Association and his many contributions to Norwegian-American activities in the Midwest.

Vecoli, Rudolph J. "The Formation of Chicago's 'Little Italies.'" *Journal of American Ethnic History*, 2: 5–20 (Spring, 1983).

Wiken, Erik. "New Light on the Erik Janssonists' Emigration, 1845–1854." *The Swedish-American Historical Quarterly*, 35: 221–238 (July, 1984).

Wright, Rochelle. "From Emigrant to Immigrant: America and Americanization in Scandinavian Song and Tradition." *Scandinavian Studies*, 57: 310–324 (Summer, 1985).

# From the Archives

## by Charlotte Jacobson

*Andersen, Magnus*

Translation by Karl B. Schultz of two chapters of *70 aars til-bakeblik*, a book by a Norwegian sea captain which was published in Oslo in 1932. The chapters excerpted deal with the voyage of the *Viking* from Bergen to the Columbian Exposition in Chicago in 1893 and later down the Mississippi River to New Orleans.

*Anderson, Mons*

Clippings about an immigrant from Valdres who came to Milwaukee in 1848 and moved to La Crosse in 1851. He established his own business in 1856 and became known as "The Merchant Prince of La Crosse." Of special interest are information about the house he purchased in 1865 and a coin which he had minted with his lion trademark on one side.

*Boyum, Arne*

Translation of a journal covering everyday happenings in home, church, and community which was kept by an immigrant from Balestrand, Sogn, who left Norway in 1853 and was ordained into Eielsen's Synod in 1858. He served the Arendahl congregation, Peterson, Minnesota, 1876–1896. He was president of the Hauge Synod, 1876–1887.

*Brosten, Andrew (Einar)*

Translations of letters to his relatives in Norway from an immigrant who came to the United States in 1881. He wrote from Illinois and Iowa, but finally settled on a farm in Griggs county, North Dakota.

317

*Fjelde, Herman Olaus*

Papers of a physician from Ålesund, who emigrated to the United States in 1889. After receiving a medical degree from the University of Minnesota, he practiced medicine in Minnesota and in North Dakota. He was a man of many interests who worked tirelessly for the preservation of the Norwegian heritage of his countrymen. He helped establish Det norske Selskab and Søndmørelaget. He was also instrumental in the erection of statues in the United States of famous Norwegians.

Dr. Fjelde came from an unusually gifted family. His father, Paul Michelet Fjelde, was a woodcarver. His brother, Jacob Fjelde, became a well-known Norwegian-American sculptor. Jacob's son Paul also became a noted sculptor. Dr. Fjelde's sister Pauline was a painter, needlework artist, and weaver, who had mastered the art of Gobelin tapestry.

*Gjerde, Jon*

Reprint of "The Effect of Community on Migration; Three Minnesota Townships, 1885–1905," published in the *Journal of Historical Geography*, vol. 5, no. 4 (1979), by a Norwegian-American scholar at the University of Minnesota. The area studied is Renville county, Minnesota.

*Gulbrandson, Esther*

Papers of a teacher of Norwegian at St. Olaf College who was active in promoting study and interest in everything Norwegian and Norwegian American. Especially interesting are papers connected with the program "Coffee Hour," conducted by the members of the Department of Norwegian over radio station WCAL. There are also transcripts of letters between St. Olaf College students and Norwegian seamen during the years of World War II.

*Gulliksen, Øyvind*

"John Lie og Amerika," the story of a Norwegian novelist and poet who lived in Fyresdal, Telemark, 1846–1916, and who was one of the most popular writers among first-generation Norwegian Americans. In 1898–1899 he visited the United States and published a volume of poems, *Helsing til Amerika*. He also gave occasional lectures, but because of ill health the visit was not a great success for him.

*Hagen, Monys Ann*

"Norwegian Pioneer Women; Ethnicity on the Wisconsin Agricultural Frontier," a master's thesis at the University of Wisconsin, 1984.

*Hansen, Edward*

Papers concerning the life and work of an immigrant from Mandal, who came to Chicago in 1904. In 1915–1931 he operated Den Norske Kafe, which became a center for fellowship among Norwegians in Chicago. Much of his time, interest, and energy was devoted to church and charitable enterprises. He was the first business manager for *Norsk Ungdom*, which began publication in Chicago in 1913. In 1926–1927 he published a weekly, *Chicago Tidende*.

*Hansen, Oskar J. W.*

Newspaper items and photographs of the work of a sculptor who emigrated to the United States from Vesterålen in 1910. In 1961 he was awarded the President's Medal of Merit for a sculpture at Yorktown, Virginia, commemorating Washington's victory over Cornwallis. His most famous work is the *Winged Figures of the Republic* at Hoover Dam, "said to be the largest cast bronzes in the world."

*Hardanger Fiddle Association of America*

Descriptive material about an organization seeking to preserve interest in the traditional eight-stringed violin which is the national folk instrument of Norway. An earlier organization, Spelemanns Laget af Amerika, founded in 1914, died out at about the time of World War II.

*Hildahl, Hild Naes*

Letters and a memoir "Listugfarmen," written by a woman who emigrated from Kragerø in 1937 to Roseau, Minnesota, after her marriage to a Norwegian-born farmer who had settled there. She tells about her life in Norway and the contrast to her life in Roseau. She had been trained in handicrafts and as a hobby began making dolls illustrating Norwegian fairy tales. The hobby grew into a business, and she traveled all over the United States, showing, selling, and lecturing about her dolls.

*Hoen, Peter L.*

*My Life*, Dyre Dyresen's translation of an account written by an immigrant from Nordrehaug in Ringerike. After coming to Chicago in 1971 he was converted to the beliefs of the Seventh-Day Adventists. He spent the rest of his life as a layman working among the Scandinavians of this denomination.

*Johnson, Nikolai*

"Hawaiian Adventure," a brief account by an immigrant from Drammen who came to Hawaii in 1880 as an indentured servant.

After a few months he was released from the indenture by his father, who paid the passage money.

### Kalevik, Erwin

Two accounts, *Kallevig Reunion* and *Georgeville, Minnesota, from 1860–1903*, edited by Kalevik, who at one time was a resident of Georgeville, Stearns county, Minnesota. The Kallevig reunion was held at Willmar, Minnesota, where descendants of three brothers, Alias, Johannes, and Olle Kallevig, gathered in the area where these men had originally settled in the 1880s and 1890s.

### Langseth, Peder Olsen

"Norske Settlementer og Menigheter i Sherburne, Benton og Mille Lacs Countier, Minnesota," written by Langseth together with A. Larsgaard and R. J. Meland. All three men had been pastors of congregations in this part of Minnesota.

### Lofthus, Orin M.

*Pioneers in the Norwegian Settlement,* a compilation of information about the families who came to Albany, Wisconsin, beginning in 1849. The statement is made that this is intended as "a layman's history of the entire settlement," which covers "members of various family groups through three or four generations." The work is in manuscript form, but has been copyrighted.

### Munch, Peter Andreas

Records pertaining to the Norwegian-American interests of a sociologist who was born at Nes, Hedmark, and received the first Ph.D. in sociology from the University of Oslo. He came to live in the United States in 1948 and after teaching for some years at the University of Wisconsin, St. Olaf College, and the University of North Dakota, he taught for twenty years at Southern Illinois University at Carbondale.

In 1939 he had been part of a Norwegian scientific expedition to Tristan da Cunha, an island in the South Atlantic. This led to his publishing numerous articles and books about the island, the best known being *Crisis in Utopia,* published in 1971.

In 1970 he and his wife, Helene Munch, published *The Strange American Way,* based on their translations of the letters of his grandmother, Caja Munch, and on excerpts from the autobiography of the Reverend Johan Storm Munch, who had served parishes at Wiota, Wisconsin, and the surrounding area, 1855–1859.

After Dr. Munch's retirement from Southern Illinois University in 1979, he was elected a member of the Norwegian

Academy of Science for his contributions to the field of sociology. He died in 1984.

*Nora Lodge, No. 1, Riddere av det Hvide Kors. Sons of Norway no. 415.*

Additions to the papers of a Norwegian cultural and benefit society in Chicago, consisting of historical information, legal documents, and five volumes of membership, secretarial, and financial records.

*Norsk Leseforening, Chicago*

Secretarial and other records of a women's reading club, founded in 1898 to foster interest in the literature of Scandinavia and particularly of Norway. The club often made financial gifts to charitable enterprises in the Chicago area.

*Norwegian-Danish Methodist Episcopal Conference, Richland Congregation.*

Records of a rural Richland county, Wisconsin, congregation, which in 1945 became part of the West Wisconsin Conference of the Methodist Church. The congregation was organized by a group of Norwegian immigrants in 1856. Because of declining membership the church was closed in 1981.

*Odegard, Ethel J.*

Papers of a Norwegian American who had a distinguished career in nursing before her retirement in 1951. She was at one time executive secretary of the Nurses' Examining Board, District of Columbia. Her article "Farewell to an Old Homestead," dealing with her home in Merrill, Wisconsin, appeared in *Norwegian-American Studies*, vol. 26.

*Olson, Irving*

A covering letter and an interview conducted by Janet Rasmussen with a resident of the Norse Home in Seattle, Washington. Olson had emigrated from Laksevåg, near Bergen, to Boston in 1907, where he joined the Norwegian Society and Norumbega.

*Overn, Anton Gustav Helgeson*

"A Pioneer's Proclamation; Uncompromising Truth; Unfailing Love," the translated sermons of a pastor in the Norwegian Synod, 1879–1905, who served congregations in Illinois, Wisconsin, Minnesota, Missouri, and Utah. The translations were made by a son, Alfred Victor Overn.

*Pedersen, Ole R.*

An autobiography translated by Pedersen's daughter Marie Peterson in 1974. It is the story of childhood and youth in Valdres, the journey to Brown county, Wisconsin, in 1873, and family, church, and pioneer life in that county.

*Pederson, Luke Molberg*

"Nineteenth Century Social Change in Lesja, Norway," a paper written by a history major in the College of Liberal Arts, University of Minnesota, 1980.

*Quie, Albert*

Papers of a Norwegian-American politician from Dennison, Minnesota, who served in the Minnesota Senate, 1954–1958, and was congressman from the Minnesota First District, 1959–1978. In 1978 he was elected governor of Minnesota and served a four-year term.

The papers deal with his Norwegian heritage and background, and tell of his visit to his people's home area in Norway.

*Rogney, Nellie*

"Alone on that Prairie," excerpts from a memoir written about 1910 by a woman who recalled the difficulties of life on a homestead in Rosebud county, Montana. With her Norwegian-American husband she had gone to Montana in 1914. The story ends tragically with the murder of her husband in the early 1920s.

*Rovelstad, Trygve*

Papers about the work of a Norwegian-American sculptor in Elgin, Illinois. His designs for a pioneer memorial in Elgin and for a huge statue to be placed in the Chicago harbor were never executed because funds were not available.

In the 1940s he was medalist and sculptor for the United States Department of War. He designed their Combat Infantry Badge and was instructor in sculpture at the United States Army University near Oxford, England. He designed and edited the commemorative American Roll of Honor, which was placed in the American Memorial Chapel, St. Paul's Cathedral, London.

Many of his statues, badges, and medals are to be found in the Chicago area.

*Royal Norwegian Navy War Veterans Association*

"The Sea Breeze," a newsletter, 1972–1983, of the United States Branch of S.S.H. Veteranforening, a social organization of citizens of Canada and the United States who served in the Norwegian Navy during World War II.

*Sønneland, Sidney Gaylord*

Additional papers given by Mrs. Sidney Sønneland concerning her mother, Caroline Stuverud Short. Of special interest is the story of Mrs. Short's pilgrimage to France as a Gold Star mother.

*Thomason, Thomas*

Copies of *Slægtregister*, an account by an immigrant from Arendal who came to Dane county, Wisconsin, in 1861. In 1867 he moved to Stevens county, Minnesota, which was frontier country. The journals cover family history, his youth in Norway, his experiences as a seaman, the journey to America, and the kinds of work he engaged in. He intersperses his accounts with philosophical observations and poems, some of which are of his own composition.

*Tillotson, Christi*

Letters written to a Norwegian immigrant living in Clinton, Wisconsin, in connection with her gifts to Opheim for an old people's home and to Vossestrand for a children's home in Voss.

*Wefald, Knut*

Letters written by a resident of Yttre Vefald, Drangedal, Telemark, to his son Knud, who had emigrated to the United States in 1887 and who became a distinguished Minnesota politician.

Papers of the son, Knud Wefald, are also in the collections of the NAHA Archives. During the past year many additions have been made to these papers. Included are an account from 1903 concerning a trip to Norway, poems that he wrote in both Norwegian and English, and extracts from the *Congressional Record* during his term in the United States House of Representatives.

# Contributors

John Higham, John Martin Vincent Professor of History at the Johns Hopkins University, has written or edited an impressive number of significant works. His study *Strangers in the Land: Patterns of American Nativism 1860–1925*, published in 1955, is a classic on this subject and has appeared in many editions. Higham's masterful examination of American ethnic history, *Send These To Me: Jews and Other Immigrants in Urban America*, in 1975, was released in 1984 in a revised version.

Carl H. Chrislock, professor emeritus of history, Augsburg College, and a member of the Association's board of publications, is a recognized expert on Progressivism in the Middle West. He is currently researching the papers of the Minnesota Commission of Public Safety, in existence from April 1917 until 1918, and preparing a book on the Commission for the Minnesota Historical Society.

Christen T. Jonassen is professor emeritus of sociology at the Ohio State University and the author of six books. His most recent work is *Value Systems and Personality in a Western Civilization: Norwegians in Europe and America* (Columbus, 1983).

Arlow W. Andersen, professor emeritus of history at the University of Wisconsin-Oshkosh and a member of the Association's board of publications, has written widely on Norwegian immigrant life. He has just completed a book-length manuscript on American government and politics in the Norwegian immigrant press during the period 1876 to 1925.

John R. Jenswold is a graduate student of history at the University of Connecticut. He is completing a doctoral dissertation on the Norwegian-American urban experience titled " 'The Hidden Settlement': Norwegian Americans Encounter the City, 1880-1930."

Deborah L. Miller is research supervisor at the Minnesota Historical Society in St. Paul. In 1985 she was the recipient of a Norwegian government fellowship that allowed her to study Norwegian-American photographs in Norwegian collections.

Odd S. Lovoll is the Association's editor. He is currently on a two-year leave of absence from his academic position at St. Olaf College to research and write a history of the Norwegians in Chicago from the 1830s to the 1930s. His most recent publication is *The Promise of America: A History of the Norwegian-American People* (Minneapolis, 1984).

Orm Øverland is professor of American literature at the University of Bergen and editor of *American Studies in Scandinavia*. He is currently researching Norwegian-American literature and preparing a book on this topic.

Ingrid Semmingsen was professor of American history at the University of Oslo. She pioneered in emigration studies in Scandinavia with her two-volume work *Veien mot vest* (The Way West), 1941 and 1950, and she continues to lecture and publish in this field. Semmingsen has contributed to this series in the past.

Janet E. Rasmussen teaches in the Scandinavian Area Studies Program and is Humanities Dean at Pacific Lutheran University, Tacoma. She is preparing a book based on oral interviews titled "New Land — New Lives: Scandinavian Women in the Pacific Northwest."

Einar Haugen, emeritus Victor S. Thomas Professor of Scandinavian and linguistics in Harvard University, and a member of the Association's board of publications, has published and lectured extensively within his field and the related areas of Norwegian-American history and literature. In 1983 he published *Ole Edvart Rölvaag*.

Rolf H. Erickson is the Circulation Services Librarian at Northwestern University Library and Second Vice President of the Norwegian-American Historical Association.

C. A. Clausen is a member of the Association's board of publications and a regular contributor to its publication program. Since volume 19 in 1956 he has prepared lists of recent publications of interest to the Association's readers.

Johanna Barstad is a librarian at the university library in Oslo. She has published a list of the holdings of the university library pertaining to Norwegian-American subjects, *Litteratur om utvandringen fra Norge til Nord-Amerika* (Oslo, 1975).

Charlotte Jacobson is the Association's archivist. She continues to receive and process significant historical documents.

Norwegian-American Historical Association

# Officers

330

# Publications

Doctrinaire Idealist: Hans Barlien, by D. G. Ristad; Norwegian-American Emigration Societies of the Forties and Fifties, by Albert O. Barton; Emigration As Viewed by a Norwegian Student of Agriculture in 1850: A. Budde's "From a Letter about America," translated by A. Sophie Bøe, with an introduction by Theodore C. Blegen; An Immigration Journey to America in 1854, a letter translated and edited by Henrietta Larson; Chicago As Viewed by a Norwegian Immigrant in 1864, a letter translated and edited by Brynjolf J. Hovde; The Historical Value of Church Records, by J. Magnus Rohne; A Norwegian-American Landnamsman: Ole S. Gjerset, by Knut Gjerset; The Icelandic Communities in America: Cultural Backgrounds and Early Settlements, by Thorstina Jackson.
ISBN 0-87732-006-3                                    Out of print

**Volume IV.** Northfield, 1929. 159 pp. A Contribution to the Study of the Adjustment of a Pioneer Pastor to American Conditions: Laur. Larsen, 1857-1880, by Karen Larsen; Report of the Annual Meeting of the Haugean Churches Held at Lisbon, Illinois, in June, 1854, translated and edited by J. Magnus Rohne; The Attitude of the United States toward Norway in the Crisis of 1905, by H. Fred Swansen; Immigration and Social Amelioration, by Joseph Schafer; The Mind of the Scandinavian Immigrant, by George M. Stephenson; Three Civil War Letters from 1862, translated and edited by Brynjolf J. Hovde; The Sinking of the "Atlantic" on Lake Erie, a letter translated and edited by Henrietta Larson; An Account of a Journey to California in 1852, by Tosten Kittelsen Stabæk, translated by Einar Haugen.
ISBN 0-87732-008-X                                    Price $8.00

**Volume V.** Northfield, 1930. 152 pp. An Early Norwegian Fur Trader of the Canadian Northwest, by Hjalmar R. Holand; Immigrant Women and the American Frontier, Three Early "America Letters," translated and edited by Theodore C. Blegen; From New York to Wisconsin in 1844, by Johan Gasmann, translated and edited by Carlton C. Qualey; Social and Economic Aspects of Pioneering As Illustrated in Goodhue County, Minnesota, by Theodore Nydahl; Norwegian-American Fiction, 1880-1928, by Aagot D. Hoidahl; Bjørnson and the Norwegian-Americans, 1880-81, by Arthur C. Paulson; The Beginnings of St. Olaf College, by I. F. Grose; Some Recent Publications Relating to Norwegian-American History, compiled by Jacob Hodnefield.
ISBN 0-87732-009-8                                    Price $8.00

**Volume VI.** Northfield, 1931. 191 pp. Illustrations, map. Norwegians in the Selkirk Settlement, by Paul Knaplund; Claus L. Clausen, Pioneer Pastor and Settlement Promoter: Illustrative Documents, translated and edited by Carlton C. Qualey; Lars Davidson Reque: Pioneer, by Sophie A. Bøe; A Pioneer Pastor's Journey to Dakota in 1861, by Abraham Jacobson, translated by J. N. Jacobson; The Campaign of the Illinois Central Railroad for Norwegian and Swedish Immigrants, by Paul W. Gates; Norwegians at the Indian Forts on the Missouri River during the Seventies, by Einar Haugen; The Convention Riot at Benson Grove, Iowa, in 1876, by Laurence M. Larson; Bjørnson's Reaction to Emigration, by Arne Odd Johnsen; Alexander Corstvet and Anthony M. Rud, Norwegian-American Novelists, by Albert O. Barton; The Norwegian-American Historical Museum, by Knut Gjerset; Norwegian Migration to America before the Civil War, by Brynjolf J. Hovde; Some Recent Publications Relating to Norwegian-American History, II, compiled by Jacob Hodnefield.
ISBN 0-87732-10-1                               Price $8.00

**Volume VII.** Northfield, 1933. 139 pp. Illustrations. Social Aspects of Prairie Pioneering: The Reminiscences of a Pioneer Pastor's Wife, by Mrs. R. O. Brandt; The Fraser River Gold Rush: An Immigrant Letter of 1858, translated and edited by C. A. Clausen; O. E. Rølvaag: Norwegian-American, by Einar I. Haugen; Some Recent Publications Relating to Norwegian-American History, III, compiled by Jacob Hodnefield; A Hunt for Norwegian-American Records, by Carlton C. Qualey; Ole Edvart Rølvaag, 1876–1931: In Memoriam, by Julius E. Olson.
ISBN 0-87732-13-6                             Out of print

**Volume VIII.** Northfield, 1934. 176 pp. Tellef Grundysen and the Beginnings of Norwegian-American Fiction, by Laurence M. Larson; The Seventeenth of May in Mid-Atlantic: Ole Rynning's Emigrant Song, translated and edited by Theodore C. Blegen and Martin B. Ruud; Johannes Nordboe and Norwegian Immigration: An "America Letter" of 1837, edited by Arne Odd Johnsen; The First Norwegian Migration into Texas: Four "America Letters," translated and edited by Lyder L. Unstad; Norwegian-Americans and Wisconsin Politics in the Forties, by Bayrd Still; The Emigrant Journey in the Fifties, by Karl E. Erickson, edited by Albert O. Barton; The Political Position of *Emigranten* in the Election of 1852: A Documentary Article, by Harold M. Tolo; The Editorial Policy of *Skandinaven*, 1900–1903, by Agnes M. Larson; Some Recent Publications Relating to Norwegian-American History, IV, compiled by

Jacob Hodnefield; Fort Thompson in the Eighties: A Communication.
ISBN 0-87732-014-4                                      Price $8.00

**Volume IX.** Northfield, 1936. 131 pp. Immigration and Puritanism, by Marcus L. Hansen; Svein Nilsson, Pioneer Norwegian-American Historian, by D. G. Ristad; The Sugar Creek Settlement in Iowa, by H. F. Swansen; Pioneer Town Building in the West: An America Letter Written by Frithjof Meidell at Springfield, Illinois, in 1855, translated with a foreword by Clarence A. Clausen; A Typical Norwegian Settlement: Spring Grove, Minnesota, by Carlton C. Qualey; Marcus Thrane in America: Some Unpublished Letters from 1880–1884, translated and edited by Waldemar Westergaard; The Missouri Flood of 1881, by Halvor B. Hustvedt, translated by Katherine Hustvedt; The Collection and Preservation of Sources, by Laurence M. Larson; Some Recent Publications Relating to Norwegian-American History, V, compiled by Jacob Hodnefield.
ISBN 0-87732-017-9                                      Price $8.00

**Volume X.** Northfield, 1938. 202 pp. Language and Immigration, by Einar I. Haugen; Two Early Norwegian Dramatic Societies in Chicago, by Napier Wilt and Henriette C. Koren Naeseth; A School and Language Controversy in 1858: A Documentary Study, translated and edited by Arthur C. Paulson and Kenneth Bjørk; A Newcomer Looks at American Colleges, translated and edited by Karen Larsen; The Norwegian Quakers of Marshall County, Iowa, by H. F. Swansen; The Main Factors in Rølvaag's Authorship, by Theodore Jorgenson; Magnus Swenson, Inventor and Engineer, by Olaf Hougen; Some Recent Publications Relating to Norwegian-American History, VI, compiled by Jacob Hodnefield.
ISBN 0-87732-019-5                                      Price $8.00

**Volume XI.** Northfield, 1940. 183 pp. *A Doll's House* on the Prairie: The First Ibsen Controversy in America, by Arthur C. Paulson and Kenneth Bjørk; Scandinavian Students at Illinois State University, by Henry O. Evjen; Stephen O. Himoe, Civil War Physician, by E. Biddle Heg; A Pioneer Church Library, by H. F. Swansen; Norwegian Emigration to America during the Nineteenth Century, by Ingrid Gaustad Semmingsen; Jørgen Gjerdrum's Letters from America, 1874–75, by Carlton C. Qualey; The Introduction of Domesticated Reindeer into Alaska, by Arthur S. Peterson; The Unknown Rølvaag: Secretary in the Norwegian-American Historical Association, by Kenneth Bjørk; The Sources of the Rølvaag Biography, by Nora O. Solum; Some Recent Publications Relating to

Norwegian-American History, VII, compiled by Jacob Hodnefield.
ISBN 0-87732-022-5                    Price $10.00

**Volume XII.** Northfield, 1941. 203 pp. Norwegian-American
Surnames, by Marjorie M. Kimmerle; Norwegian Folk Narrative
in America, by Ella Valborg Rølvaag; A Journey to America in the
Fifties, by Clara Jacobson; James Denoon Reymert and the Nor-
wegian Press, by Martin L. Reymert; Recollections of a Norwegian
Pioneer in Texas, by Knudt Olson Hastvedt, translated and edited
by C. A. Clausen; Norwegian Clubs in Chicago, by Birger Osland;
Buslett's Editorship of *Normannen* from 1894 to 1896, by Evelyn
Nilsen; Ole Edvart Rølvaag, by John Heitmann; Ole Evinrude and
the Outboard Motor, by Kenneth Bjørk; Some Recent Publications
Relating to Norwegian-American History, VIII, compiled by Jacob
Hodnefield.
ISBN 0-87732-024-1                    Out of print

**Volume XIII.** Northfield, 1943. 203 pp. Pioneers in Dakota Territory, 1879–89, edited by Henry H. Bakken; An Official Report on
Norwegian and Swedish Immigration, 1870, by A. Lewenhaupt,
with a foreword by Theodore C. Blegen; Memories from Little
Iowa Parsonage, by Caroline Mathilde Koren Naeseth, translated
and edited by Henriette C. K. Naeseth; A Norwegian Schoolmaster
Looks at America, an America letter translated and edited by C. A.
Clausen; A Singing Church, by Paul Maurice Glasoe; A Nor-
wegian Settlement in Missouri, by A. N. Rygg; Carl G. Barth,
1860–1939: A Sketch, by Florence M. Manning; Pioneering on the
Pacific Coast, by John Storseth, with a foreword by Einar Haugen;
Materials in the National Archives Relating to the Scandinavian
Countries; The Norwegians in America, by Halvdan Koht; Some
Recent Publications Relating to Norwegian-American History, IX,
compiled by Jacob Hodnefield; Notes and Documents: Norway,
Maine, by Halvdan Koht.
ISBN 0-87732-025-X                    Out of print

**Volume XIV.** Northfield, 1944. 264 pp. A Migration of Skills, by
Kenneth Bjørk; An Immigrant Exploration of the Middle West in
1839, a letter by Johannes Johansen and Søren Bache, translated by
the Verdandi Study Club; An Immigrant Shipload of 1840, by C.
A. Clausen; Behind the Scenes of Emigration: A Series of Letters
from the 1840's, by Johan R. Reiersen, translated by Carl O. Paulson and the Verdandi Study Club, edited by Theodore C. Blegen;
The Ballad of Oleana: A Verse Translation, by Theodore C. Blegen; Knud Langeland: Pioneer Editor, by Arlow W. Andersen;
Memories from Perry Parsonage, by Clara Jacobson; When America

Called for Immigrants, by Halvdan Koht; The Norwegian Lutheran Academies, by B. H. Narveson; Pioneering on the Technical Front: A Story Told in America Letters, by Kenneth Bjørk; Some Recent Publications Relating to Norwegian-American History, X, by Jacob Hodnefield; Notes and Documents: Karel Hansen Toll, by A. N. Rygg.
ISBN 0–87732–026–8                                            Out of print

**Volume XV.** Northfield, 1949. 238 pp. A Norwegian-American Pioneer Ballad, by Einar Haugen; Our Vanguard: A Pioneer Play in Three Acts, with Prologue and Epilogue, by Aileen Berger Buetow; An Immigrant's Advice on America: Some Letters of Søren Bache, translated and edited by C. A. Clausen; Lincoln and the Union: A Study of the Editorials of *Emigranten* and *Fædrelandet*, by Arlow W. Andersen; Thorstein Veblen and St. Olaf College: A Group of Letters by Thorbjørn N. Mohn, edited by Kenneth Bjork; Kristian Prestgard: An Appreciation, by Henriette C. K. Naeseth; Julius B. Baumann: A Biographical Sketch, by John Heitmann; Erik L. Petersen, by Jacob Hodnefield; Scandinavia, Wisconsin, by Alfred O. Erickson; Some Recent Publications Relating to Norwegian-American History, XI, by Jacob Hodnefield; Notes and Documents: Norway, Maine, by Walter W. Wright.
ISBN 0–87732–030–6                                            Out of print

**Volume XVI.** Northfield, 1950. 218 pp. Hvistendahl's Mission to San Francisco, 1870–75, by Kenneth Bjork; Oregon and Washington Territory in the 1870's as Seen through the Eyes of a Pioneer Pastor, by Nora O. Solum; From the Prairie to Puget Sound, by O. B. Iverson, edited by Sverre Arestad; Life in the Klondike and Alaska Gold Fields, letters translated and edited by C. A. Clausen; From the Klondike to the Kougarok, by Carl L. Lokke; Some Recent Publications Relating to Norwegian-American History, XII, compiled by Jacob Hodnefield.
ISBN 0–87732–033–0                                            Price $10.00

**Volume XVII.** Northfield, 1952. 185 pp. The Struggle over Norwegian, by Einar Haugen; Brother Ebben in His Native Country, by Oystein Ore; Norwegian Gold Seekers in the Rockies, by Kenneth Bjork; Søren Jaabæk, Americanizer in Norway: A Study in Cultural Exchange, by Franklin D. Scott; First Sagas in a New World: A Study of the Beginnings of Norwegian-American Literature, by Gerald H. Thorson; Controlled Scholarship and Productive Nationalism, by Franklin D. Scott; The Second Twenty-five Years, by Theodore C. Blegen; Some Recent Publications Relating to Norwegian-American History, XIII, by Jacob Hodnefield.
ISBN 0–87732–035–7                                            Price $10.00

**Volume XVIII.** Northfield, 1954. 252 pp. Maps. Norwegian Migration to America, by Einar Haugen; Rasmus B. Anderson, Pioneer and Crusader, by Paul Knaplund; Early Norwegian Settlement in the Rockies, by Kenneth Bjork; A Little More Light on the Kendall Colony, by Richard Canuteson; Segregation and Assimilation of Norwegian Settlements in Wisconsin, by Peter A. Munch; The Novels of Peer Strømme, by Gerald Thorson; Norwegian-American *Bygdelags* and Their Publications, by Jacob Hodnefield; Some Recent Publications Relating to Norwegian-American History, XIV, by Jacob Hodnefield.
ISBN 0-87732-037-3                         Price $10.00

**Volume XIX.** Northfield, 1956. 218 pp. The Immigrant Image of America, by Theodore C. Blegen; Boyesen and the Norwegian Immigration, by Clarence A. Glasrud; Norwegian Forerunners among the Early Mormons, by William Mulder; "Snowshoe" Thompson: Fact and Legend, by Kenneth Bjork; Norwegian-Danish Methodism on the Pacific Coast, by Arlow William Andersen; A Quest for Norwegian Folk Art in America, by Tora Bøhn; The Trials of an Immigrant: The Journal of Ole K. Trovatten, translated and edited by Clarence A. Clausen; Norwegian Emigrants with University Training, 1830-1880, by Oystein Ore; Some Recent Publications Relating to Norwegian-American History, XV, compiled by Clarence A. Clausen.
ISBN 0-87732-039-X                         Price $10.00

**Volume XX.** Northfield, 1959. 246 pp. Ibsen in America, by Einar Haugen; Still More Light on the Kendall Colony: A Unique Slooper Letter, by Mario S. De Pillis; A Texas Manifesto: A Letter from Mrs. Elise Wærenskjold, translated and edited by Clarence A. Clausen; History and Sociology, by Peter A. Munch; Beating to Windward, by Otto M. Bratrud, edited by Sverre Arestad; Pioneering in Alaska, by Knute L. Gravem; Marcus Thrane in Christiania: Some Unpublished Letters from 1850-51, translated and edited by Waldemar Westergaard; A Centenary of Norwegian Studies in American Institutions of Learning, by Hedin Bronner; Elizabeth Fedde's Diary, 1883-88, translated and edited by Beulah Folkedahl; The Content of Studies and Records, Volumes 1-20, compiled by Helen Thane Katz; "With Great Price," by John M. Gaus; Some Recent Publications Relating to Norwegian-American History, XVI, compiled by Clarence A. Clausen.
ISBN 0-87732-041-1                         Price $10.00

**Volume XXI** *(Norwegian-American Studies).* Northfield, 1962. 311 pp. Theodore C. Blegen, by Carlton C. Qualey; The Scandinavian Immigrant Writer in America, by Dorothy Burton Skårdal; Quest-

ing for Gold and Furs in Alaska, edited by Sverre Arestad; Norwegians Become Americans, translated and edited by Beulah Folkedahl; Cleng Peerson and the Communitarian Background of Norwegian Immigration, by Mario S. De Pillis; Early Years in Dakota, by Barbara Levorsen; A Pioneer Diary from Wisconsin, by Malcolm Rosholt; A Covenant Folk, with Scandinavian Colorings, by Kenneth O. Bjork; Reiersen's Texas, translated and edited by Derwood Johnson; J. R. Reiersen's "Indiscretions," by Einar Haugen; Some Recent Publications, compiled by Beulah Folkedahl; From the Archives, by Beulah Folkedahl.
ISBN 0–87732–043–8                              Price $10.00

**Volume XXII.** Northfield, 1965. 264 pp. Illustrations. A Pioneer Artist and His Masterpiece, by Marion John Nelson; Kristofer Janson's Lecture Tour, 1879–80, by Nina Draxten; Two Men of Old Waupaca, by Malcolm Rosholt; Pioneering in Montana, edited by Sverre Arestad; Seven America Letters to Valdres, translated and edited by Carlton C. Qualey; Music for Youth in an Emerging Church, by Gerhard M. Cartford; Our Bread and Meat, by Barbara Levorsen; The Independent Historical Society, by Walter Muir Whitehill; Some Recent Publications, compiled by Beulah Folkedahl; From the Archives, by Beulah Folkedahl.
ISBN 0–87732–045–4                              Price $10.00

**Volume XXIII.** Northfield, 1967. 256 pp. The Norwegian Immigrant and His Church, by Eugene L. Fevold; Some Civil War Letters of Knute Nelson, edited by Millard L. Gieske; An Immigrant Boy on the Frontier, by Simon Johnson, translated with an introduction by Nora O. Solum; The Gasmann Brothers Write Home, translated and edited by C. A. Clausen; Knud Knudsen and His America Book, by Beulah Folkedahl; Kristofer Janson's Beginning Ministry, by Nina Draxten; Knut Hamsun's America, by Arlow W. Andersen; The Romantic Spencerian, by Marc L. Ratner; Some Recent Publications, compiled by Beulah Folkedahl; From the Archives, by Beulah Folkedahl.
ISBN 0–87732–048–9                              Price $10.00

**Volume XXIV.** Northfield, 1970. 301 pp. Thor Helgeson: Schoolmaster and Raconteur, by Einar Haugen; The Letters of Mons H. Grinager: Pioneer and Soldier, collected by Per Hvamstad, translated by C. A. Clausen; The Norwegian Press in North Dakota, by Odd Sverre Løvoll; H. Tambs Lyche: Propagandist for America, by Paul Knaplund; The Social Criticism of Ole Edvart Rølvaag, by Neil T. Eckstein; A Thanksgiving Day Address by Georg Sverdrup, by James S. Hamre; Hamsun and America, by Sverre Arestad; Gold, Salt Air, and Callouses, by Thomas L. Ben-

son; Norwegians in New York, by Knight Hoover; Some Recent Publications, compiled by Beulah Folkedahl; From the Archives, by Beulah Folkedahl.
ISBN 0–87732–050–0                          Price $10.00

**Volume XXV.** Northfield, 1972. 293 pp. The *Bygdelag* Movement, by Odd Sverre Løvoll; Knut Gjerset, by David T. Nelson; Norway's Organized Response to Emigration, by Arne Hassing; The Founding of Quatsino Colony, by Kenneth O. Bjork; Norwegian Soldiers in the Confederate Forces, by C. A. Clausen and Derwood Johnson; Lars and Martha Larson: "We Do What We Can for Them," by Richard L. Canuteson; Ibsen in Seattle, by Sverre Arestad; From Norwegian State Church to American Free Church, by J. C. K. Preus; The 1842 Immigrants from Norway, by Gerhard B. Naeseth; Some Recent Publications, compiled by Beulah Folkedahl and C. A. Clausen; From the Archives, by Beulah Folkedahl and C. A. Clausen.
ISBN 0–87732–052–7                          Price $10.00

**Volume XXVI.** Northfield, 1974. 271 pp. Scandinavian Migration to the Canadian Prairie Provinces, 1893–1914, by Kenneth O. Bjork; The Story of Peder Anderson, translated and edited by Eva L. Haugen; Emigration from Land Parish to America, 1866–1875, by Arvid Sandaker, translated by C. A. Clausen; The Brothers Week, by Malcolm Rosholt; Rølvaag's Search for Soria Moria, by Raychel A. Haugrud; Notes of a Civil War Soldier, by Bersven Nelson, translated and edited by C. A. Clausen; Farewell to an Old Homestead, by Ethel J. Odegard; Georg Sverdrup and the Augsburg Plan of Education, by James S. Hamre; Factors in Assimilation: A Comparative Study, by Torben Krontoft; The School Controversy among Norwegian Immigrants, by Frank C. Nelsen; Norwegians in "Zion" Teach Themselves English, by Helge Seljaas; Breidablik, by Rodney Nelson; Some Recent Publications, compiled by C. A. Clausen.
[ISBN 0–87732–054–3                          Price $10.00

**Volume XXVII.** Northfield, 1977. 323 pp. Hegra before and after the Emigration Era, by Jon Leirfall, translated and edited by C. A. Clausen; Marcus Hansen, Puritanism and Scandinavian Immigrant Temperance Movements, by Frederick Hale; Three America Letters to Lesja, translated and edited by Carlton C. Qualey; Berdahl Family History and Rølvaag's Immigrant Trilogy, by Kristoffer F. Paulson; *Decorah-Posten*: The Story of an Immigrant Newspaper, by Odd S. Lovoll; *Symra*: A Memoir, by Einar Haugen; Erik Morstad's Missionary Work among Wisconsin Indians, by A. E. Morstad; Polygamy among the Norwegian Mormons, by Helge Seljaas; Wis-

consin Scandinavians and Progressivism, 1900–1950, by David L. Brye; Name Change and the Church, 1918–1920, by Carl H. Chrislock; American Press Opinion and Norwegian Independence, 1905, by Terje I. Leiren; The Kendall Settlement Survived, by Richard L. Canuteson; The Popcorn Man, by Rodney Nelson; An Outsider's View of the Association, by Rudolph J. Vecoli; Some Recent Publications, compiled by C. A. Clausen; From the Archives, by Charlotte Jacobson.
ISBN 0-87732-058-6                                    Price $10.00

**Volume XXVIII.** Northfield, 1979. 367 pp. Authority and Freedom: Controversy in Norwegian-American Congregations, by Peter A. Munch; *Skandinaven* and the John Anderson Publishing Company, by Jean Skogerboe Hansen; Martha Ostenso: A Norwegian-American Immigrant Novelist, by Joan N. Buckley; Norwegians, Danes, and the Origins of the Evangelical Free Tradition, by Frederick Hale; Two Immigrants for the Union: Their Civil War Letters, by Lars and Knud Olsen Dokken, translated by Della Kittleson Catuna, edited by Carol Lynn H. Knight and Gerald S. Cowden; Oslo on the Texas High Plains, by Peter L. Petersen; Dark Decade: The Declining Years of Waldemar Ager, by Clarence Kilde; Methodism from America to Norway, by Arne Hassing; Beret and the Prairie in *Giants in the Earth*, by Curtis D. Ruud; The Vossing Correspondence Society and the Report of Adam Løvenskjold, translated and edited by Lars Fletre; The Danish-Language Press in America, by Marion Marzolf; Norwegian-American Pastors in Immigrant Fiction, 1870–1920, by Duane R. Lindberg; Carl L. Boeckmann: Norwegian Artist in the New World, by Marilyn Boeckmann Anderson; Some Recent Publications, compiled by C. A. Clausen; From the Archives, by Charlotte Jacobson.
ISBN 0-87732-063-2                                    Price $10.00

**Volume XXIX.** Northfield, 1983. 402 pp. Haugeans, Rappites, and the Emigration of 1825, by Ingrid Semmingsen, translated by C. A. Clausen; Emigration from the Community of Tinn, 1837–1907: Demographic, Economic, and Social Background, by Andres A. Svalestuen, translated by C. A. Clausen; *Angst* on the Prairie: Reflections on Immigrants, Rølvaag, and Beret, by Harold P. Simonson; Emigration from the District of Sogn, 1839–1915, by Rasmus Sunde, translated by C. A. Clausen; Emigration from Sunnfjord to America Prior to 1885, by Leiv H. Dvergsdal, translated by C. A. Clausen; The Lynching of Hans Jakob Olson, 1889: The Story of a Norwegian-American Crime, by Odin W. Anderson; Emigration from a Fjord District on Norway's West Coast, 1852–1915, by Ragnar Standal, translated by C. A. Clausen; Emigration from Dovre, 1865–1914, by Arnfinn Engen, translated

by C. A. Clausen; Sigbjørn Obstfelder and America, by Sverre
Arestad; Emigration from Brønnøy and Vik in Helgeland, by Kjell
Erik Skaaren, translated by C. A. Clausen; Emigration from Agder
to America, 1890–1915, by Sverre Ordahl, translated by C. A.
Clausen; Sondre Norheim: Folk Hero to Immigrant, by John
Weinstock; Some Recent Publications, compiled by C. A. Clausen;
Index to Volumes 1–29 of *Norwegian-American Studies*, compiled by
Charlotte Jacobson.
ISBN 0–87732–068–3                          Price $10.00

**Volume XXX.** Northfield, 1985. 340 pp. O. A. Tveitmoe: Labor
Leader, by Lloyd Hustvedt; Scandinavian Settlement in Seattle,
"Queen City of the Puget Sound," by Patsy Adams Hegstad; Ole
and the Reds: The "Americanism" of Seattle Mayor Ole Hanson, by
Terje I. Leiren; Norwegians in the Pacific Coast Fisheries, by Sverre
Arestad; Reindeer, Gold, and Scandal, by Kenneth O. Bjork; The
Pioneers of Dog Fish Bay, by Rangvald Kvelstad; Three Spokes-
men for Norwegian Lutheran Academies: Schools for Church,
Heritage, Society, by James S. Hamre; The Domestic Architecture
and Cabinetry of Luther Valley, by Claire Selkurt; The Poetry of
Agnes Mathilde Wergeland, by Larry Emil Scott; Some Recent
Publications compiled by C. A. Clausen and Johanna Barstad;
From the Archives, by Charlotte Jacobson.
ISBN 0–87732–070–5                          Price $15.00

**Volume XXXI.** Northfield, 1986. 347 pp. The Mobilization of
Immigrants in Urban America, by John Higham; Profile of a Ward
Boss: The Political Career of Lars M. Rand, by Carl H. Chrislock;
The Norwegian Heritage in Urban America: Conflict and Cooper-
ation in a Norwegian Immigrant Community, by Christen T. Jo-
nassen; The Haymarket Affair and the Norwegian Immigrant
Press, by Arlow W. Andersen; "I Live Well, But . . .": Letters
from Norwegians in Industrial America, by John R. Jenswold;
Minneapolis Picture Album, 1870–1935: Images of Norwegians in
the City, by Deborah L. Miller; *Washington Posten*: A Window on
a Norwegian-American Urban Community, by Odd S. Lovoll;
*Skandinaven* and the Beginnings of Professional Publishing, by Orm
Øverland; Who Was Herm. Wang?, by Ingrid Semmingsen; "The
Best Place on Earth for Women": The American Experience of Aas-
ta Hansteen, by Janet E. Rasmussen; "Dear Sara Alelia": An Episode
in Rølvaag's Life, by Einar Haugen; Norwegian-American Artists'
Exhibitions Described in Checklists and Catalogs, by Rolf H.
Erickson; Some Recent Publications, compiled by C. A. Clausen
and Johanna Barstad; From the Archives, by Charlotte Jacobson.
ISBN 0–87732–072–1                          Price $15.00

*Travel and Description Series*

**Volume I.** *Ole Rynning's True Account of America.* Translated and edited by Theodore C. Blegen. Minneapolis, 1926. 100 pp. Historical introduction; original text of Rynning's book about America as published in Norway in 1838; and a complete English translation.
ISBN 0–87732–002–0                                         Out of print

**Volume II.** *Peter Testman's Account of His Experiences in North America.* Translated and edited by Theodore C. Blegen. Northfield, 1927. 60 pp. Historical introduction; facsimile of Testman's account of America as published in Norway in 1839; and a complete English translation.
ISBN 0–87732–004–7                                         Price $3.00

**Volume III.** *America in the Forties: The Letters of Ole Munch Ræder.* Translated and edited by Gunnar J. Malmin. Published for the Norwegian-American Historical Association by the University of Minnesota Press, Minneapolis, 1929. 244 pp. Historical introduction, frontispiece, index. A series of informal travel letters written 1847–48 by a Norwegian scholar who was sent by his government to America to make a study of the jury system.
ISBN 0–87732–007–1                                         Out of print

**Volume IV.** *Frontier Parsonage: The Letters of Olaus Fredrik Duus, Norwegian Pastor in Wisconsin, 1855–1858.* Translated by the Verdandi Study Club of Minneapolis and edited by Theodore C. Blegen. Northfield, 1947. 120 pp. Historical introduction, index.
ISBN 0–87732–029–2                                         Out of print

**Volume V.** *Frontier Mother: The Letters of Gro Svendsen.* Translated and edited by Pauline Farseth and Theodore C. Blegen. Northfield, 1950. 153 pp. Historical introduction, frontispiece, index.
ISBN 0–87732–031–4                                         Out of print

**Volume VI.** *The Lady with the Pen: Elise Wærenskjold in Texas.* Translated by the Verdandi Study Club of Minneapolis and edited by C. A. Clausen; foreword by Theodore C. Blegen. Northfield, 1961. 183 pp. Historical introduction, illustrations, index.
ISBN 0–87732–042–X                                         Out of print

**Volume VII.** *Klondike Saga: The Chronicle of a Minnesota Gold Mining Company.* by Carl L. Lokke. Preface by Kenneth O. Bjork; foreword by Senator Ernest Gruening. Published for the Norwegian-American Historical Association by the University of Minnesota Press, Minneapolis, 1965. 211 pp. Illustrations, maps, appendices, index.
ISBN 0–87732–046–2                                         Out of print

**Volume VIII.** *A Pioneer Churchman: J. W. C. Dietrichson in Wisconsin, 1844–1850.* Includes Dietrichson's Travel Narrative and Koshkonong Parish Journal. Edited and with an Introduction by E. Clifford Nelson. Translated by Malcolm Rosholt and Harris E. Kaasa. Published for the Norwegian-American Historical Association by Twayne Publishers, Inc., New York. 1973. 265 pp. Introduction, appendices, index, illustrations, maps.
ISBN 0-87732-053-5                                    Price $9.00

**Volume IX.** *Pathfinder for Norwegian Emigrants.* By Johan Reinert Reiersen. Translated by Frank G. Nelson. Edited by Kenneth O. Bjork. Northfield, 1981. 239 pp. Historical introduction, frontispieces, appendices, index.
ISBN 0-87732-065-9                                    Price $12.00

**Volume X.** *On Both Sides of the Ocean: A Part of Per Hagen's Journey.* Translated, with Introduction and Notes, by Kate Stafford and Harald Naess. Northfield, 1984. 70 pp.
ISBN 0-87732-069-1                                    Price $8.00

*Special Publications*

*Norwegian Sailors on the Great Lakes: A Study in the History of American Inland Transportation.* By Knut Gjerset. Northfield, 1928. 211 pp. Illustrations, index.
ISBN 0-87732-005-5                                    Out of print

*Norwegian Migration to America, 1825–1860.* By Theodore C. Blegen. Northfield, 1931. 412 pp. Illustrations, maps, appendix, index.
ISBN 0-87732-011-X                                    Out of print

*Norwegian Sailors in American Waters: A Study in the History of Maritime Activity on the Eastern Seaboard.* By Knut Gjerset. Northfield, 1933. 271 pp. Illustrations, index.
ISBN 0-87732-012-8                                    Out of print

*The Civil War Letters of Colonel Hans Christian Heg.* Edited by Theodore C. Blegen. Northfield, 1936. 260 pp. Historical introduction, illustrations, index.
ISBN 0-87732-015-2                                    Out of print

*Laur. Larsen: Pioneer College President.* By Karen Larsen. Northfield, 1936. 358 pp. Illustrations, bibliographical note, index.
ISBN 0-87732-016-0                                    Out of print

*The Changing West and Other Essays.* By Laurence M. Larson. Northfield, 1937. 180 pp. Illustrations, index.
ISBN 0-87732-018-7                                    Price $8.00

Norwegian-American Historical Association

*Norwegian Settlement in the United States.* By Carlton C. Qualey. Northfield, 1939. 285 pp. Illustrations, maps, appendix, bibliography, index.
ISBN 0-87732-020-9                                          Out of print

*The Log Book of a Young Immigrant.* By Laurence M. Larson. Northfield, 1939. 318 pp. Illustrations, selected list of Larson's writings, index.
ISBN 0-87732-021-7                                          Price $9.00

*Norwegian Migration to America: The American Transition.* By Theodore C. Blegen. Northfield, 1940. 655 pp. Illustrations, appendix, index.
ISBN 0-87732-023-3                                          Out of print

*A Long Pull from Stavanger: The Reminiscences of a Norwegian Immigrant.* By Birger Osland. Northfield, 1945. 263 pp. Portrait, index.
ISBN 0-87732-027-6                                          Price $8.00

*Saga in Steel and Concrete: Norwegian Engineers in America.* By Kenneth Bjork. Northfield, 1947. 504 pp. Illustrations, index.
ISBN 0-87732-028-4                                          Price $10.00

*Grass of the Earth: Immigrant Life in the Dakota Country.* By Aagot Raaen. Northfield, 1950. 238 pp. Index.
ISBN 0-87732-032-2                                          Out of print

*A Chronicle of Old Muskego: The Diary of Søren Bache, 1839-1847.* Translated and edited by Clarence A. Clausen and Andreas Elviken. Northfield, 1951. 237 pp. Historical introduction, portrait, appendix, index.
ISBN 0-87732-034-9                                          Out of print

*The Immigrant Takes His Stand: The Norwegian-American Press and Public Affairs, 1847-1872.* By Arlow William Andersen. Northfield, 1953. 176 pp. Bibliography, index.
ISBN 0-87732-036-5                                          Out of print

*The Diary of Elisabeth Koren, 1853-1855.* Translated and edited by David T. Nelson. Northfield, 1955. 381 pp. Historical introduction, illustrations, index. Available through Vesterheim, the Norwegian-American Museum, Decorah, Iowa.
ISBN 0-87732-038-1

*West of the Great Divide: Norwegian Migration to the Pacific Coast, 1847-1893.* By Kenneth O. Bjork. Northfield, 1958. 671 pp. Illustrations, maps, index.
ISBN 0-87732-040-3                                          Out of print

*John A. Johnson: An Uncommon American.* By Agnes M. Larson, Northfield, 1969. 312 pp. Illustrations, appendixes, index.
ISBN 0–87732–049–7                                     Price $8.00

*A Folk Epic: The* Bygdelag *in America.* By Odd Sverre Lovoll. Published for the Norwegian-American Historical Association by Twayne Publishers, Inc., Boston, 1975. 326 pp. Illustrations, bibliography, index.
ISBN 0–87732–055–1                                    Price $15.00

*The Norwegian-American Historical Association, 1825–1975.* By Odd Sverre Lovoll and Kenneth O. Bjork. Northfield, 1975. 72 pp. Appendix.
ISBN 0–87732–056–X                                     Price $3.00

*Guide to Manuscripts Collections of the Norwegian-American Historical Association.* Compiled and edited by Lloyd Hustvedt. Northfield, 1979. 158 pp.
ISBN 0–87732–062–4                                     Price $7.50

*Makers of an American Immigrant Legacy: Essays in Honor of Kenneth O. Bjork.* Edited by Odd S. Lovoll. Northfield, 1980. 223 pp. Frontispiece. Tabula Gratulatoria.
ISBN 0–87732–064–0                                    Out of print

*The Promise of America: A History of the Norwegian-American People.* By Odd S. Lovoll. Published in cooperation with the University of Minnesota Press, Minneapolis, 1984. 239 pp. Illustrations, bibliography, index.
ISBN 0–8166–1331–1                                    Price $35.00

*Han Ola og han Per: A Norwegian-American Comic Strip.* By Peter J. Rosendahl. Introduced and edited by Joan N. Buckley and Einar Haugen. Published in cooperation with Universitetsforlaget, Oslo, 1984. 262 pp.
ISBN 82–00–06741–6                                    Price $30.00

### Authors Series

**Volume I.** *Hjalmar Hjorth Boyesen.* By Clarence A. Glasrud. Northfield, 1963. 245 pp. Illustrations, bibliography, index.
ISBN 0–87732–044–6                                     Price $8.00

**Volume II.** *Rasmus Bjørn Anderson: Pioneer Scholar.* By Lloyd Hustvedt. Northfield, 1966. 381 pp. Illustrations, bibliography, index.
ISBN 0–87732–047–0                                    Out of print

**Volume III.** *Kristofer Janson in America.* By Nina Draxten. Published for the Norwegian-American Historical Association by

Twayne Publishers, Inc., Boston, 1976. 401 pp. Illustrations, bibliography, index.
ISBN 0-87732-057-8                                          Price $12.00

**Volume IV.** *Theodore C. Blegen: A Memoir.* By John T. Flanagan. Northfield, 1977. 181 pp. Bibliography, index.
ISBN 0-87732-060-8                                          Price $8.00

**Volume V.** *Land of the Free: Bjørnstjerne Bjørnson's America Letters.* Edited and translated by Eva Lund Haugen and Einar Haugen. Northfield, 1978. 311 pp. Illustrations, bibliography, index.
ISBN 0-87732-061-6                                          Price $15.00

**Volume VI.** *A Chronicler of Immigrant Life: Svein Nilsson's Articles in Billed-Magazin, 1868–1870.* Translated and introduced by C. A. Clausen. Northfield, 1982. 171 pp. Illustrations, index.
ISBN 0-87732-067-5                                          Price $12.00

*Topical Studies*

**Volume I.** *A Voice of Protest: Norwegians in American Politics, 1890–1917.* By Jon Wefald. Northfield, 1971. 94 pp. Bibliography, index.
ISBN 0-87732-051-9                                          Out of print

**Volume II.** *Cultural Pluralism versus Assimilation: The Views of Waldemar Ager.* Edited by Odd S. Lovoll. Northfield, 1977. 136 pp. Frontispiece.
ISBN 0-87732-059-4                                          Price $6.00

**Volume III.** *Ethnicity Challenged: The Upper Midwest Norwegian-American Experience in World War I.* By Carl H. Chrislock. Northfield, 1981. 174 pp. Illustrations, index.
ISBN 0-87732-066-7                                          Price $10.00

*Biographical Series*

**Volume I.** *Georg Sverdrup: Educator, Theologian, Churchman.* By James S. Hamre. Northfield, 1986. 218 pp. Illustrations, index.
ISBN 0-87732-071-3                                          Price $15.00